a woman's path

Jo Giese

Photographs by
Jill Johnson

Golden Books
NEW YORK

Golden Books®

888 Seventh Avenue
New York, NY 10106

Art directed by Ellen Jacob
Designed by Gwen Petruska Gürkan

Manufactured in the United States of America

10 9 8 7 6 5 4 3 2 1

Library of Congress Cataloging-in-Publication Data

Giese, Jo.
    A woman's path / Jo Giese : photographs by Jill Johnson.
          p.   cm.
    ISBN 0-307-44003-6 (hc : alk. paper)
      1. Women in the professions—United States—Biography.   2. Women—United States.
3. Women—Employment—United States.   I. Title.
HD6054.2.U6G54   1998
331.4'092'273—dc21
[B]

                                             97-40196
                                              CIP

To Dougal, who taught me the power of listening

Contents

Introduction

When we ask a person, "What do you do?," we're really asking, "Who are you?"

the living room in a friend's home buzzed with an expectant electricity as a group of professional women gathered for the first time. We'd come together because I'd been away, living in the Pacific Northwest, had just moved back to Los Angeles, and had mentioned to a friend how much I'd missed my women's group. I missed the energy, the laughter, the camaraderie and celebration of women getting together, exchanging stories.

My friend Judith Searle offered to form a group in Los Angeles. She suggested that instead of it being a social group, we should focus the discussions on our work, our professional careers. At our first luncheon, with the fourteen of us balancing plates of shrimp-and-rice salad on our laps, we each told the story of how we got from there to here. As JoAnn Matyas described her journey—from IBM engineer to Stanford graduate student to a designer who choreographs water fountains all over the world—the tone in the room changed. The casual clatter of silverware and the clinking of glasses stopped. For the rest of the afternoon the room was hushed except for the stories, one after another, of fascinating, amazing, improbable career paths.

I was drawn to these stories, pulled in by them, as hungry for them as if they held a key that unlocked secrets I'd needed to know

my entire life. I'd needed them when I was a little girl and had no idea what I would be when I grew up, I'd needed them when I was graduating from college and was still stumped by what my work would be, and I needed them now as I was navigating new pathways in midlife.

As the group broke up, with promises to meet again the following month, I remained still. Later, when I was interviewing Sister Mary José Hobday for this book, she said that at those times when she's caught a special vision, she too remains still, so the vision won't go away until she understands it. Sister Jo described these "exalting experiences that come uncalled for, at surprise moments of your readiness."

Although I couldn't have articulated it on the spot, gradually I realized that I'd been impressed by two things: the nature of the career paths and the joy that the women felt about their work. About their paths. Not one of the women had had anything resembling a direct, linear path that had moved in a single upward progression. Instead their paths had zigged and zagged, twisted and turned, gone roundabout and then *come* about. Like mine. This revelation struck home like an affirmation, a confirmation. I'd always felt that if only I had a path, a marked path, then I, too, would *know*. I would know the secret of how best to live my life. I felt that others knew, that they had an inner gyroscope, a map, and a paved road, while I was out there bushwhacking, trying to hack out a clearing.

Maybe I'd been too impressed by the crisp career plans of people I'd gone to college with, who declared a major and then actually went out and got a job in that field. Or maybe I'd been too influenced by the straightforward, predictable male model, exemplified by people like my husband, who had known since he was five that he was going to be a doctor and had never swerved from that goal.

Sometimes all my swerving and spiraling had left me feeling less than good about myself. What was wrong with me that I wasn't satisfied sticking to one job, that I'd gone from newspaper writing to magazine editing to documentary producing to television reporting to teaching to freelancing to book writing? I felt better, learning that none of the other women in the group had had the easy clarity of a singular vision, either. In fact, the stories of these successful, ambitious women revealed that many of them were groping to find their way yet again, shedding old identities, taking on new ones, transforming themselves and their work as their paths shifted and changed.

Undoubtedly, I'd heard similar stories before, but the solo voices of friends had not had the impact of a group of voices coming together like a contemporary chorus. Also, I probably heard them because I was at a professional crossroads in need of direction. After writing a book that hadn't sold, I'd found myself wandering into the Pepperdine University Career Center (more often than I'd care to admit), eyeing job listings back in television. I'd worked in network television in New York, so a producer's job for a cable show in the San Fernando Valley felt like a misstep backward. When I took the job, I put on a good face (and got a new hairdo), but inside I was wincing. I sensed that if I listened hard enough to the voices of people who had made the right connections for themselves, then I could divine my next step. Frankly, at forty-nine, I felt embarrassed to be still searching—for a connection, a success, that I hadn't yet made. Shouldn't I know by now? But then I went to the women's group, and I caught the vision for this book. I got a contract, I got to quit that rotten job, and I started having the most incredible time of my life.

For most people "a job is a job is a job." Probably only a small group are perfectly suited to what they're doing and are excited, exhilarated. But when women do transcend that job-is-a-job mentality, the joy that results is palpable. I thought, How come no one's celebrating this? Why is nobody cheering "Bravo!"?

I suspected something powerful was going on—not just in that room but across the country. And on the eve of the next century, I thought it was time to acknowledge, honor, and celebrate women who are reaching their potential, women who have managed to wrap their arms around what they love, grab hold, and not let go.

So I began a fabulous journey of crisscrossing America, listening, listening to girls and women from Alaska to Maine, from Illinois to Texas, from California to the Carolinas. Whether they're four or sixty-four, whether they're Caucasian or Japanese-American, African American, Indian, Native American, Vietnamese, Eskimo, or Hispanic, their stories have a universality that cuts across races and cultures.

When a woman in this book reveals the work she has done, is doing, and dreams of yet accomplishing, she's sharing one of the most fundamental stories of her life. She's not talking about a "job"; she's speaking about the development of herself as a whole person. She's describing the life process she had to go through to connect with the work she loves.

"What will I do?" is one of the great, puzzling questions of a lifetime, one that provokes us from our earliest days to our last. While I was in Seattle doing an interview for this book, I stood at the bow of a ferry and witnessed a family scene. Janey, three, was pleading with her mom to please let her go beyond the passenger rope out to the tip of the ferry's apron, out to where the choppy waters of Puget Sound were churning up a dark wake. Pointing to a dock worker, she said, with a pout, "Why does he get to be way up there?" "Because he works here," explained her mother. "One day

I'm gonna work here, too," said Janey. "I thought you were gonna be a waitress," teased her older brother. "Oh, I don't know what I'm gonna do!" Janey wailed, hanging her head as she swung back and forth on the rope.

The stories in this book are for the Janey in all of us, no matter what age we are. They can be taken as inspirational. But they are also instructional, directional, almost tutorial. They can be used as a road map to what works. These are stories for strength, for sustenance, for solace. These are stories to live by. One could say that the paths in this book—trails of contradictions, risks, failures, successes—are offered up as an exhilarating demonstration of what is possible.

What you won't find here is the complete journey of the person profiled. In collapsing their timeline, I intended to capture the essence of their story, a glimpse of their path.

"So, are you presuming," asked a friend, "that there's one path and only one path that's right for an individual? Like it's their destiny?" Not necessarily. Cass Peterson, a farmer I interviewed, commented, "The term 'career path' suggests a decision, somewhat early on, to make oneself into an image. A lawyer, sleek and successful. An actress, beautiful and desirable." My idea of a path is more kinesthetic, more in keeping with how Marcia Beauchamp explained that in hairdressing "there was a track and I got on it and it went. Ever since I got off it, I've had sort of an idea, but it's a whole lot less clear than hairdressing ever was."

I'm constantly asked how the women for this book were chosen. I refer to them as "women of achievement." I'm aware that the term "achievement" could be misleading because in our culture it typically means big bucks, big fame, big time. Though a few of these women are dazzling overachievers, and some are recognized leaders in their field, many are engaged in work that is decidedly humble, even low-status, when judged against more typical standards of wealth or power or prestige. But I wasn't interested in achievement in terms of the usual barometers of success. I was searching for women who had connected with that "spark" within themselves and were doing the work they're uniquely suited to do.

Consequently, some of the women were surprised to be included. For Christmas my sister had given me a massage with Madeline Martinez. While Madeline rubbed me with the softest, gentlest, most massive hands, I asked about her work—I ask *everyone* about their work—and how she'd connected with what she was so clearly born to do. In that dimly lit room, scented with eucalyptus, Madeline's story floated out, complete in one telling, as beautiful as a poem. Since I had no pen or paper to write it down, I asked if I could return and record it. "*My* story? *Me?*" she said. After Julie Brown told me her tale of adventure and adversity—of being a pilot, suffering a devastating car crash, ending up in a coma, and rehabilitating herself through deep-sea diving—she, too, was puzzled. "Are you sure I belong in the book? I don't see myself as a remarkable woman. I'm just doin' my thing, y' know?"

To grab my attention, a woman need not have dismantled traditional ideas about work like Debbie Dempsey, sea captain, or Sabrina Nickerson, tow-truck driver, or Ellen Paneok, who broke into the brotherhood of bush pilots. I was equally fascinated by the seemingly more traditional stories of Diana Labrum, pie baker, and Marcia Vaughan, children's picturebook author.

Sometimes I selected a woman because of the tortuous twists and turns in the route she took, or the place she ended up, but always I was attracted to the spirit in which she traveled. I wanted women who had found the song they're supposed to be singing, at least for that moment, and were belting out the lyrics.

In this high-tech age of video-conferencing and cyberspace chat rooms, most of the interviews were done the old-fashioned way. In person, one-on-one, face-to-face. There's an immense power and glory in a single human voice telling her story her way. After the first few interviews, I made sure to carry tissues along with my tape recorder. In speaking their story aloud, uncovering their life layer by layer, many rediscovered and reclaimed lost parts of themselves. Theirs were tears of recognition: My God, I came through *that*. Many of the interviews were so intense that the process possessed an athletic quality: athletic speaking, athletic listening. In straight journalism the interviewer is supposed to be a detached, dispassionate observer, and is sometimes adversarial. I never pretended to be anything but a participant. I had needed these stories all my life.

Once I'd done the oral interviews, it was my job to wrestle them into a coherent written form. Unlike with Madeline, the massage therapist whose story flowed out whole, most tumbled out in urgent bits and pieces, random rememberings and forgotten fragments. Aside from changing verb tenses and imposing a chronology, I left each woman's story in her voice, in her words. Aware of the exquisite gift I'd been given—the story of a person's journey—I struggled to do justice to that honor.

Then I handed the oral histories to Jill Johnson, the photographer. Because we wanted to see the women engaged in the action of doing their work, it was up to Jill to blend into the landscape, the seascape, the workplace—until they went about their business and Jill snapped the photos that appear in these pages.

We worked separately, so Jill had her own adventures. When she was marooned in Anchorage, Alaska, waiting for the rain to stop and the snow to start, she ate her first fillet of bear leg, shot and cooked by Ellen Paneok. In San Francisco, with Peggy O'Brien and

her two children, Jill was amazed that the kids let her photograph them for *six hours*.

After a year of hopscotching America, my family of friends across the country has increased. What started out as a quest turned into a spiritual journey of connection. The people in this book now populate my life. I am immeasurably changed—enlarged and enriched by these encounters. I also learned that the twists and turns, the starts and stops of a career are not necessarily dead ends and derailments, but can be the very shape of a woman's path to success. Women walk the world differently.

Recently I was back eating shrimp-and-rice salad with the group of women whose stories inspired this project. As we enjoyed what's become our monthly potluck, we went around the circle to catch up on what everyone's been doing.

A novelist with three published books admitted that she'd been going through some dark moments. Newly separated from her husband, she was convinced that she'd better find something "more sensible and secure" than writing fiction. She considered getting an advanced degree, so she could teach. "Or maybe I could be a copywriter?" she said, blushing, knowing advertising wasn't a good fit for her. The group teased out of her what she really, *really* wanted to do. Because of knowledge shared woman-to-woman, she gained the self-knowledge not to panic and slide backward out of fear, but to go forward with a heightened awareness that she was already on the right path, for her. She started on her fourth novel.

Like a series of intimate conversations around a small table, *A Woman's Path* offers the solace of a common language shared, offers the old-fashioned hopefulness that as each woman steps out on her path, whether for the first or twenty-first time, she will find the way, *her* way.

mARCIA VAUGHAN, b. 1951,
children's book author

Marcia's parents had a somewhat limited vision for their daughter's

future: her father, a lawyer, suggested she could be a court stenogra-

pher; her mother, a homemaker, suggested a telephone operator. On

a summer's day, Marcia lounges on her deck overlooking Puget

Sound. In between sips of white wine, she describes how she didn't

know right out of the gate what she wanted to do. It took until she

was thirty-one to stumble onto her path of being a children's

picturebook author.

Marcia

When I was very young I wanted to be a horse. Then I wanted to marry someone with a horse, the Cisco Kid, to be exact. Then I thought bigger. I wanted to have my own ranch and have my own horses.

In the eighth grade we were given an aptitude test. It was to help us plan our careers as we neared high school. In the eighth grade I didn't have any real career ambitions. I just wanted to be popular and have breasts. On the aptitude test I must have done something well with my hands because it turned out that I would be excellent at repairing watches.

I was pretty surprised by that because that's a skill I certainly never knew I had. It didn't make me say, "That's good to know. I can hardly wait. Is your watch working?"

Until I went to college I had this underlying feeling. It's the vaguely "not-good-enough" feeling. That I was not good enough to ever get a professional job. This was a secret thing I knew and I hoped nobody else knew.

In college I'd go into a class and get this assignment and I'd sit there and think, I don't even know how to start to do this. Then I'd struggle my way through it and get a pretty good grade. It was through doing that year after year that I found out, Whoa! I'm a pretty capable person after all. Even to this day I'll get a writing assignment from a publisher, and they'll say, "Do you want to write a series of books on insects in Istanbul?" And I'll go, "Of course I do!" Then I'll hang up and get that terrified feeling that I don't even know how to start to do a book like that. But I'll wade through it the same way I did the college assignments. College was very, very good for me.

I had decided to be a first-grade teacher because I thought I'd get to play all day with kids. I was taking puppetry, storytelling, improvisational theater, reader's theater. It was just so much fun. Back in the dorm everybody else would be studying for their calculus and their chemistry finals

> ## In the eighth grade I didn't have any real career ambitions. I just wanted to be popular and have breasts.

and I'd be memorizing *Fox in Sox* with chicks on bricks and poodles eating noodles. It's a fine, fine Dr. Seuss book and a tongue-twister. For our final we had to read it with expression and without a single mistake.

I got through student teaching but I was disheartened to realize, Uh-oh, I just did four years of college and I do not want to be a teacher. During student teaching I'd taken a group of children to the library. It was a cute library with a round braided rug and a rocking chair with cushions. I thought that this really sweet librarian was going to come and tell us stories. Instead, the Wicked Witch of the West came out and made all the kids sit crisscross applesauce. They had to be totally silent little statues while she read. I was appalled. I thought, Even I can do better than that. If I'd been really bright I would have figured out right then that I was well-suited to be a children's librarian, but it took a little longer for the penny to drop.

After graduation I escaped to Phoenix and worked in an ice cream parlor, scooping ice cream and getting mailers from the college placement office. I kept getting the teaching openings and one day there were three unusual job opportunities in a row—elementary school librarian, elementary school librarian, elementary school librarian. I went, You know, I could be an elementary school librarian.

It was a wonderful feeling. This was actually something I could do. Whew! It did mean I had to go back to college for a year of library science classes.

I got a job interview on Bainbridge Island—just west of Seattle—and I was so nervous. My interview outfit consisted of a polyester jacket and a very, very tiny matching navy blue polyester skirt. (I can't tell you how short that skirt was. I kept pulling it down.) I walked into the school district office and there sitting in the room were other interview people. One lady, I knew she was going to get the job, she had gray frizzy hair up in a bun and she was knitting and I thought, Why did I even bother to come? That's the one they're going to hire.

During the interview I talked and talked and talked. Then they asked, "What do you like to drink?" I said, "If it's during the week, I drink beer, but if it's the weekend, I drink gin and tonic." It all came out of my mouth before I had a chance to think. About a week later the principal called me up and offered me the position of children's elementary school librarian on Bainbridge Island. They liked that I wasn't an uptight person.

I loved the kids and I enjoyed the type of work I got to do. I was my own boss. I did my own planning. Nobody messed with my programs, so I was my own little entity. I was twenty-four years old and it was a real achievement—a real surprise to me that I could do a job and do it that well.

I'd probably been there four or five years and I was getting just a tad jaded. I had a favorite second-grade class, Mrs. Walberg's, and they were there at my moment of enlightenment. I was reading a folktale, *Tikki Tikki Tembo*. After so many years of being a librarian I didn't just read stories. Mostly, I acted out what the characters were doing and I made changes. If the story was too long, I edited it in my mind and made it shorter. If it was too short, I made up dialogue and stuck it in. I always thought I was making other people's books so much better.

So I was reading away and making all sorts of changes to *Tikki Tikki Tembo*, and the kids were totally into it, and all of a sudden this bossy voice inside my head said, "Marcia! Stop

I thought there would be just one door, with one career choice behind it. I've been amazed to find that there are so many doors with so many choices, so many surprises.

changing other people's books and write your own!" It was one of those moments when the lights flash and the bells ring and it's not a fire drill. I just went, Whoa! That's what I really want to do. I wore this huge smile for the rest of the day.

Then life became a tossed salad when the man-I-would-one-day-marry said, "Why don't we travel around the South Pacific and find an island to live on?" I dipped deep into my retirement account, not waiting until I was sixty-five, and we

stuffed our life's posses-
sions into two back-
packs.

There's a lot of
spare time on the ulti-
mate vacation. You can
walk the beach only so
many times, eat so
many papayas. We lived
in this little A-frame on
a lagoon and the top
loft was very small.
That's where I sat down
with a notebook and a
pen and started writing
stories. I did it by hand.
There was no type-
writer in Rarotonga in
the Cook Islands.

The first story I
wrote was *Tacky Tumu, the Boy in the Singing Shell*. While I was
writing it, I thought, I'm so brilliant. Everybody's going to
love this. I submitted it to a publisher in Australia and it
came back with a rejection letter.

I built up my writing muscles and wrote a second story.
I didn't need encouragement because I had desire, dedica-
tion, and one other really great word that starts with a *d*—
determination! Wild horses couldn't stop me. I was going to
write, and be a writer, and get published.

I found that because I'd read so many books I'd learned

how to write without ever having known it. Now, granted, I
wasn't a very good writer to start with, but I knew about
dialogue, I knew about characterization, I knew about plot-
ting. I'd learned all this accidentally by reading aloud to
children, and I'd had the very best authors as my teachers.

We left the Cook Islands and moved on to Sydney,
Australia. We'd go to a party and people would say, "What
do you do?" And I used to practice and say, "I'm a writer."
That felt real good. And then they'd say, "Really? What have
you written?" And I'd say, "Well, nothing." But it felt really

good for just a very short time to say, "I'm a writer."

In Sydney one of the first things we did was go to the Toranga Park Zoo, where we saw kangaroos, koalas, Tasmanian devils and platypuses, numbats and wombats, emus and cockatoos—bizarre, wonderful Australian animals. I thought, Why don't you ever see these animals in books?

I love what I do. It's like sitting down and playing in my imagination all day.

They are so much more interesting than lions and tigers and bears. That night I went to bed and dreamed about these animals.

The next morning I was looking up at the ceiling in the bedroom and part of me was still dreaming and this imaginary wombat waddled across the ceiling. I was saying, "He's really cute." Then all of a sudden out from behind the wardrobe a dingo ran and grabbed the wombat, and I was going, "Oh, no! Poor little wombat. I hope his friends come up with a plan to trick the dingo before the wombat gets made into wombat stew."

Wombat Stew. Hey, I thought, this is a great idea for a kids' book. And instead of being a stew that gets better and

better, this stew will get worse and worse and more disgusting and totally gross because that's the way kids would really enjoy it.

I grabbed a piece of paper and jotted the idea down. I was still in bed. I wrote it on the back of an envelope. The minute I did that, I looked at the ceiling again and now instead of one idea up there, there were ten. They were all random little bits of the story that didn't go in any order. I grabbed a notebook, and I just lay there in bed and wrote like crazy. I worked on it for two weeks and it came out so easily, that one. It's like it was in that pencil the whole time. All I had to do was hold that pencil to the paper and the story told itself.

Then came the hard part—letting go. I had the most difficult time dropping my story into the mailbox. Was it really done? Was it *good enough*?

The first publisher sent it back saying they no longer published picturebooks. That sort of rejection I could handle. The second publisher wrote a scathing rejection letter. They said they didn't think it was very well written, and I should take a writing class and learn how to write. I was so mad I slammed doors, and I was grouchy and snappy at people, but underneath it really scared me. Oh, my God, what if they're right? What if I'm not a very good writer? What if I never get anything published? That old "not-good-enough" button got pushed again.

But the angry voice in my head was louder. It said, "Oh, yeah? It is, too, a good story and I'll prove it."

Many, many months later a reply came from a third publisher that said, We have read *Wombat Stew* and think it is absolutely delightful. We would like to publish it with a first print run of 25,000 copies.

It was a moment of ultimate joy. This was really what I wanted to do. I just hadn't known it for the first thirty-one years of my life. That acceptance wasn't just a path—it was the express lane to creative fulfillment.

I've been writing for fifteen years now. I've had eighty-one books published, and *Wombat Stew* has sold bazillions of copies. (Bless its little pulpy heart.) The ratio between unpublished to published is about ten to one. I write ten stories and I sell one.

I love what I do. It's like sitting down and playing in my imagination all day. And it's challenging. It's almost like having to prove myself each time I write a book, whether it's "good enough" to get published. And if it isn't, can I rework it to make it that way?

The good part of my life is that I can set my own schedule—I usually work from nine in the morning to one in the afternoon. I work in a little beach cabin. I can do whatever I want—total freedom. The more realistic side is that I do have to sell these stories to be able to earn money to live. And the real uncertainty is that until a royalty check arrives, I never know how much it's going to be for, because I don't know how many books have sold, if any. So, there's a great financial unknown.

I used to think I had to sit in a dimly lit room with total quiet and total privacy to be able to write. But we moved back to the States after my son was born, and I found I could work in a bright room with *Sesame Street* on in the background and my son hanging on my leg. Sometimes he'd be inside the playpen playing, sometimes I'd be inside the playpen writing, where he couldn't get at me. And you know, it worked just great.

One day I was writing a story and Sam had just discovered he could open drawers and pull things out. I did not want to stop writing and I could see him, he was in my line of vision, and he was having a ball. He went to the linen closet and pulled out all the sheets and towels. He could reach up high enough that he pulled things off the hangers one at a time. He went into the kitchen and dumped out the silverware drawer, and he was starting on the pots and pans. I thought, This is probably a great idea for a book, except instead of a normal-sized baby demolishing a house I'll change him to a giant's child who demolishes a town. And it sold.

The thing that makes me craziest is that some people, who have very little to do with children's books, think that writing children's books is easier than writing adult books, both of which, I think, are challenging. But, of course, they're wrong. Because in a children's book you have so much to say in so few words that each word is like a little chunk of gold. I mean, it has to be perfect—each word and where it's placed in the sentence.

Over the years my specialty has become the humorous picturebook in which a villainous trickster is outwitted by an underdog. I think life is like that sometimes—you may not be the biggest, or the strongest, or the smartest, but you've always got a chance if you're a thinker.

I thought there would be just one door, with one career choice behind it. I've been amazed to find that there are so many doors with so many choices, so many surprises.

Debbie

DEBORAH DOANE DEMPSEY, b. 1949,
marine bar pilot

I like to make sure

Debbie's story is of a shy, inhibited girl who grew up to become a sea

captain giving orders and autographs. In the shipping industry

Deborah Doane Dempsey is a legend: the first woman to graduate from

a maritime academy, '76; the first American woman captain of a

merchant vessel on an international voyage, '89; the first woman

captain of a vessel in wartime, '90; the first woman Columbia River

bar pilot, '94. On a rainy day, with the fog almost obscuring our view

of the Columbia River, Debbie vacillates between laughter and tears as

she tells her dramatic and difficult story.

everyone knows the difference between a fairy tale and a sea story. A fairy tale

starts, "Once upon a time . . ." A sea story starts, "This is no shit." My mother doesn't think I should talk in that vein. But I don't hold back. I'm very direct. I get my hands dirty.

I've always loved the water and messin' about in boats. I was raised in Essex, Connecticut, at the mouth of the Connecticut River. It's an active sailing community, a place where everybody boats. From the time I was ten and my sister, Linda, was thirteen, we'd take off for weekends—sailing a thirteen-and-a-half-foot Blue Jay and camping along the banks. Once we were headed for Martha's Vineyard on a twenty-seven-foot Tartan. There was fog, eight- to ten-foot ocean swells, and we ran off our chart. All we had left to use was a Texaco road map. And I guarantee that a road map doesn't show much of Rhode Island Sound. We pulled into

Vineyard Haven after dark. That was cool! We did that!

Having to make do on the water is an incredible discipline. I have this dream of a sailing school. My school would be: load the boat up with twelve- and thirteen-year-olds and go out to sea for five days. Don't go anywhere. Just go to sea, combat the elements, and come back. You have to produce or you're not going to survive.

My dad certainly expected that one of his five kids would take over his pharmacy. Much to the disappointment of my parents I got sick of the physical sciences. After I graduated [University of Vermont] I became a bum—delivering yachts and teaching skiing. A friend of my dad's, he'd been watching me, suggested that I go up to the Maine Maritime Academy and learn what he knew I wanted to know.

Until this person, who'd graduated from Maine Maritime, made me aware that maritime schools existed, I hadn't known about them. I'd been working at the Essex Machine Works, a propeller and shaft foundry. I didn't want to work there the rest of my life, and there wasn't much security in delivering yachts. Plus, I was tired of living at my parents'. I felt the need for direction, and his suggestion was very intriguing.

There was only one woman at any of the seven maritime academies. I sent in my application to Maine Maritime, was interviewed on a Tuesday [October '73], and that Thursday they admitted me. Because I'd already graduated from college, I entered as a second-semester sophomore, so I didn't have to go through that grueling year of being a mug and the ten days of indoctrination where you're doin' triple-time up the hill in Castine.

My parents drove me to school and they didn't think I'd last two weeks because of the pseudo-military environment. You have to wear a uniform, polish your shoes, stand for inspection. The first couple of weeks were total chaos because of the publicity and the fact that the student body didn't want me there. I was forced to eat meals in the dining hall. I'd be sitting there, alone, with mashed potatoes hitting me from one side, gravy from the other, and I'd be ducking when a plate came overhead. I was spat on at morning formation. My classmates

It's such a wonderful feeling to know what you want to do.

left bags of choice items outside my door. It never let up. During senior finals an ice ball with a rock in it was thrown through my dorm window.

I dealt with it by going AWOL to Commander Sawyer's residence. He taught nautical science, had a daughter about my age, and was building a cabin on the waterfront. I helped him. That was my escape.

I'd been a good student at college but at the Academy I was an excellent student because I loved what I was learning. Celestial navigation. There's nothing better than learning celestial navigation and using a sextant. It's such a wonderful feeling to know what you want to do and to be following up on it. It all fell into place. Castine, Maine, is a beautiful, small, seacoast port. We had this 535-foot training ship, tugboats, sailing boats. It was fantastic. I was surrounded 360 degrees by this environment—messin' about in boats—and I was doing it on that scale. A 535-foot ship. It was such a relief, and I wouldn't have to worry about my next job.

I knew what I was getting into but it's astonishing to me, even with the group I work with today, that there are males who are threatened because a woman's doing the same job a man's doing. I was a speaker at a conference on Women in Shipping. I was serving on a panel with Captain Lynn Korwatch, the first woman to sail a commercial vessel on an unlimited Master's license (she was eight months pregnant at the time), and Elizabeth Mulcahy, who runs a ship charter service out of New Jersey. A commissioner on the Board of the Maritime Pilots, probably one of two males out of a couple hundred people in the auditorium, commented to the panelists about swinging off a rope in sixty-knot winds and twenty-foot seas. He asked if we'd address the physical requirements of a woman doing a man's job. I jumped right in and said, "That's where we differ. We don't see it as women doing a man's job." I got a standing ovation.

One of my favorite stories concerns my first job as second mate. Now you're considered the navigator of the ship. You're up there messin' with the charts, all the equipment

on the bridge, laying out the courses as the Captain wants it done, using that sextant to take morning star sights and evening star sights.

I was nervous as all get out as I pulled up to the Andry Street levee in New Orleans. The Captain, who was leaning on the railing, watched me lift my seabag out of the trunk, and told one of the third mates, "Go help the cadet with her luggage." Afterward, the third mate told the Captain, "That's no cadet. That's your second mate." The Captain said, "Like hell!" He called the Lykes Shipping office and asked, "Whatcha doin' puttin' a woman on my ship?" Their response was, "Make a trip with her. You'll like her."

We sailed from Houston in pea-soup fog. I relieved the twelve-four watch after we'd already taken departure from Galveston. There are safety fairways through a horrendous number of oil rigs and I asked the third mate, "Where's the Captain? Don't you think he ought to be here in pea-soup fog? And where are we?" He said, "I think—" "What do you mean, you *think*!" I started piecing together oil rig formations, matching them with the chart. Our vessel, the *Aimee Lykes*, was as long as two football fields, was on the wrong side of the fairway, and there was incoming traffic. By then Captain Dempsey was on the bridge, checking the radar, and he was not saying anything. Finally, I said, "What do you think about hauling right?" Total silence. About thirty seconds later, he said, "Yup," and hauled ninety degrees right. Later he told me he thought, No damn female's gonna tell me what to do.

Halfway through the South Atlantic on the way to Cape Town, it changed from "What's the matter now, second mate?" to "Good mornin', second mate." Two months into the sail on the east African coast, we fell in love. I called home from Mombasa, and all Mom said was, "You're not going to get married before you get home, are you?" We had a wonderful, spectacular trip. We wound up spending a week in Mtwara, Tanzania, where the original *Blue Lagoon* was filmed. Jack and I were the only ones who had a good time, because there was nothing to do there while the ship discharged flour.

Jack was my role model. He didn't go to one of these fancy-dancy academies where you graduate third mate. He worked his way up by total experience and never forgot what it was like to sail mate. He taught me the confidence it takes to be a Master and a Chief Mate.

When we got back we faced quite a battle at Lykes. Jack told 'em, "You guys are right. I like her so much I'm gonna marry her." The pencil Captain Hendrix was holding snapped in two. He said, "She'll never sail Chief Mate for this outfit and you two will never sail together again, if you get married."

That was August and we got married four months later, December '78. Immediately Jack was yanked from his ship, the ship to which he'd been permanently assigned. For the next six months we fought Lykes in arbitrations and hearings in New York City. We were fighting for the ability to sail and work together on the same ship. A decision was never rendered by the arbitrator, but we won because the union [the International Organization of Masters Mates and Pilots] forced them to concede and reinstate Jack, and Vice President Hendrix was asked to retire.

Another six months later Lykes did a 180 and tried to get me on Jack's ship on a permanent basis, but I didn't have the union seniority to hold the job. I'd catch a job with him whenever I could. Our happiest times were when we were on a ship, working together. We'd solved the age-old mariner's problem of how to continue sailing and maintain a normal married life. We shared a cabin, which was no problem for anybody on the ship, and we enjoyed the foreign ports together. Izmir . . . Civita Vecchia . . . Singapore . . . there's a lot of romance in those foreign ports.

My most dangerous assignment was the rescue of the *Lyra*. I was assigned Captain to the *Lyra* in June '89, and had made six trips in and out of the Persian Gulf crisis [Operation Desert Shield]. After the Persian Gulf War, the U.S. government bought the ship from Lykes. Lykes thought they could save some money towing it from Baltimore to New Orleans rather than recrewing it. In fifty-knot winds and twenty-foot seas the *Lyra*, a 634-foot vessel, eighty-nine feet wide, broke her tow off of Cape Fear [January 26, 1993]. With 387,000 gallons of fuel, no power, and no crew, the dead ship was drifting onto Frying Pan Shoals. There was no way to stop her.

I'd just gotten home to Virginia, hadn't unpacked from leaving the ship in Baltimore, and my boss asked me to fly out to the ship and attempt to anchor her.

That's another case of Jack being my mentor. He delivered me to the airport, where I was to take a helicopter to the ship. I was anxious about attempting to anchor the ship. I'd never in my life anchored a ship with two anchors. In weather like that you don't anchor—you heave to or steam back and forth. Jack was telling me what he'd do because

he'd used two anchors, but he'd never been lowered by helicopter onto a dead ship—no one had. That was the very worst part—being lowered onto the deck of a ship doing thirty-five-degree snap-rolls.

Four crew members were lowered onto the deck. There's nothing blacker than a ship dead in the water in a storm at night. After we managed to drop the first anchor, the emergency generator failed. We had to let down the second without any power from the ship. Eight hours later the first anchor dug into the bottom. This rescue received every

There's nothing blacker than a ship dead in the water in a storm at night.

maritime award, and a banquet was held to honor the entire crew. Jack was there but he didn't share the podium. He considered it my show. He was a unique man.

In 1994 the Columbia River Bar Pilots recruited me. They had the state on their back to produce with affirmative action. All ports and harbors around the world have pilots who are important because they have local knowledge. A ship arrives at the Columbia River Bar, which Lloyd's of London rated as the most dangerous bar in the world. (A bar is the sand bar across the entrance to the mouth of a river where the ocean shoals up to meet it.) Without that local knowledge it's too difficult to bring in the ship, so you hire a pilot to bring you safely across the bar.

A pilot boards the ship from an eighty-seven-foot pilot boat, which runs alongside. Negotiating onto the Jacob's ladder, which can hang up to thirty feet down the side of the ship, is the most dangerous part of the job, especially since most of the work at the Columbia River Bar is done at night. Then a pilot goes up to the bridge and, since the pilot knows the depths, knows the channel, knows the bar conditions, the pilot advises the Captain what to do.

The best part about being a pilot is that you spend all your time maneuvering the ship. On a ten-day crossing of the Atlantic, you're never changing speed, doing anything, as far as ship handling. Also, with piloting, you're no longer leaving on a foreign voyage, 50 to 120 days—you're on an hour-and-a-half transit in the harbor. So, not only are you doing what you love, but every day you're home.

I could now be with Jack on a daily basis. In our eighteen years of marriage there were times when we wouldn't see each other for six months. Last summer, it was all falling into place, it was comfortable for both of us, and we bought this house. I always looked at this as our doing it together. It wasn't just me. Then Jack was diagnosed. That was awful. He died four months later of lung cancer [June 1996].

I don't have any answers right now. I'm scared of what's ahead or not ahead. What's real unattractive is coming back to this empty house. Before, whenever Jack and I weren't together, we were by ourselves, but we were never alone. Now I'm not only by myself but I'm very much alone. That's something altogether different.

I had something none of the other pilots had. I had Jack, who knew and understood every aspect of the work, and that was fun, sharing every job with someone who could advise me, support me.

After I'd been in shipping for a while, I attended an alumnae gathering at the Williams School, a day school for girls where I'd gone to high school. Everyone was listening to my sea stories, and the headmistress commented, "Deb, when you were in school here you were so shy you couldn't speak at all. Now you're nonstop!"

I told her it was because I'd found my niche, that I'm very satisfied and quite proficient at what I do. It's such a wonderful feeling to find your niche. Male or female, until you find your niche, life's difficult.

bARBARA GILLIAM, b. 1951, pastor

Barbara's early path was a steady downward spiral of sexual abuse, truancy, reform school, addiction, and prostitution. In the midst of such self-destruction, how does a person crawl out from the belly of the beast, climb back into society, and manage to connect with a professional calling? A decorative magnet on the door of Barb's refrigerator could be the prayer for her life:"Out of adversity comes greatness."

Barbara

When I was a child I had no professional aspirations. I just wanted to survive and be loved. We lived in Cedar Rapids, Iowa, America's heartland, where people are honest, hardworking, and kids never get in trouble.

My father was an alcoholic; he still is. My dad's family blamed my mother, my brother, and myself for his drinking problems. From a young age I felt that if I hadn't existed maybe there wouldn't be these problems, this extra expense. Mom wouldn't have to work so hard, maybe their marriage would have been better.

I tended to be my father's counselor. I was kind of his surrogate wife, so to speak. At about the age of eight, that's when the sexual encounters began. My mother worked nights as a pediatric nurse and at night he'd be drunk and come in and sexually molest me. Then he'd talk about their sex life.

I started having problems at school. I let air out of people's tires. I spray-painted cars. I broke windows. Obviously, at that age I couldn't cognitively say, "I'm really angry and that's why I'm doing this." When I got caught doing vandalism, my mother would ask me, "Why are you behaving this way?" I wouldn't reveal anything. I thought, *I'm* doing something wrong. There wasn't a sense that it was his fault. I rationalized it by saying, My father's a sick man. The alcohol gets to him. Therefore he's not responsible.

At that time we attended a Lutheran church and it was really ironic. We'd fight all the way to church and Dad would smell like booze from the night before. Then we'd sit in a pew, smile, get our brownie points with God, and fight all the way back home. I remember thinking, If this is what being religious is about, I don't want it.

By the age of thirteen the police were always at our home. I had a little bit of a police record for skipping school, for shoplifting, for breaking and entering. This one time I'd been pulled into court because I'd been caught with

> We'd sit in a pew, smile, get our brownie points with God, and fight all the way back home. I remember thinking, If this is what being religious is about, I don't want it.

beer in the car. The judge consulted with the probation officer and this pastor. The pastor said, "Unless you send this girl to reform school, she'll end up dead and bloody in an alley."

I became a ward of the state and was institutionalized at the Mitchellville Training School for Girls. It had the reputation that the worst of the worst went there. People stab you there. I was scared to death.

There were five cottages, maybe about a hundred girls. There were all these stupid rules, like you couldn't cross your legs. They'd come and slap your leg. Why, I have no idea. They said, "We're going to make you into the kind of women you should be." Which meant we needed to learn how to pluck our eyebrows, how to cook, how to do child care, how to sew.

When I was admitted this matron in these black shoes said, "You're going to the hospital for a few days." I figured a hospital meant a ward of people, right? This chubby woman in this white dress put me in this little room. Well, it was isolation. I sat there in a burlap gown without any underwear on, waiting to go to the hospital. One day went by, two days went by. They'd open the little door in the big door and slip meals to me. It had a little john, a little sink, a little cot. It was like a prison cell. I was freaking out, sobbing. I'd just turned fourteen. It was a sadistic, sick place.

I'd been in there about nine months when one evening a bunch of us girls were sitting outside and I saw this car driving slowly inside the grounds. I was drawn like a magnet to that car. Mitchellville was in the middle of cornfields, there was a restraining fence around the perimeter, and we were told nobody had ever escaped and made it. I was kind

of standing there staring at the driver. I thought, Man, that looks like Dad. Could it be? When the driver motioned for me to come, I knew it was my dad. He'd disguised himself as a woman—lipstick, wig, the whole bit. I had no idea he was coming to break me out. I tore off. The house mother was yelling, "You get back here!" The driveway was blocked by another car, so he floored it, drove up over this tomato patch and took half the tomatoes with us.

We rendezvoused with my mother and brother in Moline, Illinois. She said there was an APB out for me. I thought I was the most wanted criminal in the world. We hid out in an efficiency in Fort Lauderdale-by-the-Sea, Florida.

A few years later I was taking the test to get my GED, and I saw an ad for a travel agent. I applied for it and they hired me. I started to develop this ability to relate to people, sort of a sales ability. It was my first real job that I thought could be a career. For the first time I felt confident and positive. I was a pretty blonde and I got invited to a lot of cruise ship parties.

I began to drink heavily at those parties and started having panic attacks. This hospital gave me Librium and Valium for the attacks. Then I was mixing pills with alcohol. My mother was pretty disappointed in me. I'd stay out all night, partying. I was hard to corral. I'd lie to her.

I fell in love with a Jewish boy—I was really in love with him—and got pregnant. He said, "I'm not ready to be a dad." I was devastated. They'd just passed the abortion law in New York and next thing I was on a plane. I stayed with this wonderful couple on Long Island. Everything was handled nicely. I went in for an abortion. I was twenty.

The travel agency wanted to open a branch in New York City. I stayed at this nice hotel and got the office opened. I was the office manager. I worked with another lady who did marketing, and we got corporate accounts.

The more accounts I got, the more I thought I needed. I wanted to be a big travel agent. Plus, my personal life stank. My self-esteem came through what I did in my career. I was putting in long days to get strokes from people. Then, the way I dealt with job stress, or rewarded myself, was to go to happy hour, and I never left happy hour.

Something traumatic happened. The guy who owned the travel agency was a young, hotshot kind of guy. One day I was alone in the office, and he said, "I know you want it." He raped me. I never, at that point, saw it as rape. I don't know how to explain that, but because of my past I thought, That's what men do and that's what women are for. But I was really pissed off. I hit him. I tried to fight him off.

That's when the drinking increased. I took a leave from the travel agency and checked into my first hospital for chemical dependency. I spent twenty-eight days there. But I was just twenty-one, and I felt I was too young to be an alcoholic or an addict. I thought maybe I was too stressed out being in the travel business, maybe something else would make me happier. I got a job with an executive personnel company. I was a headhunter, recruiting people to be sales reps for pharmaceutical houses. Before I was selling travel, now I was selling people. Sales are sales. I was like Dr. Jekyll and Mr. Hyde. I'd work during the day, and drink and do drugs until I passed out at night. I thought, Maybe three weeks with my mom and I'll be okay.

At that point I was also making doctors' appointments. I could see seven doctors in a day, to get prescriptions. I had three surgeries I didn't need just to get the Percodan and Demerol that I was addicted to. I faked the symptoms. It was like I couldn't kill myself, so I wanted the doctors to kill me.

The first time I did heroin I was twenty-four. I took the subway down to the scuzziest area in New York City— Delancey Street on the Lower East Side. These two Puerto Rican guys and I went to a dilapidated building and they shot me up. By that point I was also doing some hooking. I'd go to the garment district and sleep with someone if they'd give me clothes and two lines of cocaine. Among hookers, I was a high-class hooker. I wasn't out on the street doing it for fifteen bucks. But the bottom line is, a hooker's a hooker. What I really wanted was a sugar daddy.

My mother gave me the name of a Christian psychiatrist. I told him, "If you give me religion, forget it." He said, "Barbara, I can't do anything until you get off drugs." He gave me the names of a bunch of drug treatment places, including the Walter Hoving Home in Garrison, New York. A few months later, I said to myself, "I'm gonna die." I got what stuff I had, put it in a friend's car, and he drove me up to Garrison. When I got to their doorstep, I was so high I didn't care where I was. I had pills and needles and everything on me. It was December 1976. I was unconscious for three days.

The Walter Hoving Home is a drug and alcohol program strictly for women. The main house was just beautiful, a lot of dark wood and a big Christmas tree with gifts under it. It's set on twenty-seven acres right across from the West

Point Military Academy. The grounds were gorgeous, with this creek at the bottom of a hill.

John Benton, who ran the home with his wife, Elsie, said about me, "I think she's mentally retarded. I don't think she's going to make it here." I wasn't detoxing fast enough and they were scared something was medically wrong. Elsie said to give me another week.

They found me a big sister, an ex–gang member named Angie. She stuck me in a dress and I went to my first prayer meeting and I about freaked out. They were praying, "Thank you, Jesus!" [The home is supported by the Assemblies of God, a Protestant Pentecostal denomination.] I hid in the phone booth and called somebody I'd worked with and said, "This is a cult. You've got to get me out of this place!"

It was a very tough program. Yet there was a love and a caring that seemed genuine. I felt like I could stop running. I also felt kind of stupid, like I was back in elementary school. You had your own little cubicle where you did your reading, and I hadn't read in a while. You'd write out things like, What does this scripture mean to you—that God forgives you and he's full of mercy? How do you need to apply that in your life today? I thought, How could he forgive me for having an abortion? How could he forgive me when I'd committed every sin in the book? Plus, I had a lot of resentment toward the church. They say, "God, your heavenly father," and I thought, If he's anything like my earthly father, why should I trust him?

I was absolutely sober. No alcohol. No cigarettes. Nothing. There's a spiritual source you can tap into that will help you do what you can't do by yourself. That's grace.

Grace is a power greater than yourself. It doesn't mean that I wasn't responsible, that I just sat there and said, "Okay, God, you do it." I had to work hard. I had to face a lot of pain. I had to make amends. There's something powerful about asking someone to forgive you, like I did with my mom because I'd stolen money from her to buy drugs.

I was there for a year and a month exactly. When I was discharged I was a Christian and I was sober. I was going down to my mom's. I cried all the way to La Guardia Airport. I'd never flown sober. This Jewish lady sat next to me on the plane. We chatted and I told her what I'd been through the past year. We held hands when we landed. She went her way to Miami and I went mine to Boca Raton.

That next morning the phone rang and this same lady, Lorraine, was calling from Miami. She didn't know my name but she'd remembered the Walter Hoving Home. She'd talked to Elsie Benton and said she'd met this girl on the plane and needed her phone number. She said to me, "You mentioned on the plane that you might be wanting to go to college. I was so impressed with what's gone on in your life. Do you have the money to get there?" I said, "No." She drove all the way to Boca Raton, about fifty miles, to give me money. Not the tuition but the travel money to get to Evangel College in Springfield, Missouri. In the Jewish faith the number eighteen means "To life!" She handed me $418 and said, "*L'chaim!* Here's to new life!"

Academically, I did so well that I got a scholarship. Instead of studying nursing, which is what I'd thought I was interested in, I felt this call to preach. Not just to preach at people, but to be in a relationship with them and give them hope.

There were times when I didn't want to stay clean. I never drank or did drugs again, but I did switch to food. With an addictive personality I often found myself wanting a double milkshake at Wendy's. I'd catch myself and say, "Oh,

you're stressed because finals are coming." That's something I continue to deal with today.

I graduated summa cum laude. All my family was there. I sent Lorraine my graduation announcement. I walked up to that stage and got that diploma. It was a miracle.

I set up a crisis center for girls, for drug addicts, in Times Square. I felt such compassion for them. They were so tough and mean. I'd walk right up to their pimps and say,

I felt this call to preach. Not just to preach at people, but to be in a relationship with them and give them hope.

"Get out of my way. I'm taking this girl off the street." Those people could have killed me, but I had this boldness.

I worked there for a year and felt I was supposed to further my education. I picked a seminary in Boston that was part of a consortium, so I also had the opportunity to take classes at Harvard Divinity School.

At the seminary I wasn't drinking or using but I was clinically depressed. I became a test case for Prozac, way back before it was approved by the FDA. I thought, Does being on Prozac mean I'm back on drugs? But it helped me pull out of the depression until I could get through counseling.

What happened in a nutshell was that I'd been staying real busy for God, busy helping others, which is a cop-out so I didn't have to deal with myself. Different Christian television shows had contacted the Walter Hoving Home, looking for women who were living drug-free to give testimony. So I'd been on Pat Robertson's *700 Club,* and on *PTL,* Jim and Tammy's show. Jim Bakker had said, "Here's this girl who's done drugs, who was a hooker on the streets of New York, and look what God can do." I felt a little exploited.

At Harvard there was a Catholic theologian and philosopher named Henri Nouwen. He took a liking to me. He had me over to his house with other students, but he just mentored me. Henri Nouwen might not mean much to some people, but to me—Henri Nouwen at Harvard Divinity School—I mean, I didn't deserve this. He'd written oodles of books, including *The Wounded Healer*. He said, "Barbara, you're a wounded healer."

In college I'd met a man named Rick and we'd stayed in communication as friends, off and on. I always thought he was a hunk. He came to Boston and we spent a week together, talking, and realized we loved each other. (Rick's in sales, computer sales for corporations.) Three months later, in 1985—I was thirty-three, he was thirty-one—we were married in Cedar Rapids, Iowa. That's where my family was from and maybe I wanted to have some good memories there. I went back to the old pastor, I went back to the reform school. I had to do that for my own healing.

The first year in our marriage, I tested Rick in little ways to see if he really loved me. I wasn't the best housekeeper. I wasn't the best cook. I didn't know if I wanted to have kids. He looked at me and said, "I'm committed to you until death do us part." I could rest in that. We've grown in that love in the last eleven years. Marriage is way beyond what I thought it would be.

Today I'm a chemical dependency therapist at Hoag Hospital, and I'm the senior pastor, *the* pastor, at North Long Beach Tabernacle. It's a small inner-city church. The congregation of Filipinos, Hispanics, and blacks is like what I was used to in New York. The church had been in this storefront for fifty-four years. When I found out they needed a pastor, I said to my husband, "After fifty-four years, do you think they'll want a female?" They had these Hispanic men and that's a cultural thing, to want a male pastor.

In October 1996, they voted me in.

I work a lot with youth. I have drug addicts walk off the street. They say, "We don't know why we're here, but do you know anything about drugs, Pastor?"

1

YNDA MARIE JORDAN, b. 1956,
scientist

It's a steep uphill ascent for a poor inner-city black girl to become a

world-class scientist. Especially since even on the cusp of the twenty-first

century, only 1 percent of American scientists are minority women.

Lynda speaks leisurely in a drawl acquired from going to school in the

South—until the talk turns to science. Then she's a woman transformed:

her speech accelerates, her eyes sparkle. During Lynda's sabbatical at the

National Institutes of Health in Bethesda, Maryland, a snowstorm slams

the East Coast. As she winds up her story of science and self-discovery,

the world outside has changed, too: the barren limbs are glistening with

snow, and the ground is shimmering in winter white.

I grew up in Boston in

Lynda

the projects, the Jamaica Plain Projects. I didn't have any idea that there was a way out.

What I saw was young poor women. My mother included. Young, poor women who were somehow disenfranchised from their mates—with children, with no education, and no money. And I was part of the struggle. Being the oldest of three children, my role was not one of a young child who was growing up and exploring. It was one of responsibility.

There's one vivid memory that changed me. It was a time when we were waiting for the welfare check to come. If you know anything about the system, you know the checks never come on time when there are particular things that are very important. For example, Thanksgiving, Christmas, Easter, Mother's Day, on those holidays which exhibit family structure, the checks tend to be late. This was one of those times—it was Easter—when we were waiting for a check and we didn't have any food. We were taking canned milk and diluting it with water so it could stretch.

Routinely the oldest child would be the one that waits, the one that has the responsibility to help the parent, the mother. So this is day number three that the check is late and I'm sitting downstairs, waiting for the mailman. And this time every apartment in the building has a representative there and we're all like, "Is he coming? Is he coming?" And when he gets there, this public servant says, "No checks, ladies. Ha, ha, ha!" It was funny to him. I put my head down and said, "How in the world am I going to go upstairs and tell her?" I was angry because it wasn't funny. To him it was like, Okay, you don't have the check, but for us it was like, Okay, here's another day that we're going to have to survive and eat and we don't know how. I was about ten years old and I decided I would not depend on the U.S. government for money. I couldn't do it. I would not live like that.

When I was eleven my mother remarried and I was devastated. We'd gotten ourselves together, put our chin up, and become a family unit—the four of us, my mother and her three children. We'd just gotten ourselves stable to the point that my mother had recently gotten her high school diploma, she had a part-time job, and we were working our way off welfare. Then all of a sudden here was this man, this man that I didn't know. It wasn't only this man. It was this man with twelve children. *Twelve children.* They bought a ten-room house with one bathroom. We slept three and four to a room. Don't make me laugh. If anybody wanted to take a bath, you had to go around and ask everyone if they wanted to use the bathroom, so you could have fifteen minutes of free time. To take a bath, really. It was a trip. We used to have to wake up in shifts. In addition, my mother had three more children. That's another story. So altogether there were eighteen children. He was working and she started working full-time. She took care of children—in the home. More children. I'm serious.

I was overwhelmed and angry. I started smoking ciga-

rettes and hanging out with the crowd. I'd ride the bus from where I lived all the way to downtown Boston, and I would also hang out on the corner of Blue Hill Avenue. Blue Hill Avenue was a long strip that was well-known in the black community. It was a place where there was a lot of drinking, a lot of smoking. I wasn't doing alcohol, but I was thirteen, fourteen years old, right on the cusp of getting ready to learn other things. There's a high pregnancy rate and I was getting ready to go to that level.

What kept me from that was the Upward Bound program. It was a mistake how I got there. Though I don't call it a mistake. I say it's fate. I say it's God. We were in the girls' gym and we were smoking cigarettes and the hall monitor smelled the smoke. Well, lo and behold, I did not want to get into trouble. So we split up and ran. I ran into the auditorium and there was a group of children sitting there with this big black man. I was like, Oh, I didn't know this was going on. The hall monitor came in, so I sat down like I was part of the group. This man was talking to people about joining Upward Bound. The thing that got to me was that he said, "What are you going to do with the rest of your life? Stand on a corner on Blue Hill Avenue and smoke cigarettes?" It floored me because I thought, How does this man know this is what I do after school?

The thing that's most significant is that the guidance counselors had selected who they thought should go to that meeting in the auditorium. I was not selected but I ended up going anyway. If it wasn't for Upward Bound, I would not be here. I would have been a statistic, a person with five or six children, probably on welfare, and living in the projects.

I went to Upward Bound for the first time in the summer of my sophomore year of high school. It was a six-week program on the campus of Brandeis University in Waltham, Massachusetts. These people expected me to do my best, and there was no limitation on what the best was. I learned that I was capable. I was in a college preparatory chemistry class and it was difficult—the first time I'd ever had chemistry. In our home we hadn't been able to afford a lot of toys, so what my mother had done was buy us jigsaw puzzles. You had to figure out how one hundred pieces went together to create this picture—say, a picture of a farmhouse with a boat and some trees and grass. I was used to doing my puzzles and escaping out. I attacked chemistry like it was one of those jigsaw puzzles.

They had a convocation to honor the top six kids. I was waiting there in the auditorium to see who these six children would be because this program was *hard*. We worked from six o'clock in the morning until eleven o'clock at night. They chose the six people who had the highest average. And I was one of them.

For the first time I felt like, Wow, maybe I am smart. I don't know why I'm crying. I've never cried before about this. I mean, that was the first time I realized that maybe I could do something. That was the first time I saw a door open as a way to get out of my situation. Education was the way to get out.

As part of the Upward Bound program we'd filled out applications to college. Usually what happens when a girl in my family graduates from high school is that they go to Boston Business School and become a secretary, and then they go back and help out the family. In terms of my immediate family, there was no one who had gone to college before. So you can imagine, in order for me to even apply to school—this is a new thing for my family structure. Here I was, breaking all these ties, and my family did not understand. They did not understand why I had to go to school.

It was suggested to me that I go to a black college so I could be around strong black women and see them as role models for what I wanted to do in life. I went to North Carolina A & T State University in Greensboro. I was a chemistry major, but my goal was to go to medical school. A lot of kids think if you mess up your first year, it's over. I was not an A student my first year. People need to know that.

For the first time I felt like, Wow, maybe I am smart.

I was playing around and still making B's in chemistry and enjoying partying. It's good to make A's, but if you don't, don't cry over spilled milk. Pick yourself up and keep going.

My junior year I went to a Harvard University summer program. I was going on rotations with doctors and I was squirming. But when they talked about biochemistry, I let everything else go. The teacher talked about medicine at a different level. He talked about diabetes, and the malfunction in glucose metabolism as it related to diabetes, and I was excited.

I matriculated at Atlanta University and did my research at Morehouse School of Medicine in Atlanta—that's one of three black medical schools in the country—and again it was biochemistry, the biochemistry of diseases, that excited me.

Chemistry is the study of molecules. What makes it so significant is that we're studying chemistry of the biological system. We're seeing how reactions occur inside the cell. And the most fantastic part is that we're relating it to living things—plants, animals, and most important, humans.

I was completing my master's and I was going to get me a job somewhere—at a pharmaceutical company, a chemical company. But I'd also filled out the Minority Locator, the student locator service of the GRE, and they contacted my school. My chemistry professor called me into his office and said, "MIT's interested in you applying for your Ph.D." I didn't play him any attention. I'd gone to school for six years. I was twenty-three years old. I was on my way out to get me a job and have a life.

A few weeks later, he paged me in my dorm on Saturday morning and literally brought me to his office, locked me in a room, and left me with the MIT application. He was an MIT graduate himself, and he said, "You're not leaving here until you fill it out." If you've ever seen the application, it's crazy it's so long. He came back about one o'clock and threw in a box of chicken so I could eat.

I come from poor inner-city blacks. I remember one time, this is when I was, say, around eight or nine, I had a conversation with my mother on one of our outings. There's a bridge that separates Cambridge from Boston, and there's a saying in the Boston community that "the bus stops at the bridge." If you want to get to the other side, you have to walk. My mother and I did a lot of walking in the summer. We were sitting there on the Cambridge side of the Charles River. There's some benches there and you can get a breeze.

I'd turned away from where it looks toward Boston and said, "Ma, what's this?" She said, "That's MIT." I said, "What's MIT? It's so nice, it's so beautiful." She said, "That's where rich white people go. Don't worry about it. You'll never get to go there." She was being real, to her.

And then these people invite me to go there.

My mom was elated. She was like, "I don't believe it. You must be smart if you're going to MIT." It took her all that time to realize it.

My first day at MIT I was at a graduate get-together. I'm sitting there and I'm waiting and I'm seeing all these different people and I wait and I wait and I wait. And I look and I look and I just keep waiting for someone else to come. I didn't realize it at the time, but I was waiting for other black people. I didn't know until they said, "Let's sit down," that the whole class—about sixty to seventy people—was there. I looked around, and said, "Oh, my God, I'm *it*."

That was the first time in my life that I'd felt like I was a minority. There was one Chinese woman. She looked at me and I looked at her, and I mean, we clung. Only three African American females have graduated with a Ph.D. in chemistry from MIT to this day. I was one of the three.

The thing that's important to me is that during that difficult first year, this guy, this chemistry professor who took me to his office and gave me that tremendous application, he came to my lab and visited me. He was from Atlanta and he'd just show up in Cambridge. This is significant because I was going through a whole lot of crap and it was a crucial moment. I'd say to him, "Why am I doing this?" He'd say, "Your degree is not just for you. It's for other people."

What he meant is that from my success I'd open doors for other minorities. It wasn't only the fact that I was an African American female, but that I was an African American female from a low sociological background in the Boston area. All those things were significant at MIT, and are still significant at MIT today. There is still this ideology that intellect is correlated with finances.

I don't know how to explain how it is being black and poor in America, but it's like if you're successful then you're pioneering a role for someone else. That was enough to keep me going.

There was a point at MIT when I was working on my dissertation research and I finally felt, I'm Lynda Jordan, a scientist. I wanted to figure out how this particular flavin played a role in the electron-reduction process of this enzyme. My adviser had one postulation of how it worked, and I had another. And mine worked. That was fantastic. Those things legitimate you, and you say, Okay, I'm a scientist.

In 1985, when I was twenty-nine years old, I was accepted to do postdoc work in Paris as a Ford Fellow at the Pasteur Institute. For the first time in my life I was working with a woman, a female scientist, who was married with children, who is an M.D./Ph.D., and her husband is an M.D. A man who has no problem with cooking dinner while she's in the lab, which is wonderful.

I'd been in Paris for about ten months when I got married. He was a musician. This is very interesting. I think girls who want to go into science need to know this. One of the things young girls think about is who they will marry. Some of my colleagues in science, my male colleagues in particu-

lar, say, This is not related. I say, Yes, it is. Because that child's choice in a man is going to make a significant impact if she's going to be able to make an investment in a scientific career, or if she's going to give it up.

In the twenty-first century, I hope men are able to accept women who are smarter, who have chosen different types of careers, and men are able to take that nontraditional role of maybe doing the cooking because tonight she's running this experiment with this compound and it took her six months to synthesize it and she's right in the middle and she

To be a scientist you have to be a risk-taker.

has three more hours to wait, and if she leaves, it's shot. And to understand that it fell on your birthday and I got your present and I love you, honey, but I won't be home until eleven o'clock. Can you handle it?

What happened in my marriage was that he could not handle that I didn't have a conventional life. He was a musician, so if I had a late night in the lab, when I was coming in, he was leaving to go out to play.

Bastille Day, July 14, is a big day in France and it's a beautiful thing and I wanted to spend time with him, but I had to do this experiment. I couldn't let my collaborator down. And so we made this wonderful lunch and put it in a picnic basket and brought it to my lab. That was one of the good times. I put him at the computer where he was learning how to type the lyrics to his music while I was working in the laboratory. It was definitely easier for him when I was the one sitting there waiting for him to finish his work—like I did a whole lot of times when he was in the studio—rather than him waiting for me to finish my work. It's difficult for women who are scientists—whether they are geologists, astronauts, or oceanographers—unless their mates are scientists, and that doesn't happen a lot.

My husband is still doing lyrics, but not with me. The marriage between music and science stopped in 1989. My husband had difficulty accepting that I—Doctor Lynda Jordan—was the intellectual heavyweight in our relationship.

When I was thirty-one and separated, I came back and started building a lab at North Carolina A & T State University where I would continue studying PLA$_2$. PLA$_2$ is involved in various diseases like asthma, arthritis, diabetes.

It wasn't like I just came in and ran a lab. I had to build a lab. We had nothing. I went there on Sundays, put on jeans and a scarf over my head, and cleaned out crud myself. I wanted a facility where we'd have the opportunity to perform top-notch research. It was a continuous process, but I raised over a million dollars.

Now a lot of people are offering me positions at the administrative level at other universities. I'm at a crossroads because in academia when you get promoted you go into administration, a deanship. But I'd be going away from my heart. I don't want to leave the bench.

I want to be considered an intelligent human being, an intelligent, full-figured, short-haired, African American woman who is making a documented contribution to society and to science. This is important. Let's be real. When you think of a scientist, who do you think of? You don't think of me. When you think of an African American woman, what comes into your mind—an entertainer. Maybe Ella. Or Josephine Baker. After I returned from Paris, one of my colleagues at this Beta Kappa Chi National Science Honor Society meeting told me, "You look just like a gospel singer." I said, "I am a scientist! I am with you! I am your colleague!" Scientists come in all shapes, sizes, colors, and heights.

To be a scientist you have to be an independent thinker, you have to be a risk-taker. You have to go beyond what anyone thinks would work, and you go on your own heart and your own intuition, and you try it anyway. You have to be willing to sacrifice everything.

There was a lot of sacrifice in a family that did not know how to support a first-generation college student, that did not know why I couldn't come home for Easter, that did not know why I had to go out and do something like this. Breaking through my socioeconomical background and feeling isolated and alone—it's been some sacrifice. All for the love of science. For the love, check this out, of doing what you believe that you were put on this earth to do.

Is all the sacrifice worth it? Is it worth it? It's worth every bit of it when I see my first student get a Ph.D. and she didn't even know she was capable of it and she's not thirty years old and she's doing her postdoc at Rutgers and she's married successfully and her husband's taking a nontraditional role. It's worth it. It's worth it. It's worth it. It's hard but it's worth it.

t

TAMARA ZAKIM, b. 1980,
high school senior

I play basketball with a team, and it's never one person's fault if you win or lose. It's all of you together and it's more than just a sport, it's a social interaction. We're always supporting each other. Even though I do other things, like I work hard in school and I play violin, basketball is what's really kept my life together. With all the pressure I put on myself, it serves as an outlet for my everyday anxieties and frustrations. Playing on a team makes me focus not only on myself and my skills, but on the group, and the cooperation that's needed to work together. I hope I play basketball the rest of my life.

I'm six feet tall and I'm still drinking milk. I hope I'm going to grow another inch. I'm stretching myself because I'd like to be able to dunk. Dunking is very glorious and glamorous.

Tamara

j

JULIE BROWN, b. 1964,
scallop diver/
lobster fisherman

It took Julie five years to break into the brotherhood of lobster

fishermen. Now in summer you'll find her hauling lobsters along

with the men of Maine. This woman, who admits she's always

liked doing something different, lives with two kitties on Vinalhaven

Island, pop. 1,500. The message on her answering machine sets the

tone for her current life: "You've reached the rustic but scenic

boathouse of Julie Brown. Hard tellin' where I am. Probably I'm

up to my butt in fish bait . . ."

My job is all about flow,

Julie

ebb and flow. I live in an old boathouse. It's about twenty by thirty feet. It's built on posts and at high tide it's located maybe five feet from the ocean. During a storm the ocean comes up onto my lawn.

Vinalhaven Island is a big piece of granite in the middle of the ocean. I can hear the waves crashing and the wind blowing. And when I get caught in the grip of a northeast blow with forty-to-sixty-mile-per-hour winds, the wind blows under my house and it shakes. I rent this house and it has no running water, so I get my water from a spigot downtown. It's primitive. To take a hot shower, I heat the water on the stove and put it into a twenty-gallon plastic container. Then this boat bilge pump that's powered by a car battery pumps it through a hose with a little plastic showerhead. I try to shower every day. I smell terrible from the fish bait.

When I was a little girl I always wanted to be a pilot. I pursued that fiercely and soloed on my sixteenth birthday. I was in a program called the Civil Air Patrol. It's kind of like the junior air force. The summer I was sixteen I was chosen as the young person from Maine to go to Laughlin Air Force Base in Texas. We went through undergraduate pilot training with a class of fighter pilots. I have a picture of myself standing beside a T-38 fighter trainer. Life was wonderful. I was totally convinced that I wanted to be an Air Force fighter pilot. At the time, there weren't women fighter pilots, and I've always liked challenges. I'm very much a tomboy.

At twenty-one, I got my commercial pilot's license, but I didn't graduate from college because my grandmother had Alzheimer's and I wanted to come home to take care of her. While I was home, I was waitressing and putting out résumés. I wanted to fly Medevac, like Life Flight, where I might pick up a sick child at one hospital and fly her to a different hospital. I thought the state police would be a good place to start doing something like that. I'd just passed my physical fitness test, my written exam, and my oral boards to fly for the Maine Police Academy. It wasn't where I was going to end up, but it was a steppingstone. Then I had the accident, and that kind of shot that in the butt.

Since I'm head-injured I remember nothing about this, about flying, period. I lost all memory of anything prior to the accident. My parents have shown me pictures and I kept a diary, so I know about this, but I don't remember it.

At the time, I was waitressing at China Hill, a restaurant in the next town. I was headed to work at the restaurant. It was in January. There was a big snowstorm, a lot of slush and ice underneath the slush. The roads were extremely slippery. I was twenty-three and I was in a brand-new two-door Ford EXP, a light front-wheel-drive, cute little car. My first car I ever bought. It wasn't a year old. I started sliding, and coming down over the top of this hill was a truck loaded with cement. Because he was so heavy the road didn't feel that slippery to him, but he couldn't avoid me. I wasn't thrown from the car since I had my seat belt on; they think the sunroof, instead of popping out, popped down, and I impacted with it.

I had three stitches. That's it. I had no broken bones. I simply had massive head trauma. I was in a coma, and they wouldn't lay odds on my survival.

After a month and a half, I came out of the coma. I was tucked tightly in a fetal position and was very much like a child. Lying in bed in rehab, I overheard a neuropsychologist tell my mother that she should consider putting me in an institution. Mom said they were so happy to have me they'd gladly deal with anything because they loved me. I think deep down, even though I wasn't good at the time, that gave me an incredible amount of strength. My parents never faltered in their support. That's a debt I can never repay. A lot of families aren't close like that, and that's sad. I was also very lucky. A lot of people with extensive head injuries don't recover as completely as I have.

I had to be taught to walk and talk and do everything—tie my shoes, tell time, eat. I couldn't sit up without being tied to a chair. I could track my progress. I could say to my mother, "Momma, I feel about three today." And before long, "I feel about ten today." I went through all the stages of childhood again, right through puberty. The whole nine yards. It's amazing, the power of the brain.

After I was released from the hospital, to get out of the house and to start functioning on my own a bit, as part of my therapy I'd go lobstering with this man. He was an older man who adored me. It was like going to haul with your father. I couldn't drive, so Mom would take me down. That winter he took two divers scallop diving. I'd always loved the water, and I grew up pretty much on the water. I loved to get on that boat, a thirty-two-foot classic fiberglass lobster

When I took that first tentative breath underwater, the air came out so sweet and so easy.

boat, and help with the divers. I'd run around with a towel and dry their faces.

I saw what the divers made and thought it would be wonderful to have a job where you earn that kind of money. What they make depends on the weather, visibility, how many tanks of air they dive, how they're feeling, and if they swim into a mess of scallops or not. But usually it's several hundred dollars per day. I was back at the restaurant, making in the ballpark of $6.50 an hour. I was hostessing because the manager thought it would be easier for me to seat people

and not have to remember all the things on the menu and their prices.

By the end of the season, it's a six-month season, I said to the divers, "Next year I'm going to be a diver." "Oh, yeah, right," they chuckled.

Fishing in Maine is a traditional male industry. There were no women divers in my area. It's difficult to break into as a woman, especially if your father doesn't fish, or your boyfriend doesn't fish. It's hard to stand on your own two feet and jump in all alone.

I took lessons to get certified as a diver. I was in a swimming pool with my class, and the first time I took a breath off a tank with a regulator, it was a total rush. Because, you see, when you're underwater your brain is saying, Hold your breath. That's what you're always taught. When I took that first tentative breath underwater, the air came out so sweet and so easy. I loved it immediately.

It became an all-consuming desire, a passion. And I felt better about myself under the water than I did on the surface. Underwater, you see, the fish didn't care that I was head-injured. On land, I was aware that everybody was comparing me to who I was before the accident, someone I couldn't even remember. I had people say, "Hi, Julie," and I didn't know who they were. I'd get teary and confused and scared. My mom encouraged me to say, "I've had a terrible accident. Please forgive me, but I don't remember who you are." Some people would say, "Of course you know me. Guess!" That was horrifying. I couldn't guess. I'd never seen that person before. In fact, I had, because they were my next-door neighbor.

I became a certified diver and when the season opened, I was right there. That was November 1, 1987. I'd gone to the bank and taken out a loan for $2,000. I had my own mask and snorkel and fins, and the loan paid for an Arctic dive suit, weight belt, four tanks, and my BC [buoyancy compensation] vest.

I was very, very excited and sure I was going to swim into all kinds of scallops, like I'd seen on the boat the winter before. That first day I dove three tanks of air, shallow, like thirty to forty feet, and got seven scallops all day long. I was so fascinated by the bottom that I couldn't see the scallops. I was having a wonderful time. However, seven scallops won't pay many bills.

With those seven scallops I was thinking, Oh, no, I've made a terrible mistake. But I loved diving, so I knew I had to put in the effort to be good at it. By the end of the season I was averaging forty-five to fifty pounds, bringing home $150 to $200 a day.

Now I can pretty much hold my own. I'm not the best diver, and I don't bring in the most scallops. It depends on how the scalloping is, what kind of bottom I find—meaning is it sand, is it mud, is it a big shelf, is it a rocky ledge?

It was rough getting accepted by the guys. I was called a lot of unflattering names, like bitch, the whole nine yards, the nasty stuff. A lot of guys wouldn't have me on their boat because a woman on a boat's bad luck. I was still diving for the old man, but if we saw someone out there we knew and pulled alongside to chat, I couldn't step on the other boat.

The other divers told me that if I was going to whine and bellyache I could stay home. I took that seriously, and once when I broke my arm, I didn't say boo. That day my mother was with me because she used to come and watch and make sure I was okay. I slipped in the boat and broke my arm in two places. Because of the head injury, I have a high tolerance for pain, and I kept diving. All I knew was, Boy, I've really given myself a good bang, and it was difficult reaching with that arm to pick the scallops up. But, you see, I didn't whine on the boat. I was afraid if I said anything they

A lot of guys wouldn't have me on their boat because a woman on a boat's bad luck.

wouldn't let me come again. It wasn't until Mom and I were on our way home that I decided I ought to have my arm checked out. I was sick to my stomach, my arm hurt so bad. My car was standard and Mom couldn't drive it, so I drove to the hospital, and was that awful.

I didn't let them put a cast on because I couldn't dive with a cast. After some lengthy discussions in the E.R., they agreed to put on a plaster half-splint that I could take on and off.

I didn't go back to that boat where the guys said, "Don't whine." I went to another boat where the guy said, not thinking I'd ever dive with a broken arm, "You can get on this boat if you can put your dive suit on all alone." The wrist seals are very tight, and I had to really drive my arm in. It brought tears to my eyes but I toughed it out. Once I was in the water the pressure made the arm okay.

On a typical scalloping day I'm on the boat by six o'clock. We head out, sometimes in the dark, to where we're going to dive. The air temperature can be anywhere from in the thirties to the teens. The water temperature's probably in the low thirties. There's a barrel with hot water on the boat so we can warm our hands, or you can get into the barrel and warm your whole body. A lot of times when we're diving, ice cakes are floating on the surface around us. It's very, very cold. Without hot water on the boat I personally couldn't stand it. The dive gear covers everything but my cheeks, and they don't have much feeling. Sometimes when I come up my face is blue. But it's not so bad that I can't stand it. Weather permitting, I dive as much as I can—four to seven hours, sometimes seven days a week.

I love it down there. The serenity and the beauty. The thing I like the most is that you don't hear anything and there's this fluid motion of the plants swaying with the sea, and the colors are muted but beautiful. If you take the time to look around, it's like being a guest in another world.

I came to Vinalhaven Island on a boat with a bunch of divers in the winter five years ago. I'd been diving and making money at it six months of the year, but the other six months I'd been working in restaurants and I hated it. All I did was talk about my diving and how I couldn't wait to get back to the ocean. I wanted to work on the water year-round. In the summer in Maine, that's lobstering. And Vinalhaven has some of the best fishermen in the state. They go at it hard, and they're serious. I came to a place where I could learn how to do this. It's very much like going to school to learn how to fish. Because it's an island and the workforce out here is smaller, their choice of who they're going to take on a boat is limited. The guys were more receptive to having a woman. I was lucky to get a stern site my first year.

That means I worked the back of the boat. The captain drives the boat, picks up the buoy, puts it through what's called a pot hauler, like a winch, brings the trap aboard, and slides it down the side of the boat to the sternman. The sternman takes the lobsters out, dumps the old bait, rebaits the trap, picks out the sea urchins and trash, and slides it to the very back end of the boat. When you've picked up all the traps for an area, you start setting them back in the water. That's what a sternman does.

I'm not a lobsterwoman, a lobsterperson. I'm a lobster-man. A fisherman. A sternman. They're just words. I never got caught up in that jargon.

I started to set up something like a college syllabus for myself of things I wanted to learn that would make me a more well-rounded fisherman. I haven't gone yet, but I have a chance to go on one of the herring carriers and watch them catch the fish we use to bait the lobster traps. Right now I'm working at a lobster-buying station because I want to see that end of the business. Although I took a drastic cut in pay from what I made sterning, I can still pay my bills, and I'm learning an awful lot.

This year I'm hauling my lobster traps by hand in a twelve-foot rowboat. I have seventeen traps on seventeen separate lines. I row probably half a mile and if the wind's blowing, it's choppy. The other day I was rowing, and my little rowboat was taking water over the stern. It was rough. But it's a way for me to gain respect.

Normally people fish where they're from. I was born in Surry, up the coast two hours from here. I have a birthright to fish the waters around Surry, but I have no birthright to fish in Vinalhaven. But here there are so many lobstermen who can teach me, where in Surry there are only four or five lobster guys, and they do it as a sideline. Here, that's what they do—they lobster. They make a whole year's pay in the spring–summer–fall. They go hard and don't have time for foolishness.

It's taken me five years to set traps here, and if I were here for the rest of my life I'd never be able to fish more than two hundred–three hundred traps. What I want is to have a thirty-six-foot brand-new lobster boat with eight hundred to a thousand traps. I can never grow to that point here. I'd have to go back to Surry.

When I get my first big boat it'll be called *Grandpa's Legacy*. In my family the only one who ever fished was my great-grandfather, and he fished all his life. He was a very old man when I got to know him, and we had conversations about fishing and the ocean. Somewhere deep inside I think he knew I had that love.

MEGAN GLOUNER, b.1965,
high-tech contract worker

Megan had no idea how her liberal arts education (French/art) would translate into a career in a high-tech world. After working in marketing communications, she landed at Microsoft. She's a new breed of worker: a professional full-time temp. People who work this way can also be called contract employees, independent contractors, part-timers, freelancers, leased employees, contingent workers. Whatever the name, Megan describes how this work that was once considered low-status—a last resort in between jobs—has become mainstream, and how it suits a mom like herself with a preschool daughter.

Megan

my dad came to this country from Ireland and started from absolute scratch. From him I learned that you're a fool and a lazy slacker if you don't take advantage of everything that's available here.

At fourteen, I had my own paper route for eighty-five dollars a month. Right when I graduated from high school, I got a summer job at Philadelphia Steak 'n' Sub, a deli. I scrubbed toilets, bussed tables, washed floors, and took out the garbage. I never, like, rose to the lofty position of fry cook or cashier, which I could have handled. It was awful, but I was making my own money.

After I graduated from college [Scripps], I tried so hard to get into advertising. I interviewed with every single agency in Seattle and most in Los Angeles. In the meantime I sold shoes at J.C. Penney, where they expected you to give up your whole life to sell a ten-dollar pair of Keds.

After trying for a year to get into advertising, I thought, I've got to get started. At a telecommunications company, this guy, bless his heart—he was like a guardian angel—hired me. I was happy to have my first real job, but humiliated to be a secretary. I'm embarrassed to say this because now I have the utmost respect for secretaries, but on Secretary's Day when people came by my desk with flowers, I said, "Please! I'm not a secretary. I'm an administrative assistant." I've grown up a bit since then and have learned that you're no better than anything you haven't done before. Even if you have a college degree, you can't just jump in at the higher-level jobs. You gotta start at the bottom, and that was a real rude awakening for me.

With "secretary" tattooed on your forehead, you are totally pigeonholed. I was sitting there, making $18,000 a year [1990], and thinking, This is not going to cut it. My husband and I went through a lot of thinking, and I read the book *What Color Is Your Parachute?* I was drawn to marketing because it drew upon my strong communications skills. My husband convinced me that a job in sales could be a springboard to where I wanted to go in

My girlfriends and I have always talked about how you can make work work for you.

marketing. For one awful year I was a sales rep selling pagers. But there's something that you gain from just being in the workforce. It isn't even actually skills, but just how to conduct yourself in different situations.

Exactly one year later, I got my big break: a marketing job with a high-tech government contractor. Finally, at twenty-six, I had arrived. I had my own office, and I was like a high-powered career woman, working until seven-thirty every night. I could make a contribution. I could talk to people, not as their subordinate, but as their equal.

My girlfriends and I have always talked about how you can make work work for you. After I had my baby, I went through an introspective time. My friend Marni, a graphic designer, said, "Don't worry. You'll find your way."

When Madeleine was five months old, I was ready to go back to work, but I did not want to go through a big drawn-out job search. I hate looking for full-time employment, hate sitting in a room and begging for a job. I went to a job fair here in Seattle and left my résumé with a firm that specializes in placing high-tech professionals in temporary positions. I was so ho-hum about the interview with the agency that I didn't even get dressed up because it was "just a temp agency." When they called me with this perfect marketing job at Microsoft, I was like, Wow! This is exciting! Two weeks later I was working at Microsoft as a contract employee.

Microsoft's so cool. I work forty hours a week, make good money, and have total control over my time. (Maybe I'd be a little bit more worried if my husband didn't have medical benefits.) This way of working gives you that extra freedom, and also gives you a chance to be in control of your time and your career path. If you find the work's not challenging anymore, or you've gained some new skills, you can start something new, get a different contract on a new project.

CAROL WIOR, b. 1948,
fashion designer

NIKI WIOR, b. 1973,
fashion designer

A self-made woman, Carol turned $77 and three sewing machines in her parents' garage into a multimillion-dollar business in the garment industry. She holds a U.S. patent on Slimsuit, an engineered swimsuit that was honored in the Smithsonian's "Mothers of Invention Tour." Her success— her company manufactures over a million swimsuits a year—carved out a path for her daughter to enter the business.

CAROL: When I was

Carol & Niki

small, like three or four, I truly wanted to be somebody. Somebody famous.

I always have. I was never comfortable with anything you might call normal or regular. I remember telling my father that when I went to work I wanted to walk into an elevator and the lady, she'd be wearing a pillbox hat, she'd say, "Good morning, Miss Weddell." I'd seen that in a movie and I liked the respect people who worked in offices received.

In grade school I wanted to be in the fashion industry and open up a boutique, which I ended up doing, and actually, that's how I ended up in manufacturing. I didn't end up going to college. I was very motivated. I thought I'd get a jump on it and by the time my friends got out of college, I'd have four years on them. If I had to do it over, I'd highly recommend going to college because I paid dearly in mistakes for my lack of education.

My first job was working at a bank. I started out as a receptionist and got promoted to secretary. One day I was picking at the keys on the typewriter and thinking, Is this what I want to do for the rest of my life? No. I loved clothes. I thought it would be so glamorous and wonderful to work in fashion.

I started looking for a job in that field. I applied at Lerner Shops and got a job as an assistant buyer. One day I went with a buyer to visit a manufacturer. I liked the industry but I thought it was retail that I liked. As we were sitting in the showroom—like right now you can hear the machines out there going *bzz, bzz, bzz*—I said to the manufacturer, "What's that sound?" He said, "That's the factory." I said, "Can I see it?" He was shocked that I wanted to go out into the factory instead of sitting in the elegant showroom. I went into the factory and that was the lightbulb. I said, "Oh, my goodness, you have all this? This is so exciting!"

I still love to hear the sound of the machines. It's like music to my ears. There's something about the excitement of watching the garment being passed from machine to machine, from sewer to sewer, and all the intrigue of it. The intrigue of starting out with a piece of fabric and turning it into something somebody can put on their body and wear. The intrigue of watching your idea go from the initial concept in your head, and then watching it being manufactured, and then watching it go through your shipping department, and then watching it go out the door. And the next thing people are buying it and you say, "Wow!" I love it.

In the garment industry you can be a buyer, a manufacturer, or a retailer. My original concept was that I'd open a chain of boutiques and do the manufacturing for my own boutiques. As I look back now, that was a pretty ridiculous idea. It's hard enough just to open up a retail store, and it's hard enough just to manufacture, but to try and do both at one time is pretty outrageous.

I opened up this boutique out in the middle of nowhere in San Dimas. I couldn't afford Beverly Hills rent, so unfortunately I went to an area I could afford, but there weren't any customers. Within six months I ended up closing.

It was disappointing—very—but before I went out of business I started manufacturing. I had an item—a ladies' caftan—that sold very well. I thought, I'm sitting in this store, waiting for these people to walk in and buy something. Why don't I make these caftans and sell them to the big department stores?

I did what I've done all of my career in the garment industry—I saw a need. I didn't really like the caftans because I couldn't really understand them. I personally was not a caftan customer, but it was a way to get in.

My parents had a garage and they allowed me to put three sewing machines in there. The original deposit into my company bank account was all the money I had: $77. I hired some ladies that could sew. I called on Lerner's and they said they'd take 120 pieces. I was so excited. I couldn't hand-cut 120 pieces, so I called this man who had a cutting/contracting service and asked if he'd be interested in going into business with me. He laughed and said, "Maybe we should have lunch first?" We went to lunch and I said, "Here's what we'll do. Somehow I'll get the money. I'll design the items. I'll sell them and deal with the customers. You run the inside and see that we ship it and produce it." We shook hands on it and became partners. I was probably twenty-two.

He had a Quonset hut he was operating out of. Within maybe six months, we needed a bigger building. We'd just signed a lease on a much larger space when he said he didn't like the business and wanted out. I was devastated and so frightened. I thought my whole life was over.

My first major year in business was crazy: my partner

left, I got married to Niki's father, became pregnant with Niki, and they discovered a tumor in my breast they thought was malignant, so they wanted to induce labor. I was living on such a shoestring that I could hardly afford to eat, let

CAROL: I did what I've done all of my career in the garment industry— I saw a need.

alone be doing all of this. But I was lucky. The tumor was benign and I had a healthy baby. I was very, very fortunate.

Niki's dad and I divorced shortly after that and I was a single mom for about six years. I tried to be a good parent. I always felt guilty having to leave her, having to make business trips. And she was an only child so she didn't have any brothers or sisters to play with at home. Because of that a lot of the time she went with me. I'd simply call my customers and say, "I don't think it'll be a problem, but may I bring my daughter to a meeting or two?" A lot of them were working mothers themselves. They understood. But really, a lot of the men were terrific about my having a three-year-old accompany me. She'd have her coloring book and be doing her thing while I'd be selling.

The next six years, from when I was twenty-three to twenty-nine, I did extremely well. By the time I was thirty I'd made enough money on the caftans and a simple black dress that the Millionaires' Club asked me to join. (I was shipping a million dollars in volume.)

I was making dresses and dabbling in swimwear when a customer I knew—actually her husband was a dress buyer of mine, and she was a swimwear buyer—said she was going to Hawaii on business and said, "Why don't you go with me?"

I was on vacation but my real motive was to get fresh ideas. I was on the beach and saw all these people in swimsuits, and they weren't comfortable. I went to one of the large department stores on the island and introduced myself.

NIKI: I wanted to do young stuff for skateboarders and surfers—that's my target audience.

I said, "I'm thinking about doing some swimwear. Do you care if I hang out in the department? I'd like to hear what people have to say." The woman said, "Fine, go ahead." I listened and took notes.

The next day at the pool my suit was riding up in back,

and I was trying to hold my stomach in, and I was tugging on the front of the leg. I looked around and everybody else was pulling and tugging and was really unhappy. I went up to the room right away. I had the thought, What if I took a piece of elastic and stretched it around my body to hold my stomach in? It would hold my buttocks up a bit, and what if I put in underwires, instead of big hard snowcone cups? I couldn't wait to get back to L.A.

I made over a hundred prototypes and it was not working. The problem was that I had two different stretches—an inside of 22 percent Lycra™, with a different stretch fabric on the outside—and I couldn't stabilize the bra. I had pattern makers tell me, "Forget it. It's impossible."

I'd read an article on Henry Ford and it said that when he was inventing, I believe it was the V-6 or V-8 engine, his engineers said, "Forget it, Mr. Ford. It won't work." He said, "It's got to work," and he kept sending them back to the board. One night at about two in the morning, I was lying in bed and I was thinking about this. I was so close, and then the solution dawned on me. The next morning I redid the work of the technician, and bingo! The suit was incredible.

At the same time, my dad had become very ill and was dying. In his primary business he was a general contractor, but he was always coming up with ideas, inventing new things. My getting a patent on the Slimsuit was really in honor of him, because he'd never had a patent. When I applied for my patent I found out that of all the patents only four percent are obtained by women.

NIKI: I remember being young and traveling with my mom and loving what she did and wanting to do what she did. I loved going to the fashion shows and watching her things coming down the runway and knowing that it was my mom, and I was sitting right next to her. And the applause, I loved it. I'd be in meetings with her, listening and trying to be quiet and behave, and she'd run around in her suit and was all-powerful. She'd take me to dinners after the meetings. I'd be out all night long with her and up early in the morning. She'd order room service. I'd get hot chocolate and pancakes and then we'd go off to the showrooms. It was a lot of fun.

CAROL: I wanted Niki to be a brain surgeon. I didn't want her to be in this business because I didn't want her to have all the crazy pressures I have. In another sense, you know, you're building something and you think, Gee, who am I going to leave this to?

The fashion industry's a lot of pressure and very little glamour. Time goes very fast. The clock's always ticking. You're doing delivery date to delivery date, deadline to deadline. Buyers are calling asking where's their shipment. No matter how good you are, no matter how terrific your people are, there's all these crazy little emergencies.

When Niki was nine I'd designed this solid-black swimsuit and it was a huge seller. I brought it home and said, "Niki, you know what would be beautiful, if we did something hand-painted on this suit." She sat down and drew a Hawaiian orchid. I sent it out and had it screened, and within six months that was a 65,000-unit suit.

NIKI: I think I was younger than nine. It was at nighttime and she was in her usual mode of having sketching paper spread out across the kitchen table and trying to design. She'd designed her wedding invitation and it had an orchid on it. I thought it was the most beautiful thing I'd ever seen. I said, "Why don't we put that on the swimsuit?" Even then she was very supportive, like, "Show me, Niki. Do it, Niki." I don't know how I knew how to do it—probably because I was always drawing. She was always drawing and I just wanted to be like her.

CAROL: Niki got caught in the middle of my second divorce and funds were just ridiculous. I was penniless for about six months. In 1991 I had to start the business over from scratch. Niki didn't have the money to go to college, so she started out here with me, helping out.

NIKI: We hadn't actually nailed it down where I was going to college, but all my friends were going to Wisconsin and I didn't want to be left behind here in L.A. But I didn't have the heart to leave my mom. She'd been there for me my whole life, so the one time she might ever really need me, I couldn't leave.

Money was very tight and I had no friends left here, so I just started going to work with Mom every day. I started with order entry. I was saying, Okay, we have ten thousand suits on order here and nine thousand suits there. The wrong job for me. I was way off. Then I repped her line. I'd make appointments with each store to bring her line down and show it. It was pretty much trial and error, figuring out what I wanted to do. I started working in design with a dress. It has the same patent as the Slimsuit. It was like Mom said, "I don't have anyone to design this. Design it."

I wanted to do something a little more junior, more my customer. My mom's customer is contemporary missy. Missy's a middle-aged woman, usually a mom although it doesn't have to be. Contemporary's a young working woman. I was eighteen. I wanted to do young stuff for skateboarders and surfers—that's my target audience.

The transition came when a bikini company went out of business. For years they'd made the cutest little swimsuits. I told my mom that there was a niche in the market. She knew the line I was talking about, a line my girlfriends and I wore all the time. Right then people at the conference table were like, "Niki, why don't you do something?" I was like, "Yeah, why don't I do something?" Everyone was asking, "What are you going to call your line?" Little Hazel—my pug—was sitting right there and I said, "Hazel!" It all came together in like four minutes. (The dog's so confused now because everyone's always saying her name.)

Hazel's very young and fun and junior. I bring in crazy, wacky things. A '60s-style bikini brief that looks like a boy's Speedo with FOXY written in rhinestones across the rear. And I made swimsuits like little girls' underwear with ruffles on the butt, like we used to wear. Mom looked at them and went, "They look like little girls' underwear." I said, "That's right!" She may not like it, she may not get it, but she tries.

Hazel was launched in 1993. My first and second years were a lot of fun. There were some frustrations because it didn't take off right off the bat. And because I had such a large shovel—I had my mom behind me—I dug my hole very deep. The hole's pretty much a debt, fabric-wise—hundreds of thousands of dollars. You have to order three thousand yards of fabric, minimum. I can probably make fifty thousand swimsuits with that, especially my teeny-tiny bikinis. Mom makes missy swimsuits and they take a yard of fabric.

Mine, I can fit five in a yard. I should have known this, I guess. I don't know how I didn't. But I do now.

Being the boss's daughter isn't easy. I think maybe you lose the respect of other people because they think the door's been opened for you. And it has. So, you fight other battles you wouldn't have to fight.

CAROL: Niki doesn't take advantage of me. With Niki, it's almost reversed. Like yesterday, she was in my office and she started to cry. I said, "What's the matter?" She said, "I just can't wait until I can have my own building and be on my own one hundred percent." I said, "Your own building? Don't you like it here? I love having you. I like looking at your face—"

NIKI: —until I got my lip ring. I pierced my lip, just three weeks ago. My mother's mortified. It's going to look better as soon as it starts healing.

I want to be really independent. I mean, everything's run the way my mom wants it run. Like if we have to share a showroom together at one of the shows, it's decorated the way she wants it decorated. We have two different markets. My buyers walk right by her stuff and wouldn't even think Hazel's in there. Like there I am, trying to be cutting edge, and I'm sitting in a tiki thing with Mom. It's like, my mom's been designing swimsuits for a long time and she's never had a swimsuit in *Sports Illustrated*. I had three [February 1997]. That's like the Holy Grail for swimsuits.

A million people would kill to be in my situation, I'm sure. But after Hazel grows, I've talked to my mom, and I'm going to do my own thing. She doesn't realize how much more proud she'll be of me when I succeed on my own.

COLONEL JEAN PEPPLE, b. 1938,
auctioneer

Jeannie bloomed right where she was planted on a farm in

Pennsylvania and forged her path alongside her husband. I

found her in the auction barn kitchen doing double duty as cook,

stirring a pot of ham stew. "It's for the auction people tonight,"

she said. "They're country and they like a good ol' homemade

ham pot pie." At a sale Colonel Jean starts off describing an item

in her regular voice. "Green sofa. Splits in two. Good for an

apartment, girls." Then she takes off like a racehorse, electrifying

the audience with her voice and personality.

Jeannie

i was born up here at this farm, in that house. So I'm almost back where I started. We worked on the farm, my mom, my dad, and myself. We had cows to milk and there'd be field work to do. I think what is good is that we all growed up together as a family, where today I don't think you have that. I was really close to my dad. I'd get in the truck and ride with him wherever he went.

When I was in high school I got a job as a nurse's aide at our local medical center when it opened up. I loved it. I always wanted to be a nurse. In between all this I had a baby boy and that sort of put a damper on me going on to college to be a nurse. I stayed with my grandma and she helped me. I'd get up in the morning and make my formula and then I'd go to school and play basketball. I kept on playing basketball. I never let that ruin my life.

A few years later, when Pete and I married, there was no work here on the farm, so we went to Bristol, which is right out of Philadelphia. I could hardly handle it. I was so homesick I called home every day. I don't think I had the friendliness there that we do here. The neighbors couldn't have cared less who I was. I'd keep all the blinds in the house closed because I just had a fear of living

It's not an easy job to be up there and holler.

in the city. Pete worked for U.S. Steel until my father had the heart attack. With two farms and his health like that, my mom said she was going to sell this farm. I said, "I'm coming home."

We came back and had 182 acres. I says, "What are we going to do for a living?" And Pete said, "Let's turn the barn, since we're not using it"—we had no cattle or nothing—"let's turn it into an auction barn."

In Bristol we'd had sort of a routine. I gave my kids a bath in the evening and put them in bed, and Pete would go down the road to a little auction. He'd come back with maybe a little crock—I have the first one he ever bought. He loved to dig in and get a crock or a piece of furniture that could get to look cute in your house and that didn't cost a fortune, because we were pinching pennies.

to waitress, hostess, and I loved to cook. I'd go in there when they needed me until we got our business going. I started with Mr. Culler as a clerk, writing the items down as he called them off and collecting the money, which is just as important, almost, as the auctioneering.

We started seeing our auctions were going to go good. Pete says to me one night, "Why don't you go to auctioneer's school?" That was a Thursday and he says, "The

That's what got it in our heads to start this, when we came home and had no job. Pete took a survey by looking in Chambersburg, which is twenty-five miles over the mountain. "If they can have a sale, why can't we have a sale?" That's what got him.

We had a gentleman, Mr. John Culler, a fabulous auctioneer, call sales for us. I'd been working off and on since high school at the Howard Johnson's. It was on the Pennsylvania Turnpike and it wasn't far because there was a shortcut through the woods. I loved working in food. I loved

school doesn't start out in Kansas City, Missouri, until Sunday night." We do things like that. On the spur of the minute, without thinking for two months what you're going to do. This was twenty-one years ago, in 1975.

Within two days I was on my first plane flight to Kansas City. Another thing that's sort of strange is that there were only four women and two hundred men in the class. I didn't know anybody. But I'm a person who's never met a stranger. So I just smiled, and of course I had a room away from everybody else because of being a girl.

Every person's just as important if they have a sale that's worth $30,000, or if their mother's stuff is only going to bring $1,000.

The first day of class you learn a tongue-twister. I talk fast anyhow, so that helped me a lot:

Betty Bawter bought some butter but she says this butter's bitter. If I put it in my batter, it will make my batter bitter. So she bought a bit of better butter, put it in her bitter batter, so 'tis better Betty Bawter bought a bit of better butter.

I called home and told Pete this tongue-twister on the telephone, which blowed his mind. I practiced night and day until I learned it. I figure if anybody wants to do something bad enough they'll do it.

I learned my chant by going, "I made a one-dollar bid, to two-dollar bid, to bid three, to bid three, to four . . ." You get a rhythm. At school I was so wound up I don't think for two weeks I ever got tired.

In the state of Pennsylvania you must apprentice under an auctioneer for a year. When I came home from school, there was a farm sale up the road. The gentleman I was apprenticing under, Mr. Culler, who worked for us, said, "Why don't you get up there and call?"

Legally, I was not allowed to do that. All I did was get on top of an old farm wagon—I'll never forget this—and the first thing I sold was a three-prong pitchfork. The guys were fabulous. They bid more money than it was worth. Any little tool, I sold it. They bid, bid, bid. The hands just flew. That made me happy because it gave me confidence. I was the first woman auctioneer in three counties.

I love being an auctioneer onstage. Up there you've got control. What I mean by that is you've got to get control of your whole audience. You've got to be the person to keep their interest. You've got to be a little bubbly. You can't be a person that doesn't get up in the morning and get with the program. It's not an easy job to be up there and holler. Your voice has got to hold up for a lot of hours. But it's a career that'll last you a lifetime. There's always going to be sales.

Of course, I know a lot of people by name. I recognize them sometimes when they walk in by saying, "Hi, John, it's nice seeing you tonight," and I keep on going. They like to be honored and acknowledged. After you're in this for so long you just about know all your faces. You're the person they're looking at, too. And I tell you what, they look you over from A to Z. They'll say, "Oh, I love those earrings. They're real pretty." I have a complex that at all times I want to look my best.

I get my hair done at six A.M., so I can be in the beauty

parlor and be back here to the barn and open up before any-body's missed me. It really is a 1950s hairdo, an upsweep with curls on the top. The reason my hair's like this is I can be mowing my grass and an attorney calls to make an appointment to meet a family for a sale. I have to be in a suit and look like I've never had to do any labor work. In an hour I can look completely reversed.

What I like best about the job is when you're working with people who are very depressed because they've lost a loved one. We're called out to their house to appraise a mother's items. You have to know how to handle a family. There's a little bit of tension because this girl thought she should have that, and that person thought he should have that. You have to go in and comfort them and be their friend, as well as be the person that sells the things most precious to them. It's a little more than you see, being an auctioneer. Every person's just as important if they have a sale that's worth $30,000, or if their mother's stuff is only going to bring $1,000.

I love it when the phone rings and they say, "We'd like you to come look at our items." To Pete and me that's won-derful. We love to rummage through clunky old barns and tell them what they have. We try to be as truthful as we can, and try not to take the best stuff and not the junk.

We outgrew the first auction barn. People stood up out-side and couldn't get in. The new place has a seating capacity of five hundred, and we do fill it up. Our audience comes from all over. Some of the people are from the city and they have got cabins back here, summer cottages. And when we don't have a sale they just drive us crazy. That's something

for them to do, to get up here, bring their friends. It's a recreation for a lot of them.

Pete is the honcho of the auction, and he loves that auction barn so good he's got his TV out there, he's got his coffeepot on, and he works in that auction, barn seven days a week.

We keep adding on and adding on. I turned the barnyard into Kobweb Korner. Think of an old farm barn, upstairs and downstairs completely carpeted and paneled with smalls, small items plus furniture. And we built a miniature golf course, Barnyard Golf. That was Pete's idea to supple-ment if the auctions are slow or the shop's not real busy. I also cook for the people who come to the auction. I learned how to work the grill so good at Howard Johnson's.

I really should have someone to help me in the office because I work awful hours. The phone never quits ringing, and I do all the bookwork. The auction's just a small part. When the sale's over then the clerks and the cashier stay until everybody's checks are done, and sometimes we're here until two A.M. There really isn't enough hours of the day for me. I run myself thin. Everyone keeps saying to me, "You can't keep it up." I had an eighty-one-year-old great-grandmother that washed the windows in our house out on the roof of the house. She was active until she passed away. I think I'm going to be just like her. I'm just going to go until I can't go no more.

JANET MARIE SMITH, b. 1957,
urban developer

Even on a winter's day when the baseball diamond is covered with snow, Oriole Park at Camden Yards in downtown Baltimore, which opened in 1992, looks friendly and inviting. How did Janet Marie's path lead to this field—a developer who works in sports? As she describes her life as an executive with the Orioles and the Braves, her suitcase stands nearby, ready to be scooped up for her weekly commute to Atlanta.

I tend to think of my work

Janet Marie

in terms of the results. And I've been very happy with the results.

It's a funny little role that I've carved out for myself. My job category doesn't fit neatly into a pocket. Architect is tempting because I have a degree in that field. But architect implies that you design and draw, and I don't. Even last week when we opened Turner Field I had to correct a TV reporter who said to me, thankfully before we went on the air, "I'm going to introduce you as the architect of the stadium." I said, "Let's get that right. I'm not." Yes, I'm an architect and maybe that's shorthand when someone's only got thirty seconds to do an interview, but it's inaccurate. And it does a disservice to the people who busted their tails doing all this other work to suggest that it's been a singular endeavor on my part just because I had the good fortune of being at the crux of the project.

Urban planner is also tempting because I have a degree in that, too. It cuts a little closer to what I do, but it doesn't address the full breadth of things I'm responsible for. If someone said to me, "She's an urban planner," I'd assume that she did master plans for different communities. I do one project at a time and I do the whole piece of it—from the design to planning to financing to occupancy.

In my world, project management, project director, are titles that are used frequently. Although those are the titles that people who work with me have. Real estate developer is good, except people who do real estate development, typically, are thought of as doing commercial work, and I don't do that. Sometimes I'm put in the category of sports executive. While that's accurate, I don't trade players. I don't negotiate contracts. Urban developer—there, maybe that's the term. That's closer. That's more accurate than architect or urban planner.

I've learned the strength and confidence and competence that I have now. As a little kid I was more like the ugly duckling. I wasn't the smartest, I wasn't the prettiest, and I wasn't the natural leader. I don't think I ever really knew what I was going to do. My organizational skills have always been good, though. I can remember going to the grocery store with my mother and I'd drive everybody crazy because I'd line up all the cans on the shelves. Organization has always been of paramount concern to me.

My father's an architect, and when I was a high school senior he was on the advisory board of the new school of architecture at Mississippi State. In the traditional rebellious mood of a seventeen-year-old, I didn't want to do what my dad did. So I refused to even consider architecture. I thought I was interested in engineering and art.

My dad suggested, strategically, but it was a wise suggestion, that I go up to Mississippi State—that's where I'd chosen to go to school—and take a look at both the art school and the engineering school. The art school was fine but there wasn't enough action for me. And the engineering school—it seemed so musty in that building that I couldn't fathom that that was the right path for me. The architecture school was pumping with energy. They had the music turned up and students were on the drawing boards. I was completely sold. The fact that this was a new school at Mississippi State, just one year old, gave it an energy that most schools of architecture don't have and most schools on Mississippi State's campus didn't have. I'd hit it at a critical moment, and there was a little pocket of energy that was just unbelievable.

Somewhere about my second year I knew I wasn't cut out to be an architect. My studio courses were almost always C's. I was never satisfied with my designs, so it made it difficult to commit to drawing them up. Even when I was satisfied with the design, the steps involved in drawing it up were so tedious. I hadn't thought about it until just this minute, but I realize now that's probably one of the reasons why what I do is good for me and why I do it well. I can look at a design someone else has produced and know whether it will result in a good building, and then while they're spending the next six days drawing it up, I can go and do a million other things. My preference is to snap my fingers and have it done.

Since there wasn't anything else I wanted to do, I was determined to go through the six years. There's the adage that the A students teach, and the B students work for the C students. I'm amused by that now, but it didn't seem so funny then. I mean, it was frustrating that things didn't come easily, and I was always up all night trying to complete what seemed like meaningless assignments.

What's truly important in all this was the summer I spent in New York City. I had a professor at Mississippi State, he taught the business and contractual end of architecture, and I excelled in that stuff. There I was in Starkville, Mississippi, which is about as far away, culturally, from New York as you can get, and I told this professor, who'd come from New York, that I wanted to go to New York. He wasn't a warm and fuzzy guy—he was a tough cookie, which is one of the reasons I liked him—and he taught me how to go about looking for a job.

I sent out a jillion letters with my résumé and followed up with phone calls and got three or four interviews out of those fifty or sixty letters I sent out. I ended up working in the marketing department of a huge architectural firm under the tutelage of an incredible woman, Katie Carton Hammer. She offered me the job sight unseen. Maybe she didn't think it was that big of a deal for a ninety-day intern. How bad could I be? Maybe that's the way she viewed it, but for me it was incredible.

One of the things that became crystal-clear to me that summer in New York was that the kind of thing I was interested in—the way cities come together—didn't happen because an architect conceived of a building and then developed designs and got it built. I was much more interested in the big picture of the city than in individual buildings. That is important because when I went back to New York after I graduated, I was able to say, "I don't want to work in an architect's office. I want to work on an urban development project." I was interested in civic spaces and their ability to play a role in revitalizing a city.

My first real job out of school was coordinator of architecture and design for Battery Park City. Probably nobody

else wanted the job, because who knew if that parcel of land—for years it had been a sandbox—was going to turn into anything? It was a ninety-two-acre landfill on the tip of lower Manhattan, and for twenty years they'd been doing master plans and having groundbreakings to try and get it off the ground.

I was madly in love with New York City, and I thought to be a part of building an appendage to the greatest city in the world was the most unbelievable thing that could have happened to me. I was exhilarated by it. I was twenty-three, but if I'd been fifty-five I would have been blown away.

In many ways getting a job like that is timing. Timing and place. Six months earlier the director wouldn't have been interested in hiring anyone for that role. Six months later it would have been filled. The projects I work on have a finite number of people you can put on a team, and they have a three-, four-, five-year cultivation time, so it's not like a law firm where the pressure grows and they add attorneys.

My job was to coordinate the master plan and design guidelines, which were done by an architectural firm, and translate them into design requirements for the developers. At the end of the day, the buck stopped with my boss—the director, Amanda Burden—not with me.

We wound up building what's now known as the World Financial Center, a million square feet of office space, and about two thousand units of housing, Rector Place Housing. If Battery Park had been a dead end I might have learned a lot, but people wouldn't have said, "Wow!" One thing that's been nice for me is that three of the four projects I've worked on have been built.

Toward the end of my work at Battery Park City I went to graduate school and got my master's in urban planning, which gave me the skills and the intellectual hunger to explore the financing and the real estate side of a development. The first time I had responsibility for those additional areas was at Pershing Square. It's a relatively small park—probably six to eight acres in the middle of downtown Los Angeles. I was eager to give L.A. a try. In '84 when I moved out there, the Olympics were there, and there was this great moment in time when L.A. seemed to have a chance to be a world-class city. So I was curious. What do you know? You're twenty-seven and you can afford to be curious about these things.

At Pershing Square my responsibilities grew from overseeing the design to also developing the financing, working on site issues and political issues that had to happen in order to pull it together.

After four years in L.A. I felt that what I cared about was more valued in older East Coast cities. You look at Boston, Philly, New York, Baltimore, cities that grew up in the 1700s, the 1800s, and they have an older fabric that they're interested in preserving. They come with this mind-set of treasuring that built environment and its translation into today's world. So I was eager to come back because I felt what I cared about professionally was here, somewhere here. I could go anywhere—it was just me and my kittycat.

This is sort of a little dream story. My husband Bart says there's something in this story that I'm not telling because it sounds too charming, but it's true. It was 1988 and I was flying to speak in Philadelphia at a conference on public park development. Before I went to Philly, I flew to Baltimore to watch the Orioles play the Yankees. I've always loved major league baseball. I didn't grow up loving it because they didn't have major league baseball in Mississippi, but by the time I lived in New York, I was going to a lot of Yankees games, a lot of Mets games. I loved the way that in baseball, more than in any other sport, it reflects the city and reflects people's attitudes.

So I flew to Baltimore. I'd always sort of liked Baltimore. The Braves, who were my favorite team, had terrible years in the '80s, and in 1988 the Orioles had a worse record than the Braves. (The Braves lost 106 games, the Orioles ended up losing 107.) I wanted to see the Orioles play in their home park the year that they were worse than the Braves. I went by myself.

I was there watching the game and I'd say, "I missed that play, how'd you score that play?" In the course of this, the people next to me said that the Orioles were going to be building a new park downtown. I thought, Gosh, I can't believe that. Every other team that's building a new stadium is going out to the suburbs. I put that away in the baseball/recreational side of my head.

I was back in L.A. and I knew that the Pershing Square project was going to end. I started looking to see what other projects were out there. One facet of my work that I think would cause most people concern is that I don't have a safety net. I finish a job and then I go to something else. That lack of security is a choice I've had to make in order to do the kinds of jobs that I do. It's a trade-off. I started thinking about the Orioles stadium project. I sent them a letter. I sent variations of that same letter to a lot of other people at different projects. I was ready for something different.

The first time I saw Camden Yards it was a railroad station with a lot of old warehouses. I interviewed with Larry Lucchino, he was a part owner and president of the Orioles, and he said, "We need some help, but does it really make any sense for you to come on staff for four years?" I said, "Yes, I do it all the time." He said, "You'd move to Baltimore?" I said, "Yes!"

Nobody ever said I had to fit into a box, and I believed it.

Larry wanted an old-fashioned urban ballpark that would be as magical as Forbes Field, or Ebbetts Field, or Fenway, or Wrigley. America loves specialists and I'd never worked in baseball, or in sports, so he was appropriately cautious. No one in baseball had built an old-fashioned park. In many ways Battery Park City had been a similar project for me. It was a new appendage to lower Manhattan, but it was designed to have the style of older New York neighborhoods. So I felt I'd been through that process before.

What was really exciting for me was when I realized that I could do what Larry wanted me to do. What he wanted had not been done before; the team at the table could do it with the right leadership, and I thought I could provide the information that would make that happen. He was the leader. Let me be real clear on that. I think of myself as more of a director and a facilitator, and I rely on my boss to lead it.

I'd been working there for not more than just a few weeks, and we had some real head-to-head conversations with the state authority that was acting as the developer about things that we considered fundamental to the success of the building if we were going to achieve our desire of being an old-fashioned urban ballpark. They ranged from the building siting, how it met the street, and particularly the steel structure. I wanted very badly for it to be a steel truss system, and the engineers who worked for the architect were equally adamant that there was no way to do that steel truss system within our budget. It either had to be a concrete system or post and beam. And so literally for weeks we debated that issue. I thought about it twenty-four hours a day. If we hadn't been able to do it that way I would have always felt we'd missed out on one of the fundamental features of the design that makes it as good a piece of architecture as it is. Certainly it's the single feature that's been mimicked by Cleveland, Denver, Arlington, Atlanta, and San Francisco. I mean, every baseball park that's been built since then has used exposed steel trusses, just like we did.

Opening Day was April 2, 1992, and I couldn't wait for the first game to be over. The thing that worried me the most was that somehow the pitcher would get on the mound and he'd say, "Holy Mackerel! Something's not right!" I couldn't think of what it might be because we'd done wind studies on the playing field to make certain that there wasn't any backlash off of the warehouse that would make it like Candlestick reversed. But until a first official

> There's a lot of people, even today, who assume that once you've become a mom it alters your ability to think straight.

game had been played, I wasn't certain it was going to be a major league park. The Orioles won the game. It was incredible. Rick Sutcliffe pitched a 2–0 shutout game.

That was a real honeymoon year for me. The ballpark opened in April and I got married in November. Bart loves baseball, too, and we'd dated during the time I was building the park, so we shared a lot of the struggles with it. I didn't think about how marriage would fit into my career. I saw a chance to spend my life with this incredible man, and we were hoping we could have a family.

In '93 I started going down to Atlanta periodically to work with the Braves on Turner Field while I was still finishing up with the Orioles. I was five months pregnant with my son when I was offered a full-time job as vice president of sports and entertainment facilities. I think that's a nice statement for women. There's a lot of people, even today, who assume that once you've become a mom it alters your ability to think straight.

My husband works in Baltimore, and it's important to me and to my family that I have one home. I don't live in two places. I live in Baltimore and work in Atlanta. On Tuesday mornings I usually leave my house at five A.M., and I can get to my office in Atlanta by eight o'clock. It's three hours door to door. I work there Tuesday through Thursday, and those are intense times. I'm in the office until midnight and I sleep next door at the hotel. Both of our children (ages one and three) go to day care in the mornings, and the three days I'm away a family friend picks them up and stays with them until my husband gets home. I have an office at home and work at home when I'm here in Baltimore on Mondays and Fridays. For my son, this is part of his routine: Mom goes to work, she'll call me tonight, Daddy will be home for dinner.

I don't pretend that this is an ideal scenario. I'm not sure there is any ideal scenario when you're a parent with a job. I mean that. I know that in terms of number of hours I probably spend as much or more time with my children as a mother who works in an office five days a week, nine to five. You work nine to five, you're gone eight to six, five days a week.

My marriage has put limitations on my career, but they're well worth the trade-off, and they're also welcome. I don't know how many of us really like living without bounds, and I like the bounds of my marriage and my family.

There are a lot of, let's call them alternative, or nontraditional, fields in architecture, and I think women and minorities are far quicker to find those. We've been brought up not feeling we are pigeonholed. If you listen to the way people, they don't mean it maybe, but they talk to young boys, they talk to young men, and say, "Do you want to be a doctor? Do you want to be a lawyer?" They talk to women, and it's a much broader spectrum of things they can do. That could be a blessing or a curse, depending on which way you look at it. But I think women are just brought up thinking they can do anything. They can be anything they want to be because there aren't any stereotypes, and if there are, they've been largely rejected by most professional women. So the world is just bigger and women are probably more creative about twisting things around, maybe out of necessity and maybe out of imagination. I think one reason all the jobs I've had have been self-defined is that nobody ever said I had to fit into a box, and I believed it.

k

KAITIE WEBNER, b. 1989,
second-grader

SARAH WEBNER, b. 1989,
second-grader

KAITIE: I thought we'd do the same thing because we're twins. But we decided we wanted to do different things. Sarah wants to be a dolphin trainer and I want to be a teacher.

SARAH: On career day I was hot because I was wearing a wet suit because that's what a dolphin trainer wears. And I wore a whistle. If I can't be a dolphin trainer—maybe I didn't feed the dolphins every time or I forgot to do the trick and I lost my job—I'd really like to ride a horse in the circus and do tricks.

KAITIE: I could probably do the same thing.

SARAH: I know someone who does two things. My teacher works at Disneyland and teaches us. She told us Mickey is her friend.

KAITIE: My biggest dream is that work will be fun . . . In college they help you with what you need to do to get a job at Disneyland.

Kaitie & Sarah

mADELINE MARTINEZ, b. 1964,
massage therapist

Madeline's is the story of true Texas grit. A pathfinder hobbled by poverty and family circumstance, she dropped out of school and drifted from job to job. While relaxing at a client's house after finishing a massage, Madeline explains that desperately seeking a better future, she found it rooted in her past.

Madeline

ibelieve my path began when I was ten years old. **My father had been in a fight at a bar and came home with his legs swollen so bad he couldn't stand. The next day he had trouble walking and asked me to rub his legs. Not really having a choice, I did as he said.** When I say I didn't have a choice, I mean that already there was a lot of resentment between us. He was a body man, he fixed cars, an American Indian [the Tunica Biloxi tribe of Louisiana], and he was one of those men who come home late and are abusive to their wives and children. But when I rubbed his legs, I forgot I was doing it out of an obligation, forgot it was him, and that I didn't want to do things for him. I felt real good. "Keep goin'," he said, urging me to continue. "I feel relief." The pain in his legs decreased, and I loved the feeling in my hands.

In my hands I feel a Great Sensation.

My first summer job was making lamps. The people were friends of my parents and they hired me to go in there and make lamps. They were called ginger lamps because they were constructed out of old glass ginger jars. It was a ma-and-pa operation, and for $3.75 an hour I made the whole lamp—from assembling the electrical components to creating little arrangements of grass, moss, flowers, shells inside the glass. Each one was different, with its own pretty setting, and I got to do it my way.

A year later my parents went through a divorce and I didn't get to graduate like normal people. We lived in a refinery town outside of Houston, and during lunch hour my mother sold her tamales to the refinery workers. Because it got to be too hard for me to go to school in the day and work fast food in the evenings, I dropped out of school.

I worked for all sorts of small businesses—answering the phones, typing, doing the payroll. I began working for a chiropractor where I did X-rays, set up appointments, and handled insurance claims. The mailman would come in to deliver the mail, and since the chiropractor was out on his lunch hour, the mailman would complain to me. "My shoulder really hurts." Pointing to where he carried his mail bag, he'd ask, "Could you rub it?" Not really

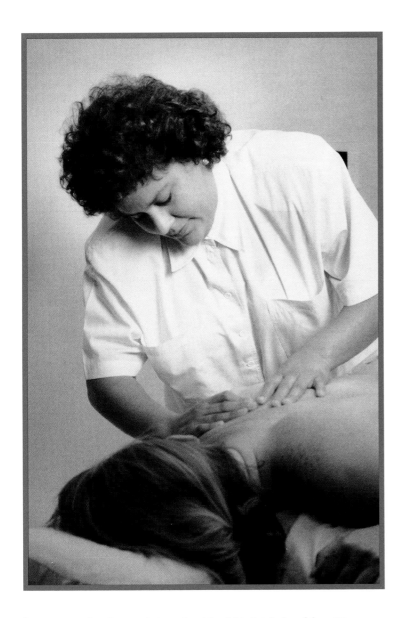

who worked in the office. On our lunch hour we'd massage each other, and she believed in my ability, too. That's when it hit me that all my other jobs—doing payroll where all the different little columns had to be right, handling insurance claims—were head stuff. I wanted to work with my hands. People would come into the chiropractor's office and complain about their body and, like with the mailman, I wanted to touch them and make them feel better.

About that time my husband and I went on a Christmas vacation to his country of Honduras. His eighty-four-year-old mother had arthritis in one of her legs so bad it was curving in like a bow. I told Ercella, my mother-in-law, that the next time I saw her I'd be able to work on her, help her feel better. I don't know why I said that. I hadn't even signed up for massage school, but I must have known that was to be my path.

I enrolled in massage school at the beginning of the New Year, 1989. The first day when I massaged a fellow student I had the same feeling in my hands as when I was ten years old rubbing my father's legs.

The feeling in my hands when I go over a body's hurt spots is unbelievable. Knots change and loosen, people experience relief and relax. In my hands I feel a Great Sensation. Sometimes after I've worked on a knot for five or ten minutes, the body will allow me to go deeper, and then it's like a small miracle when the body lets go. It's like a joy, a healing, a change for the better. That's what I mean by the Great Sensation I feel in my hands.

Massage is a healing. I can feel I'm giving something back to the person—not just relaxation. It's like there's a

knowing what I was doing, I rubbed his bad shoulder. He said it felt so good, said I ought to go into massage. His encouragement changed my life. There was also this lady higher power working through me to give this person what they need, even though they're not aware of it. They don't need to be aware of it. I'm a channel for them to receive whatever it is they need to move themselves forward or let go. I can't get into this with each person, but I know and I believe. I hope that, not hope, I *know* that when I'm done something has happened.

I met my husband when I was twenty and married him three months later. He's a Latin man who's had to accept that I work on men who have no clothes on. From his culture to accept this, he's had to overcome a lot. After I enrolled in school, and finally got my table, I gave him a massage. I draped him with the sheets and he experienced the same thing my clients do, so he understands what I do.

We're both goal people. We want a better life for his family in Central America, for my family, and for ourselves. We don't want to reach sixty and have to struggle and worry about how we're going to live. We want to have a nest egg.

Now I'm my own company and I'm on call at a salon, but mostly I make house calls. My business is all word-of-mouth. What I'm thankful for is that whoever I work on, they call back. For financial reasons they might not call back that week, or that month, or in six months, but eventually they call back. The fact that I don't have to work forty hours a week to make $230 is good. (When I left the chiropractor I was making $8.75 an hour, and now I make between $50 and $100 an hour.) What's better is that I'm doing something I like. It makes me happy and gives a little peace to the other person, too.

I'll only be able to go so far with massage because I only have so much energy in myself. It's not just my hands, it's my body, too. I put forth to each individual all this energy, and I'm drained after a massage. I can do four, really three, comfortably in a day, so I have a little extra time.

One of my clients, I've known this lady for four years, wanted to open a furniture store. She asked me to go on a buying trip with her to buy Honduran mahogany. She believed in my ability to make this happen. She spoke no Spanish at all, so I got to use my Spanish. I did the interpreting and found the sources. It was great. I did it. The furniture's here. The store is open. And also it connected me with something my husband does. He does upholstery. Before we were separate. I had my massage and he had his upholstery. I want something that I can do together with my husband, something that we have a little bit in common.

I enjoy what I do but I feel like there's something more. I'll continue more training to enhance my massage. I'll be going on more buying trips. But I think I can do something even more.

gRACE TSUJIKAWA-BOYD, manufacturer

On a table outside Grace's office, lovely calla lilies swoop from a vase over a small sculpture of a rhino. Stuck to the rhino is a Post-it scribbled in Grace's handwriting: "Company Mascot—he's tough, he's rough, he's grown a thick hide." Grace is a rare mammal herself—a woman manufacturer. In thirty years her Seattle company has grown from making hand-crafted flower pots to producing high-tech dies for fighter jets.

Grace

i've always been very achievement-oriented. I sort of wonder myself why I've had to be an achiever. I think it had a lot to do with the way I grew up, and having to be as good as my brothers. During the war years we were persecuted, all the Japanese people were. I have vague recollections of being locked up in Idaho. After the war was over and we returned to the Coast, I always felt that we'd done something wrong. When you're a child you can't rationally think this out, why you're being locked up. As a child you think if you do something bad, you get locked up. So we had to prove that we were really good people. We had to achieve to make ourselves worthy, or better, to show that we were not bad guys.

I think that had a lot to do with how I operated when I got to junior high school. I practically had a nervous breakdown because I felt I had to be everything. I competed scholastically as well as socially. I was secretary of the student body, vice president of the Art Club, president of whatever. I must have had half a dozen different offices when I was a junior and senior in high school. I was driven.

I married Mr. Boyd when I was twenty-one. By then I'd dropped out of college and gone to work at Boeing as a graphic illustrator. It wasn't a great time in my life. We didn't have money. I mean, I lived from hand to mouth, seriously. I'd go to work and I wouldn't even have lunch.

Unfortunately, our marriage lasted only four years. After my husband and I divorced, I worked double shifts. I'd drop my daughter, Kelle, off at day care, work from eight to four-thirty as a graphic illustrator at Boeing, pick her up at day care, drop her off at my aunt's, and my aunt would give her a bath, give her dinner, and get her ready for bed. I'd work a second shift at a job shop at Boeing doing technical illustration until eleven o'clock at night, and then I'd pick up Kelle, carry her home, and put her in her other bed. That was really tough. The toughest. I didn't even own a car of my own.

> I really like selling a product I can wrap my arms around.

I shared one with my brother. I was really broke.

I worked for the Boeing Company for nine years. At that point I decided that Boeing was a male-dominated company and that no matter how hard I worked—I was working sixteen hours a day—I wasn't ever going to get an advancement into a management position. There was absolutely not a chance. If I wanted to get ahead and if I wanted to use what I felt were my talents, I needed to go do it myself.

While I was at Boeing, I'd read about a husband and wife who started a company making architectural pottery, producing large planters for hotels, corporate offices. I was just in love with the idea that I could do something like that, only I could probably do it better because I was an artist and a designer.

I was working days at Boeing, and nights and weekends I started making sample pots one by one in the basement of my home. I had a little kiln in my kitchen and one in the backyard. I could fire only one or two pots at a time.

There's a misconception that I inherited my father's business. I did not. My brother did. In traditional Japanese families that's pretty typical that the males in the family carry on the family business. The boys get to inherit the business and the girls get to do the dishes. That's the way it was. As a girl child between two brothers, you grow up in Asian homes and oftentimes, although your parents probably love you equally, they don't treat you equally. Women or girl children are treated differently than male or boy children. It didn't stop me and I didn't carry a grudge about it forever, either.

My father manufactured small red clay flower pots. They weren't even glazed. They were the red clay flower pots they use in greenhouses. Although I grew up with my father in the pottery business, it was totally unrelated to what I did later. I wanted to make production pieces and enter the commercial marketplace. I had no intention of making hand-thrown art pieces. I wasn't really a craftsman, a sculptor. My art had to do with painting and oils and graphics.

I told Merle, this artist I'd been dating, "Look, I'm really getting close to where I want to get involved in this one hundred percent. I'm thinking about quitting my job, and I need your expertise because I don't know how to build equipment. We're going to have to go to the junkyard to get equipment together. So, how about it?" He became my partner in the sense that his investment was his time, labor, ideas, and his ability to put equipment together with junkyard stuff. It was my responsibility always to find financing and to market the product.

I hoped for a niche market: Fortune 500 companies with a lobby. I was so excited about getting in business that it never occurred to me I wouldn't be getting a paycheck every other week. I had blind faith that we could generate these pots and sell them.

I approached banks for financing. In 1968 the female role in the workplace was as a second-income person. If you weren't a homemaker, you were a secretary, a bookkeeper, an interior designer. That kind of work. That was more feminine. Manufacturing was a man's job. I'd grown up in my father's plant and was comfortable in it, but I found a lot of resistance, like, "You have a great story, little girl, but we can't lend you any money." Sort of patting you on the head. I ended up using my credit card to charge glazes, clay, and plaster, the components I needed to make pots.

With a loan from the Small Business Administration in 1969, we had enough to build a dryer, a kiln, and move into a five-thousand-square-foot warehouse in Pioneer Square. At that point we were beginning to sell a few pots. It never occurred to me to be afraid. And I know we were very poor because I remember night after night eating fried potatoes. Once I was so embarrassed. I can specifically remember one time my brother came by with a friend of his and it was dinnertime and we didn't have any dinner. I was humiliated that we couldn't even offer for him to stay for dinner. We had no groceries.

When you don't have money, the only thing you can do is put in long hours. I used to work anywhere from fourteen to sixteen hours a day, seven days a week, and I did that for years. I had tremendous energy. And if you don't have financing, if you don't have money, your support comes from friends who network you to other friends.

When I first started producing product, I was told we needed a sales rep. I had some really good friends who were interior designers and they gave me names of reps. The reps asked, "Where's your catalog? Where's your factory? Where's your customer list?" Of course, I didn't have any. I had only a couple of customers. But a few sales reps were willing to educate me on marketing and tell me how to make a sales call.

Once I established myself in Seattle, I was able to go to Portland, Boise, Spokane. I'd drive everywhere. I'd make eight to ten calls a day on designers, architects, landscape architects, furniture dealers—anyone who could buy, sell, or display our pots. A lot of times I got stood up, but I had a job to do and I went for it.

Everyone has certain regrets. My regret is being a single parent starting a new business. I mean, something has to go. There's only so many hours in the day. When Kelle came home from school, I was there in the basement, but one-on-one personal time was lacking because I was so occupied

The opportunities are greater now than ever, ever, ever in our history for women to go into manufacturing businesses.

with my second job. If you're working that hard, you're cheating your kids. I haven't made a helluva lot of mistakes in business, but in my personal life I've made a few. Merle and I lived together for fifteen years, but we never married. Maybe we should have. Maybe if I'd done the family thing, it would have filled in the void and given my daughter more stability.

A woman who has not been the single-working-supporting-breadwinner for a family can never understand the sacrifices both sides, the mother and the child, have to make. I know there are a tremendous number of single parents now, but I'm not for it. I think it takes two parents to raise a child.

In retrospect, I don't know how I could have done it differently. No one gave me money to start my business, and no one supported me for ten years while I built it. I put every minute of my waking hours into this business. When you really look at a working mother in my position, it's unrealistic. If you're bankrolled by somebody, have an eight-to-four-thirty job, and have funds to support a nanny, that's great. But how many of us do? What I can do is pass this information on to another working mother. I can tell her the price of my path.

My daughter's in her mid-thirties now. She was in a band, and there are a zillion bands in Seattle, and let's put it this way, she couldn't support herself in the band and needed a job. She came here, and now she does customer service. We're close in proximity, working in the same building, but not close. The downside is that I worked so hard to achieve the various milestones that I sacrificed my relationship with her. When Kelle was a little girl, she said, "Oh, Mommy, I want to grow up to be beautiful like you." When she got older, she said, "I don't want to be like you. I don't want to be driven. I don't want to spend fourteen hours a day and Saturdays and Sundays at the office." When she started working here, she said, "I'm an eight-to-four-thirty person. I want to forget about this place when I leave."

In the beginning I didn't realize the big picture, as it

related to my daughter or the business. When I quit my job at Boeing, I pictured our products being real popular in the city of Seattle, and that would sustain my business and provide me an income. I don't think I realized I had to go regional, national, and international in order to sustain the business. The goal was just to be a successful businessperson. I never thought I'd have my own building worth $3 million. I never in a hundred million years imagined I would be involved in engineering, because in 1979 I barely knew how to craft a pot, let alone get involved with high-tech ceramic dies for aerospace.

In the 1980s the business built tremendously. We were fourteen weeks back-ordered, sales were over a million dollars, and we expanded into this 56,000-square-foot warehouse. There was this warm and fuzzy feeling that we were making money. By the late '80s, business flattened when a huge company began importing terra-cotta planters from Italy.

I made a successful transition into ceramic dies, or forms, because I was willing to start from scratch again. I said, Okay, I have all this equipment—dryers, kilns, forklifts, overhead cranes. I'm hiring a consultant from the University of Washington to study what other business I can go into.

The consultant hit upon the idea of ceramic tooling. That meant we'd extend our knowledge of working with ceramic products into producing molds for shaping titanium and metal alloys. Ultimately, our plan was to commercialize our product into areas like transportation, sporting goods, and medical products.

Boeing was already investigating ceramic dies as a method of making airplane parts, and since they were right in our backyard, theirs was a natural market where we could introduce this new technology immediately. Very honestly, no one's ever asked me why I'm building dies to form parts for a fighter plane that's going to be used in defense. In the very beginning we targeted the commercial side of Boeing, and that led us to the defense side.

Whether Boeing uses our ceramic dies to form parts for the F-22 or they use steel dies, it doesn't matter. Someone is going to make that aircraft. My contribution to that aircraft is that it costs less to form this piece my way, and that's taxpayer money that's being saved. The money has already been allocated to build this aircraft, and all we're saying to the Air Force is that we can provide these dies at considerably less money.

The government, especially the Air Force and the Department of Defense, is very supportive of women entering nontraditional fields of manufacturing. The opportunities are greater now than ever, ever, ever in our history for women to go into manufacturing businesses. I think it's by choice that women don't. As far as I can see, there aren't many running their own manufacturing business.

To me the most exciting thing about being in manufacturing is that I'm the creator of a tangible product. It's not like a service business where you're selling something intangible. I really like selling a product I can wrap my arms around.

Sherman Baylin, b. 1958,

animal activist/stunt woman

A first-time customer wandering into Sherman's store is likely to wonder why it is not called Sherman's Pet Place, like most stores that sell pet food and offer grooming services. Gradually one realizes that the shop also serves as a lively community center— an anchor for people in the neighborhood and a rescue service for animals in peril. Thus it defies easy definition: It is Sherman's Place.

Sherman

i got to where I am quite by accident. **A couple years ago a movie-of-the-week was being filmed in the parking lot in front of my shop. I was working as a stunt woman and I was supposed to be a pedestrian who was hit by a car. I flew up in the air, rolled over, and when I came down realized I hadn't been hit by my stunt driver.** A civilian, who wasn't supposed to be in the scene, had run into me. Then Marco, this twenty-one-year-old who was already drunk first thing in the morning, rushed out of his car and screamed at the crew, "She hit *me!*"

Later that day I met with the young man's dad. The father lived up the hill from the shop and over the years we'd talk in the neighborhood, and I'd ask in passing how Marco was, and he'd always say, "Perfect. He's perfect." At our first meeting, the great façade came down and the father said, "I have a big problem." He told me how Marco had a DWI, how they'd tried Tough Love, how he'd been in and out of recovery programs, and nothing had worked. Until Marco hit me with the car, I never knew. I never knew. Especially the way he looked—he was always dressed so beautifully, short hair, his car was absolutely perfect, no signs of any frayed edges. Perfect.

A customer once said I'm like a female Robin Hood.

All three of us had big problems. The father needed a way to help his son. Marco needed to get sober. And I needed help to keep my shop going. I had nine hundred square feet, a lot of empty shelves, I took in too many animals that needed costly medical care, and I was so busy running to animal shelters that the store never had regular hours.

The father said, "Here's the deal. I give you $60,000 over the next year. Keep Marco sober and the money's yours." (The $60,000 was for improvements to the shop.)

I think it was a combination of things—that the father had known me about three years and had seen me work with some neighborhood kids and a lot of animals. He knew that I felt for even a butterfly that was hurt. And he knew that if I did something, I'd give it my best shot. The risk to me was that if I failed and I lost Marco, I'd be partially responsible for having someone who was absolutely wonderful never reach any expectation.

As a stunt woman I'm a bit of a daredevil, and I took his dare. I've thought about this, about why I took the deal. I didn't care about the money so much as I saw a person dying in front of me. From visiting and lecturing in elementary schools, I'd seen some very special healing happen with children and animals. Even the most troubled children can relate to a puppy, a kitten. I guessed Marco was just going to be an older version of that. It was going to be animal therapy, my brand of animal therapy.

Marco's father also had an idea about bathtubs. He'd been at a grooming facility in San Diego that had tubs, and he said he'd never seen so many wet happy people and wet happy dogs. The owners were washing their own dogs. All of a sudden I had one drunk and four bathtubs.

Marco was a rich boy who'd never had a thought for anyone else. When I commented that he didn't have any animals, he said, "I'm a young, good-looking bachelor. I don't need anything. I'm fine." Then this little stray was brought into the shop, and the more Marco ignored her, the more she went only to him. "I'll take her home for the night," he said, "but I don't want a dog." The next morning she was sitting on his lap, her paws on the dash. "Look! She's steering!" he said, and asked what would be a good name for a pit bull. Soon it was Marco and Molly this, Marco and Molly that.

Marco manned the front desk and answered the phone. He'd bring in things to eat. He'd say, "Look at the lovely dessert I made." Strawberries dipped in chocolate. "We can nosh on these during the day." He always brought in two separate plates—his and mine. One day he was carrying on, eating all these strawberries. Finally, I said, "I want some of your strawberries." I bit into one. Wow! He'd shot them full of vodka. He'd bring in Diet Coke spiked with vodka.

I got so fed up I said, "I'm leaving! You run the shop, and you run it into the ground, and you tell your father, and you tell everyone else in the community." I put the responsibility back on him. I told him, "And be sure to feed and clean the animals." He said, "I can't take care of them right now." I said, "That's too bad, because if anything happens to these animals, it's on your head."

Gradually, very gradually—he had to practice a lot at being sober—he replaced his Coke-and-vodka habit with caring, one habit replaced with another. And gradually, month by month, I got my $60,000. By the end of the first year, we agreed to continue our partnership. His dad had bought him in, but Marco had earned his own way.

I grew up steeped in animals and natural history. My mom, a Jewish girl, had been raised in a Catholic convent, and every year when the other kids went home to their families, she had to have contact with something, so she turned to animals and nature. When she had a daughter of her own, she schlepped me on endless field trips to understand nature—animal behavior and human behavior. I was the only kid on the block who, at age five, could spell lepidopterology—the branch of zoology dealing with butterflies. I suppose she felt she'd overdone it when she came home one day and found me in the living room watching television with Ted, my horse.

My career as a stunt person who works with animals began by accident, too. My mom was writing for the television show *Owen Marshall, Counselor at Law,* and I was just an extra, a twelve-year-old sitting on a horse. When the horse spooked, I toppled over backward and accidentally did what turned out to be a triple gainer with a half twist. The cameraman, who caught the action on film, said to me, "You should do more of that."

Like with the rest of my career, I never went to school to learn stunts; I just started practicing. At a local stable, I'd place a mark, loosen my saddle, and practice galloping and falling off at the mark. I was just a kid and I practiced over and over and over.

The first time I was actually hired for a stunt job was for a television commercial. I was twenty-two and a fellow stunt person told me about this gig where they needed someone to roll around in the water with an alligator (his mouth was wired shut) and emerge with a piece of luggage. I got a pretty good reputation based on that commercial.

As you can probably tell, I never had a path. I'm envious of people who at ten years old know they want to be a vet, but I was never focused in any way, never had a goal, or a purpose. Everyone in my family has gone to college. My great-grandmother was one of the first women lawyers in Russia. My mother, a successful Hollywood screenwriter, was a hard act to follow. My father was a businessman. And then there was me, who dropped out of high school and felt embarrassed that I was taking up space. I didn't realize it's a gift to be able to listen and learn from people who know more than you do. You could say that I'm a later bloomer, a terribly later bloomer.

When the stunt work was slow, Mom said to me, "You need a business." At the same time a developer wanted to put in a mini-mall on a vacant lot near where we lived. We live in Malibu, which is a rural area, and for years my family and I had been fighting big development, big hotels, major projects. I'd been attending the city council meetings protesting the development of the nearby lot. Finally, the developer, who knew me because I'd become something of an institution, said, "What would it take to shut you up?" "A store," I said. I knew that the property was going to be developed, and at least his project had been downsized from three to two stories, and fifteen stores to eight. And if I had a storefront, I'd have a headquarters for my work with the animals. He allocated space for me in his new mini-mall and gave me a year's free rent.

My mother had this mother-daughter fantasy of a lovely home design shop where we'd work together and probably even wear matching outfits. I'm serious. I love her so much that I didn't want to disappoint her.

At first, she decorated the shop exquisitely with plush hunter-green carpet, and glass shelves with Lalique and Baccarat. Folks would wander in and say, "I have twelve puppies that need a home. Can I put up a notice?" Or a pregnant girl would come in who didn't have anywhere else to turn. Mother was still bringing in crystal, while I started dragging in hurt wildlife—a bird, a bunny. After about four months, I said, "Mom, let's compromise and make a country store. We'll have some nice things and some hurt animals." She said, "I love you but I need order in my life. I quit." She was very gracious about it. I think she was relieved that for the first

time she saw that I was moving toward something of my own.

After Mother moved out, I struggled—*struggled*—for three years before Marco and the bathtubs moved in. Then, to generate more foot traffic so customers would buy food and supplies, I started grooming. I signed up for a course, but they were so rough on the animals—pushing the dog's head away, with the dog yelping—that I bailed.

I did what I suppose you could call "stunt grooming." It's probably the only time I should have been killed because of the way some of the dogs turned out. Once a customer brought in two cocker spaniels who were so gorgeous that there was no way I was going to clip them. Marco and I closed the shop and took the cockers to a real groomer. Now I've read every book, screened every video on grooming, and I feel more relaxed because I clipped a dog for a show and it won a first-place ribbon.

I've come to think of the shop as an asylum for animals and people, a place where everyone can relax. Whether it's a kid who's so loaded he can't go to school, or a dog someone was going to put to sleep, or a high school teacher with a troubled teenager, we're the place in the community that folks turn to. We're not formal. People sit on the bench out front and talk with each other, or they hang out in the shop and yell above the dryers and the music. And customers love the bathtubs, especially divorced men who don't know what to do with their kids on the weekend, so they bring them in to wash the dog.

If an animal's in jeopardy and Animal Control doesn't have the personnel to handle the situation, I've asked them to please call me, and they do. I've slid down a two-hundred-foot cliff to rescue a horse, been lowered into a dark crawl space to hunt out a ten-foot boa constrictor, and during the Malibu fires of '93 and '96, I aided hundreds of animals.

A customer once said I'm like a female Robin Hood, a character who takes money—in my case, from my stunt work and the shop—and gives it away to help animals and people. That's probably a pretty accurate description, except after nine years in business I'm learning to be choosier. I'll never turn down an animal, financially, but now when people come in I listen, and if someone needs money to go to a doctor to set a collarbone, I'll give it to them, but if they want a new shirt, or to have their BMW tuned up, I've learned that's not my job.

I had no personal life away from the shop. Now I've learned balance. I've learned that it's okay not to save everyone and everything in the world. Before, I'd be up at three o'clock in the morning, thinking, Right now a cat is being used for food! I'd fill up that void because I didn't have a relationship. It's the truth. Now I have a great boyfriend and I can allow myself to pet a dog, and I don't have to save it.

I had no intention of looking like this—bedraggled and sopping wet from grooming and rescuing animals—or driving a vehicle like this—a truck with hay in the back—or owning a place where everyone hangs out. But without knowing where I was going, and without feeling too good about myself, I accidentally stumbled onto something. Sherman's Place is not just a place for animals and other people, it's been a place for me to shine. Now I'd probably be all right even without the shop. I can shine on my own.

DIANNE PILGRIM, b. 1941, museum director

Dianne was told early on that she was "not college material." Now she's the director of Cooper-Hewitt, National Design Museum, Smithsonian Institution in New York City. This scholar and art historian oversees the only museum in the country devoted solely to historical and contemporary design. Hers has been a lifelong journey of forging ahead while facing disabilities.

Dianne

i'm not just disabled. I have a serious illness—multiple sclerosis. I get a lot of "Aren't you remarkable?" and all that. That's to a large degree hogwash. For some people, like myself, my job is a salvation.

The major influence in my life in terms of work was my mother. She always talked about some mythical career that she was going to have and missed out on because of the children. She could never describe what the career was going to be. What she didn't realize is that her six kids were her career. She put tremendous energy into it. It was something she was very proud of, but in her mind it wasn't the same thing. A real frustrating thing for her was that to one degree or another, all of us kids were dyslexic. Here was a person who loved books, loved to read, and she had all these kids who were doing terribly in school. Particularly me.

Schools didn't recognize dyslexia for a long time, and certainly not the highfalutin private school I was going to. So my grades were C's. I understand now why kids have behavioral problems when they feel stupid. It's horrible to sit in a class when you feel stupid. (To this day the word "school" sends shudders down my spine.) The difficulty, and unfortunately I think it's still true today even though we know more about learning disabilities, is that no one said, "Dianne, you have a problem but it doesn't mean you're stupid."

In the tenth grade I was told, "You're not college material." [Long pause.] My mother told me. I don't know why. I think she was confused in her thinking, because I know she loved all of us and fought the battle with every one of our teachers to explain that her children weren't stupid, but we had this learning problem.

I ended up in college by sheer luck. My SAT scores were so abysmal that every place I applied to turned me down, except Penn State. In fact, in 1991 I got a Distinguished Alumni Award from Penn State, and I said, "I'm particularly grateful to Penn State for two reasons. One, you're the only college or

> Here was someone who was putting time and effort into me, and I didn't want to disappoint him.

university that accepted me." There was nervous laughter. And I said, "I'm dyslexic. I cannot take tests like SAT's or Graduate Record Exams. I was turned down flat by everybody but you. What would have happened to me if you hadn't taken me? Where would I be today?" I said, "The second reason I'm grateful is that the first person who ever took an interest in me academically and pushed me was an art history professor here."

I have to backtrack. In my parents' desperation to find something I did well, they kept saying I was a good artist. That I could draw and paint. So for my first few years at Penn State my major was creative arts, and it was painful to discover that I was pretty bad. But I'd always loved art, and art history interested me. One of the reasons we do Career Days at the museum now is that I had no idea you could major in something called art history. So anyway, in my junior year that became my major. And this art history professor actually suggested that I should go on to graduate school. Here I was not even supposed to be in college, and he was talking about graduate school.

He did things that were very painful but very necessary. He said, "If you're going to get into graduate school, you cannot get another B." He took me down to the local coffee shop and went through the blue book, word by word, where I'd taken my exam. It was very painful but I never got another B.

I don't know that I saw it at the time, but it's so clear now that without his encouragement I never would have done as well as I did. I mean, here was someone who was putting time and effort into me, and I didn't want to disappoint him. I'd never had that experience before. In fact, I'd always had the opposite. I had people who did not expect anything of me. And so they got nothing.

I was incredibly lucky about graduate school, because for some reason NYU didn't require the Graduate Record Exam. I wanted NYU because they have a museum training program with the Metropolitan Museum of Art, and I knew I did not want to teach. (With a master's in art history, your options are either to teach and write, or to go into museum work.)

What I was beginning to discover was that for me to study something I had to see it in the flesh, instead of looking at photos or slides. This realization naturally led in the direction of working with museums. But it was not like a decision, "I'm going to work for a museum." That happened slowly. I was not thinking in terms of a career, as people would think today—what am I going to do to support myself? I'm just old enough that I was in that last gasp where as a woman you didn't necessarily think you needed to support yourself. Your husband would. It horrifies me to think that's the way we thought, but that's the way we were brought up.

The last part of the museum training program is an internship where you work for one semester in a department at the Met. I did an internship in the history of decorative arts. Decorative arts have always been considered the lowest of the low in the hierarchy of the arts. Decorative arts are what we consider functional objects, things we use day in and day out—furniture, silver, ceramics, glass. Primarily they're made for functional use, as opposed to painting and sculpture, the fine arts, which are made more for personal, political, emotional, and cultural reasons.

The director of the Met always had a party for the students when their internship was up, and at the party he asked me, "What are you going to do?" I didn't have the faintest idea, and he said, "You come see me next week." He very kindly gave me a fellowship. This was in the good old days. No committee, no nothing. I started doing a lot of research on early-nineteenth-century New York City cabinet-makers.

The Met was celebrating their centennial anniversary [1970] and they had decided they were going to do a show on nineteenth-century American decorative art. Research needed to be done on the entire century. The great joy to me about all the projects I've worked on—in fact, almost my entire career—is that I've worked in areas where nobody had ever done any great work at all. For me, that was the excitement of it. It was like a detective game, trying to find out about all these things, and no one knew anything.

I got married at the tail end of this period. My husband was in American painting at the Met, but he'd accepted a job as curator of American art at the Corcoran Gallery of Art in Washington. I had to make a decision, which was hard for me because I was enjoying the work I was doing. But when you're in love . . . So I quit and moved down to Washington.

I didn't do much in Washington. I couldn't find any decorative arts jobs. The frustrating thing is, during most of the two and a half years we were there, the new director of what used to be called the National Collection of Fine Arts, now the National Museum of American Art, had just

taken over the Renwick Gallery, which would be devoted to objects and native crafts. The director and I negotiated for over a year about me becoming the first curator. One day I got a phone call and he said, "The job's yours." I said, "Great, but Jim just took a job at the Met and we're going back to New York."

The long and short of it is that jobs in decorative arts are in short supply, and I didn't have a job for a while. Then for some unknown reason, but I'm extremely grateful, the head of American painting at the Met hired me on a contract basis to do an exhibition on a private collection of American paintings. It just so happened that at the same time the City University of New York started a Ph.D. program in American painting. It seemed like the perfect thing to do. I was already spending my time in the library working on the catalog for the exhibit, so I could work on two things at the same time. I'd get a Ph.D. in American painting and whatever came up, I'd have more options—I could either be hired in an American paintings department or decorative arts department.

The next job that came up was back in decorative arts—as an assistant curator in charge of decorative arts at the Brooklyn Museum. I was in my thirties and I'd never been a curator of anything. It was pretty terrifying. There was a secretary and that was it, and a collection of over sixty thousand objects and twenty-eight American period rooms that needed to be renovated.

In 1978 everything happened at once. In May my husband moved out, and in September I was diagnosed with multiple sclerosis. By some incredible miracle, a show we

the way back I thought I was going to die because my legs were so tired. That's when I realized I had to have myself checked out.

The diagnosis of multiple sclerosis, MS, freaked me out in a whole lot of ways. Jim and I had just, not four months before, separated. I hadn't been on my own for a very long period of time. So I was quite nervous about that. Then I get this devastating diagnosis that I have this disease that's the largest crippler of young adults. Even to this day people think Jim left me because I had MS. The two had nothing to do with each other. We'd been breaking up for a long time.

were doing called "The American Renaissance" opened in October 1979.

I was thirty-seven and I'd had symptoms for two, three years before. At the time I thought it was depression from my marriage, which was breaking up. I was also having bladder accidents. Again, I blamed that on my nerves from the marriage. That summer on a business trip to Europe I'd gone to Versailles. I walked out to where what's-her-face [Marie Antoinette] had her little country place, Le Petit Trianon. On

I was told that about eighty percent of all people who get MS have "attacks." You can be perfectly normal and wake up the next morning unable to walk, or you can wake up totally blind. You can stay that way for a week or two months. You can get one-hundred-percent better or seventy-five-percent better, but you'll have this up-and-down pattern. There are ten percent who are "chronic progressives," which is the category I fall into, in that I've never gotten better. I've been in a wheelchair for eleven years, but, actually, a lot of people with MS don't ever wind up in a chair.

My mother had MS and for me to get *her* disease—I could have gotten any other disease and it wouldn't have been quite as devastating. The disturbing thing for me was that my mother had been a person of tremendous energy. She kept going and going, just like the Energizer Bunny. When MS happened to her she was going through menopause, her children were leaving home for college, and she got depressed and took to her bed. In a manner of speaking, she gave up. I was determined that for all the ways we were supposed to be alike, I was not going to be like that. In a way, her example was a great impetus for me.

The fatigue is the most insidious aspect of MS, because it's hard to make people understand what you're talking about. One of my dearest friends in the whole world just died of AIDS. He said to me, "You know, Dianne, all those years you talked about fatigue, I realize I had no understanding of what you were talking about. But now I do." Because it's not a matter of being sleepy. It's being bone-dead tired.

It would have been very easy for the Brooklyn Museum, particularly in the beginning, to say, Adios. But they were always very, very supportive. I never felt that my job was threatened because I had MS, and I was very grateful.

The first time I was approached about the director's job at Cooper-Hewitt was in February '87. I wasn't interested. It had never occurred to me to be a director.

A curator is the expert about the object. As decorative arts curator at Brooklyn I was responsible for adding to the collection, for its care and maintenance, the cataloging, the installation of the collection in galleries, fund-raising.

When you're a curator you get your satisfaction from doing something yourself. You are the one who goes out and buys the object, or you get the donors excited about doing an exhibition. You have to make a leap if you're going to be interested in directing. Because what you're doing as director is setting the mood, the direction, but other people are hands-on doing the shows.

Cooper-Hewitt approached me again a year later. I still wasn't thinking about leaving Brooklyn, because I was happy there. But in a certain way I'd learned everything about my job, and I needed to be on a new learning curve.

The Brooklyn Museum is an art museum, and to move to a design museum is very different. In a design museum you're not necessarily looking at objects as art—you're looking at them as both function and art. You're interested in the process of how they came about, as much as the end product. But it wasn't the subject matter that was the change for me. It was the job. It was 1988, I was forty-seven years old, and I went from managing five people to seventy-five, and overseeing a budget of $5 million. That was the learning curve, being director.

I realized after I got there that this was the first time in my life where the buck really did stop with me. I was *it*. In the past, there had been my mother, then my husband, and in Brooklyn there were lots of intermediary people you went to even before the director if you had a problem. I have to say it took me about a year. I sort of kept looking behind me, thinking maybe there's someone there who can help me with these decisions. Also, I was used to being part of the guys, so to speak. When you're the director you can't be that anymore, so you wind up having a very different relationship. You're the boss.

I can't know what it's like to be anything other than what I am, which is a white disabled professional woman. The disease has certainly given me an understanding I didn't have before of how we all, whether we like it or not, do have these stereotypical images and they come into our heads before we can even stop them.

One of the problems that hinders me in my job as director is that people are nervous about inviting me to their

I've never had a dream of myself in a wheelchair.

homes. And not just because their homes may not be totally accessible. People ask the silliest questions, like, How would you get here? Most people don't ask about the bathroom but they think about it. They ask, Do you go out for dinner? Of course, I go out for dinner! These are perfectly ordinary, everyday things that everyone does. I mean, if I were sitting at home and not doing anything, then I can see perhaps asking some of these questions. But how do they think I run an institution? How do they think I live alone?

It hinders me in my work because I need to continually meet new people. We have to expand our donor base. It's a major detriment, a major problem. Now I think it's hard

being a single woman, period. But if you add the disabled part onto it, people just get so uptight they can't handle it.

I don't see myself as a disabled person. I've never had a dream of myself in a wheelchair. In fact, when I visualize myself I'm always standing and I'm five foot four and a quarter inches tall. When I see photographs of myself in the chair it's like, Who is that person?

I always insist that anyone who takes a photograph of me has to show me in the wheelchair, because I think it's important for people to see that and not focus on it. It's like not focusing on whether someone's black or white, male or female—we're all just people.

I'm a museum director and I just happen to use a wheelchair, but so what? For nearly thirty-eight years I was a relatively healthy person, and I haven't changed. I'm basically the same human being I was before. Just because these things have happened doesn't take away from the talents I have to offer.

On the one hand, I certainly never thought I'd get multiple sclerosis and end up in a wheelchair. But on the other hand, never in my wildest dreams did I think I'd be director of the National Design Museum. I didn't anticipate either of those, and they happen to be interrelated. One is not a very terrific thing and one is incredibly exciting.

Aja

a JA METOYÉR, b. 1983,
eighth-grader

I would like to be a makeup artist. But I don't just want to be a makeup artist, because they don't make enough money for doing what I want to do. So I want to have my own makeup line, and I want to be a professional actress. My aunt's a makeup artist for the studios and she deals with a lot of famous people. She's always laughing and smiling and she's never bored.

My aunt took me to her job at this makeup place. I saw people making foundation to match their customers' skin. That was pretty cool.

I want to go to college and major in business. In school we did a project on the stock market, and about nine out of ten times I made all the right decisions. I want to have my own business and I want to be more than comfortable because you can lose your money so quickly, even if you're rich. I need to make sure I have money put away everywhere, just in case anything were to happen. Like what if my business caught on fire and the insurance place wouldn't pay for it? I'd be stuck.

The day we did this photo, I did the model's makeup perfect, like everything matched on her. She had on a lavender-blue dress and her eye shadow was navy blue with soft purple. My aunt told me I'm a natural. She's afraid that I'll take her job because I'm really good.

My mom says I have the brains for all the stuff I want to do.

j

JUDITH BLUESTONE, b. 1944,
neurodevelopmental specialist

Now a gutsy woman on a mission, Judy speaks quietly about her shaky begin-

nings. She was born with brain damage, and by healing herself she has learned

how to help other brain-damaged people. Susie Hepner, past director of the

Head Injury Re-Entry Center at Evergreen Hospital in Kirkland, Washington,

says, "It's so hard to articulate what Judy does. I've had patients with brain

injuries, and the families have been torn up, taking their kid to three or four rehab

centers, and I say, 'Okay, Judy, can you work with this person?' They have dramatic

outcomes with her that they don't have with anyone else."After three decades of

working with neurological impairment in both the United States and Israel, in

1994 Judy opened the doors to her own institute in downtown Seattle.

Judy

there's a black-and-white etching on the wall opposite my desk. It's of an elderly man, his skull is open, and inside the skull there are all these little systems of gears interacting with one another. He has one of his hands—a strong, powerful hand—holding this skinny screwdriver, and he's going in to make adjustments to those gears. An artist in Israel, who knew of my work, called one night and said, "I just finished this thing. I think I did it for you. Come get it."

When I work eighty- to ninety-hour weeks, people tell me I'm a workaholic. I say, "No. I'm a passionaholic."

What I see in it—and I'd never hang it in our clinical area because it could be frightening to our clients—is that there are ways that we can get into our minds, brains, sensory areas. No matter how old we are, no matter how scarred we are, no matter how many deformities and problems we've had, we can get in and make little adjustments that will make us functional and keep us going. It's what we do here at the Institute. Of course, we don't peel back the skull.

What we do through noninvasive means, using absolutely no high-technological means—the highest technology we use in an evaluation session is a penlight—is study how a person's nervous system has developed. We do that by asking people to do things. They think we want to see *what* we've asked them to do, like drawing a circle on a blackboard. Basically we want to see *how* they're doing it. The body tells you so much when you know how to read it—the things it avoids doing, the things it seeks, the ways it moves. It gives you a mirror to what's going on in the brain.

I describe myself as a detective. At the clinic we have a few formal tests that give us some clues as to how the eyes are working, which gives clues to what parts of the inner ear are working and what's not. But by looking at how a patient uses the basic neurological subsystems—light, taste, odor, touch, sound, the sense of their body in space—I can figure out which parts of the person's brain are immature, what parts are damaged, what parts are there but not connecting properly with other parts. Then I *gently* reorganize the system. Neural rehabilitation.

I'm constantly told by other professionals that I "see" what others can't. I believe that's because I've personally struggled with being brain damaged. My path was one of a person born with systems too damaged to process experiences as others do. Prior to my conception, during my whole gestation and early development, my dad, a research chemist, worked on substances which we now recognize as mutagenic. He did a tremendous job getting food to millions of people—that's what he was about, pesticides, insecticides, and growth hormones. He was bringing them home on his clothing, storing vials of them in the basement, spraying our yard experimentally with different chemicals. He put food that was grown with them on our table.

Parts of my skull stopped growing prenatally and other parts continued to grow abnormally. By the time I was seven, I'd lost my hearing because of abnormal brain growth. My nose had "fallen" into my mouth, which made me look like I didn't have an upper lip. I slobbered and could barely chew until I was seventeen or eighteen.

The boundaries between my path and others were lined with barbed wire and huge "No Trespassing" signs. I know people were repulsed, frightened, threatened, nauseated. In junior high school I was told by the other girls that I could not sit at their table because they couldn't stand that I was drooling what was basically Gerber's junior food, and having to do some strange things to get it around and get it down. One girl said, "See that table in the back? That's where you sit, facing the wall." I still cry now over that pain, whether

it's for me, or a client of mine who has that experience. You can't force people to accept you.

In the neighborhood the word got out that parents with

special-needs children could use me as their babysitter. I had an affinity with the severely brain injured, the castaways, the kids they couldn't leave with anyone else. We had fun. No problems. They understood me. I understood them.

I speak of my painful past not to engender pity, and not to blame my dad, who's in his eighties now, but only because that past determined my life's work. In college I thought about going into journalism, but realized, Nope, almost anybody could write that article, that story. It wasn't me. I needed to be in touch with what felt whole to me, and anything other than using my special abilities to work with people with neurological disorders felt splintered. I'd already been doing this as a special-needs babysitter, reaching the unreachables. I didn't know exactly where I was going, but I wanted to work with people suffering from learning and behavioral problems. I wanted to take their problems back to their most basic root—the brain and the nervous system.

In grad school [Counseling and Behavioral Studies: Neurological Impairments] I was in an assessment class with other students and a couple of professors who had years of experience. A family came in with their three-year-old. The child looked psychotic. When someone talked to him, he'd look for them up in the ceiling. I was studying this thin, pale, blondish boy with big frightened eyes, and thinking, Come on, guys, he has severe figure/ground problems. He can't see the person for the background. Ours was your typical evaluation room with puzzles, pictures, desks, and there was too much clutter for that little boy. As an experiment I suggested we take him into a room that was as plain as possible. It was a revelation. With no visual clutter he could see the car keys and pick them up.

The family home was Early American Colonial with frilly patterns, floral wallpapers, curios. The child, who suffered from an immature visual system, could not pick out foreground from background, so the dresser spoke to him. He couldn't see his mother for the couch. I told the parents that if they wanted their son to see them, they should replace the wallpaper with a solid color. They should reupholster the couch in a plain fabric. This is not the advice you're supposed to be giving. You're supposed to recommend treatment with a speech-language pathologist, or you give medication to reduce hallucinogenic experiences. But he wasn't hallucinating. My professors, who'd been doing this for so long, had missed the diagnosis and the prescription. I was in that assessment class to learn how to give standardized tests and come up with the recommendations those results yielded. It was a defining moment for me because it was proof that I had an ability to go beyond those "tests" and provide solutions that, to me, were obvious and logical.

The most important event in my metamorphosis was moving to Israel. I was a newly divorced, single mom, and the woman at the Jewish Resettlement Agency said, "Don't come. We're a nation of families, not single mothers, and there are no jobs for you." I told her I'd create a market for what I do.

I spent eleven years in Israel. In 1989 a program I designed received Israel's National Prize for Early Childhood Education. The award was for the early diagnosis and treatment of an at-risk population in Givat Olga. This was the third generation of kids who were not learning, more than 50 percent were being retained in kindergarten, and then most were going directly into special education, without ever seeing a normal first-grade classroom. Most of the children had at least one parent or grandparent incarcerated or on the street selling drugs. Givat Olga was a horrendous little pocket of unsolvable problems. The state department of education had tried program after program, bringing in specialists, and nothing had worked. I looked around this community of about 400 young kids, and said, "Sure. This is do-able."

We taught twenty preschool and kindergarten teachers how to integrate therapeutic activities into the school day. One teacher was unable to do circle time because the moment she'd start to show an object, a problem boy would turn, put his feet on the child in front of him, and lean back on the child behind him, which disturbed everybody. I came in before circle time and watched this little boy painting at an easel. He did two things: he started painting with his right hand and when there was something at the far left side of the page that he wanted to paint, he would switch his brush to his left hand; when he made a sun-type object, he didn't switch hands, but to make the other half that would have gone beyond his physical midline, he would move over to the left. His right hand never crossed beyond his nose, belly button. At circle time this child was sitting so his left side, left hand, and left leg were facing where the action was. When the teacher showed an object, he turned fully so he could take it in with his right side, the side he operated from.

I told the teacher to put him on the opposite side of the circle and she'd have no problems. She protested that my solution was too simple, but when she changed his seat, the problem ended. To help him cross his midline and take in information from a whole world, we introduced activities that the entire class could do. You know how teachers hand out something and say, "Take one and pass it to your neighbor"? We had her say, "This time everybody sit on your left hand, reach to your right to take the paper, look at it, and pass it [crossing their midline] to the person on your left." It's not a big deal. Just by incorporating little bits daily into the curriculum, we got developmental things to occur. And the

My mission is to move hundreds and thousands from dysfunction to function, from despair to hope.

kids didn't know they were getting therapy.

We got kids going into first grade and succeeding. The following year the program was introduced in Benyamina. When the parents saw what was happening, they asked, "If I did some of those activities, would it help me?" Some parents got off the street and got the Israeli equivalent of their GED. We turned that neighborhood in Benyamina around at the end of the second year.

I've been accused by professionals of having a talent and an intuition like they've never seen. But that means that only I can do this work, that it can't be taught or replicated. That's why when I returned from Israel to finish my doctorate, instead of going into private practice, I opened the HANDLE Institute [Holistic Approach to Neuro-Development and Learning Efficiency]. My purpose is to figure out what it is that I do, to write it down, codify it, and teach it to my staff and interns. My mission is to move hundreds and thousands from dysfunction to function, from despair to hope.

We're a shoestring operation where most salaries are deferred. It's not easy. I've been doing a lot on plastic, saying to myself, If we don't ever make it to the point where I can pay me and I can pay this off, people have declared bankruptcy for much less important reasons. I'm doing this to be able to keep our doors open and serve this population. When I work eighty- to ninety-hour weeks, people tell me I'm a workaholic. I say, "No. I'm a passionaholic."

Our holistic, drug-free approach treats the problem at its root rather than month after month masking problems with drugs. We treat adults with bipolar disorder without lithium. We treat children with ADD—I call it Attention Priority Disorder—without Ritalin. We treat people with Tourette's without clonidine.

Recently, we saw a twelve-year-old boy who was severely autistic and had a vocabulary of about twenty words, all made up of two-word phrases that he'd blurt out, like "Taco Bell!" "Video Ranger!" "Cap'n Crunch!" This boy wasn't yet dressing himself, was rarely feeding himself, had no eye contact or touch. His parents brought him in for an evaluation. He was of average height, very thin, ghost-like in appearance, frail, pale, cautious.

I moved him through exercises on the floor, taking his body through certain motions—tipping to one side, coming back, tipping to the other, slowly opening up pathways. Each time I thanked him for his cooperation and let him know that I knew this was difficult for him. I did a face-tapping exercise and explained this would help with enunciation, getting words out, being understood. I told the parents to do these exercises with him twice a day.

The next day the father came to a seminar I was giving. He was crying, totally emotional, hugging all these complete strangers, saying, "I have to tell you what happened!" He said that his wife was doing exercises with their son—it wasn't thirty hours after they'd seen me—and when she tapped on his face, their son started to make strange grimaces. She was used to talking to him, asking him questions, even though she'd never gotten an answer. She asked him, "Am I hurting you? Do you want me to stop?" He said, "No. Need to talk better." She nearly passed out, and finished the activity with tears in her eyes. Then the wife called her husband at his office, told him what had happened, and before she hung up, asked their son, as she had hundreds of times before, "Do you want to talk to your dad?" In the past, he wouldn't have held the receiver, let alone gotten it close to his face. He took the receiver from her, held it correctly, and said into the phone, "I love you, Daddy. I love you, Daddy."

We do this for families every day.

MARCIA BEAUCHAMP, b. 1955,
nonprofit project coordinator

In her dining room in Sonoma, California, with packing boxes stacked for her next move to Nashville, Tennessee, Marcia talks about the "growing pains" of drastically changing her career in midlife. In a voice that's still heavy with Oklahoma, she describes how she cut hair for eighteen years in Tulsa, and how she's now navigating a very different cutting edge: she's training progressive communities across the U.S. how to include religion in their curriculum.

Marcia

from the time I was ten or eleven years old, I used to love to play with people's hair. I used to go with my mom to her beauty operator. She had a salon in her home, a garage that had been turned into a little salon. I can remember watching this woman back-comb my mother's hair, and somehow learning it, memorizing what she was doing, and trying to understand how it was working.

Doing my mother's hair, it satisfied—I can get real psychological about this, having the benefit of a lot of years—it probably satisfied a feeling in me of pleasing her in a way that I often didn't. Almost always it took place in the kitchen. I'd seat her at the kitchen table and erect a little mirror in front of her, so I could see what I was doing and she could watch me. And it was something that only I could give her. She couldn't do it for herself. It made me feel special and necessary.

Even early on it was about much more than hair.

In high school when I found out that by the time I graduated I could have a license to be a cosmetologist, a hairdresser, I could think of nothing more wonderful. I was also a kid who could not wait to be an adult, who could not wait to be on my own, to have my own stuff, to be out of the house.

My tenth-grade counselor took out my transcript, and said, "Honey, you don't want to do that. You make straight A's. You could go to college." But as far as I was concerned, this was my dream. Of course, when I talked to my parents, they also, because neither of them had graduated from college, couldn't imagine anything more wonderful than that I'd get out of school and have a trade. They didn't have a moment's thought about giving me permission to do it. They thought I'd be fabulous at it.

I got this little kit. It was an old-fashioned hard suitcase with brass corners, and it was packed with pink hairnets, those little foam things you put over your ears when you sit under the hair dryer, a set of purple rollers, combs, scissors. I loved the half-size rollers because they let you get into those hard-to-reach places. Obviously, I was now prepared to be a professional because I had all this stuff.

Not for a moment did I question what I was doing. I knew exactly what I wanted to do and I wanted to be the best at it. Actually, the personal side complicates this whole story and I should stick that in. I was dating a boy in high school, and so part of what made all this so right was that I wanted to go out and be an adult and get married. He was nineteen, I was seventeen. I talked to my dad because I had to have his permission, and my dad, he said if I finished cosmetology in the summer at a private school so I had credentials and could go to work, he'd let us get married.

That summer I went to the Robert's Beauty Training Center. That's where I got my experience working on real people. That was also my first little taste of—how do I want to say it—a vision of what excellence might mean in that profession.

One woman stands out in my mind from that experience. She was "the woman no one wanted to do," and, of course, they always gave her to the new kid on the block. The reason no one wanted to do her was that she had a nerve disorder and had lost a great deal of hair. Her scalp was excruciatingly tender. You can imagine trying to put hair like that in a roller and put a clip in and not hurt her. But she stayed with me until I left there. Because I listened to her and tried to respond to what she had to say.

Even early on it was about much more than hair. It was about communicating, listening, understanding, and being able to translate that into a service. The communication piece got to be the key. I couldn't have articulated it back

then, but if I had a conversation with someone, I could discern what they wanted. Someone would come in with straight-as-a-stick dark brown hair and show me this picture. At the time it could have been of Olivia Newton-John with blond wavy hair that flipped back from the face. I had the ability to say, "We can't do it exactly that way, but you like it coming off your face? That's what you're looking for?" I was able to go through questions and answers to the point where there was something in there that I could do to make them happy.

My first job was at a little shampoo-and-set salon. That's where I realized that I didn't know anything. I did this child's haircut and I thought it looked fine. It was just a blunt bob thing. The owner of the salon came over, looked at it, and put her comb in the hair, and as soon as she did that, I thought, Oh, God, this is horrible! It looked different when she pulled her comb through it. It was uneven and awful. I was embarrassed that I'd gotten a license and didn't know any more than I did.

But I was so gung ho that I'd do whatever it took to learn. It was the beginning of the blow-dry era, and I knew I wanted to be in a progressive salon. I found an opening for a starter hairdresser in this department store where they had trainers from Sassoon in New York. After a month I'd done so well that the woman who was doing the training suggested that I could go on and be a trainer for the company. That excited me no end. The problem was that I had to pay my own way to New York and come up with the money to stay somewhere for three or four days during the training. I'd just turned nineteen, my husband and I had used every bit of our savings we had in the world to buy a house, and I didn't have the money. My parents didn't have anything extra. I couldn't do it. I had to say no. It was awful to say no to that. In a way it became the thing I always wanted to do, because I couldn't take that opportunity when it was offered.

I kept my sights on being a trainer. A new salon offered me the manager's job. I was twenty and a half years old. It was in the nicest shopping center in town and I built up an incredible following. I was booked two weeks in advance—that was really something—and I was making good money with no college education. Then my marriage broke up. I was doing well, but my husband could manipulate me to feel guilty about it. He'd done a number of things professionally, he was a salesman, and he'd gotten involved with someone else and I learned about it. I mustered up the courage to get out of the marriage. It was very hard to do. I had the feeling that I'd probably married him because I'd wanted to be an adult and get out of the house. It had never occurred to me that I could do that on my own.

About the same time my direct boss said, "This guy just applied for a job. You should think about hiring him. He has a wonderful résumé." I said, "A hairdresser with a résumé?" He was a real disco-looking guy, unbuttoned shirt, gold chains, the whole bit. He was full of himself, a Warren Beatty *Shampoo*-style person. But he did have this incredible résumé and this Vidal Sassoon training. I saw him as someone who could teach me something about haircutting. He'd been someplace that was like Mecca.

Eventually we started a relationship. He wanted to open his own salon. I still wanted to travel, see the world, and be

a trainer. We became partners in the Chic salon, we were running this business together, and we decided to get married. At its height, we had sixteen operators, manicurists, facialists. One of the things that Charles and I were good at was feeding off each other's energy. We saw major possibilities. We talked all the time about our place being *the* place to go in Tulsa. I felt we were on the doorstep of making something happen. I had not had that feeling before, because I'd always worked for someone else. We were going to give our

To think that we're all Protestants, Catholics, and Jews is just not so anymore.

employees paid vacations and health benefits. Of course, that was not done at the time in beauty salons. We did all of that.

I did it alongside my husband and it did not affect the marriage well. I'm not sure we so much married each other as we married that business. It was our family. It was our life, every hour of every day. It still is for him. We never really did take any time away to create a relationship that was separate. That was our mistake.

An exclusive department store with marble floors

opened across the street, and we were riding on their tails. The bigger we got, the way I saw it, the more structure we needed for the business to run well. I wanted to write a policy manual for new employees. I wanted procedures to be clear and everyone to adhere to them. That included Charles. We ended up in a mom-and-dad situation in the salon where dad was easygoing, wanted everyone to like him, and mom always ended up being a bitch. It was horrible. I was short and edgy. It wasn't my dream anymore.

I was twenty-eight years old and I'd had two divorces. It gave me pause. I started to think maybe I wasn't good at the relationship part. Maybe I'd just be by myself.

I opened my own salon, Capelli, but it wasn't fulfilling the way it had been when Charles and I had done Chic. For the next two years I felt like I was walking in the same place I'd been before, only this time it wasn't half as much fun.

The other part of this is that I'd been going to school part-time all these years, taking courses. I think what was accumulating in me was a broader worldview, and the triviality of what I did was getting to me on a fairly regular basis, especially when I had a picky customer.

I started seeing myself at fifty, and I thought, I cannot stand here and do this for another twenty years. I'll be bitter, or diminished, or stunted. It started to feel more like, Okay, I've done all I can do here. This was as far as this job would take me and it wasn't far enough. It felt like a wake-up call and a time to look around for a solution. What else had I been turned on by that I could go and do?

It wasn't like I sat down one day and recognized all this. It evolved over time, and little things started coming to me.

About the same time I met John, my husband-to-be, and he was a very encouraging factor. He'd recently changed his life and he said, "You can do anything you want. You're not stuck doing this."

I was also having my own spiritual journey and that included going to the Unitarian church. The minister had traveled widely and taught a course on the world's religions. In his travels he'd picked up all these figurines of deities from different religious traditions—a goddess from the Hindus, a medicine person from an African tribe, a collection of Buddhas. World religion really interested me, but what would I do with something like that?

One day I was reading the Sunday *New York Times* and there was this article about several states that had passed legislation requiring their public schools to offer Cultural Religious Studies. The idea is that the U.S. is becoming more pluralistic, and the only way we're going to solve our problems is to understand each other better. The way to do that is to teach kids in public schools about the world's religions. Not from an indoctrinating point of view, but *about* the religions. I thought, Here is something I can do. That was a moment of revelation.

When I told people, their typical response was, "You're certainly not going to do that in Oklahoma, or Arkansas, or anyplace in the Bible Belt." Or, "I can't imagine any public school's going to allow you to teach about religion." Or, "That's illegal."

It's not illegal. In fact, the Supreme Court decision that banned state-mandated prayer in public schools advocated the "objective" teaching about religion in public schools.

I became a full-time college student, which I paid for with the sale of my salon. John had moved to Little Rock, Arkansas, to be with his kids. With all the courses I'd taken, I entered Hendrix College, which is twenty minutes from Little Rock, as a junior. It was weird. I'd lived by the clock for so many years. Every forty-five minutes somebody new would sit in my chair and I'd have to be ready to talk to them and perform. I had to get used to being the observer in the class, not the actor on stage.

I got a B.A. in philosophy and religion. I had this adviser who was a theology professor and he came up with five graduate schools for me, including Harvard. Harvard was the only school that was an absolutely perfect fit: their Religion in Secondary Education program offered a master's in theological studies.

The day I got the acceptance letter from Harvard—with a good scholarship—I called my mother. "Sit down. You're not going to believe this." I was crying, so she thought something horrible had happened. I felt like Miss America.

It was about the second week of school in late September [1993], and it was so traditionally New England. The trees were changing colors and I was crossing Harvard Yard—I'm getting goose bumps now even talking about it—and I was thinking, I'm a student at Harvard. All of a sudden everything was bright. I've always had a sense that I was supposed to do something special. Being at Harvard meant that I had a chance, that I was in a position that maybe I could make a mark, do something worthwhile.

How do you teach about religion in the public schools and do it right? You have to be careful—that was part of what we were taught. Some people would say you sneak the religion in. I prefer to say that there's a naturally occurring opportunity. It's not an adequate education if it's not included. In a junior-year social studies class it's inadequate to teach the history of Africa without including the spread of Islam across the African continent. You can't teach about the founding of America without teaching about religion. I care so much about this because I think freedom of conscience is extremely important, and pluralism is growing. To think that we're all Protestants, Catholics, and Jews is just not so anymore. This sort of education helps us live with our deepest differences.

One of the things I did while I was at Harvard was work as a field researcher for the Pluralism Project, a project that studies the presence of the world's religions in the U.S. and what happens to Hinduism or Buddhism when it gets rooted in U.S. soil. It was incredibly enlightening to go back to my home state of Oklahoma, the buckle of the Bible Belt, and find the Hindus, the Buddhists, the Muslims.

I went through some really rough moments making this career change and had an incredible crisis of confidence while I was practice teaching. I totally bombed. I wondered, Have I made a wrong turn? Do I want to do this? I faced professional fears that I'd never experienced in eighteen years.

My goal had been to teach about religion in secondary education, but teaching wasn't a good match for me. Then in September 1996, the Freedom Forum First Amendment Center [in Nashville, Tennessee] needed a coordinator to work on their Religious Liberty Project. The Religious

Liberty Project focuses on the bitter conflicts that divide many American communities and schools. The goal is to help Americans move from battleground to common ground, and to build bridges of dialogue between groups on opposite sides of the debate. I could not have designed anything more perfect than that job.

The decision to take the job was complex. John recognized that this was an opportunity that I couldn't pass up, much like the Harvard one was. It was this or keep bumping around and be eighty and hate myself because I'd passed up this opportunity. That's what it came down to.

When I was younger and I wanted to be a hairdresser and I got that kit, there was an awful lot of need for exterior recognition of being good. I didn't feel that way about this. And, in fact, I haven't gotten much support, mostly because of the relationship issue. We'd moved to Sonoma [in Northern California] only a year ago but we'd already made good friends. (John's social and he gets out and makes friends easily.) Most of our friends here didn't understand how I could do this. First of all, we already lived in paradise. Why would I want to leave Sonoma to go to Tennessee, of all places? And then, since John had to stay here, why would I want to endure that kind of separation, for any job? And at my age? If I were twenty-two, that's a different thing, then you go where the job is. But at forty? Why?

I had to do all kinds of soul searching to come up with my own answers to those questions. My answers have had a lot do to with contribution. What I said earlier, feeling I was supposed to make a mark somehow, and seeing this work as the culmination of everything I'd done in changing my career.

I've taken to this work like a duck to water. One of the things I'm doing is leading workshops in communities around the country. Working in teams, we help educators navigate contentious waters and understand what's constitutionally permissible. We're trying to help people achieve civil discourse, rather than civil discord.

I liked hairdressing because there was a beginning and an ending and I could evaluate how well it went immediately. This is similar. These workshops are a day long, two days long, and I'm able to evaluate immediately how well it's gone. I have to be able to listen to people. Probably I'm drawing on skills I developed a long time ago. It's good to feel I've made a bridge.

In fact, I was in my hometown last week. We did a two-day seminar in Tulsa for several of the public school districts there. The workshop took place in a hotel that shares the parking lot with Chic, the beauty salon I owned with my ex-husband. I could look out the window of the hotel where we were doing the workshop and I could see my old beauty salon. It really was full circle.

**M**AXINE KELLEY, b. 1953, *licensed general contractor*

JAMILLAH SIMMS, b. 1972, *construction manager*

AKILAH (Keekee) SIMMS, b. 1974, *office manager*

Maxine & Jamillah & Keekee

With a light snow dusting Chicago, Maxine and her daughters are gathered in the living room of her apartment. Theirs is the story of one family's evolution out of the cycle of poverty, public aid, and pregnancy and into a mother/daughters construction business. The hard-hatted women of the Diving Remodeling Company are rehabbing themselves as they rehab houses in northeast Chicago. On the eve of moving into a home of their own, Maxine's construction boots are planted on the threshold of a new life.

mAXINE: I believe before you can really get your business going, your home life, your foundation, has got to be together. That's why I'm closing on this house.

KEEKEE: It's a home. There's an upstairs, a downstairs, and Mama's going to remodel the basement. All of us live in different places now. We pay roughly $1,800 a month for rent. There's a lot of money being spent out.

JAMILLAH: The house to me represents unity, okay? We'll have eight people. Me and my two kids, Keekee and her three kids, and Mom.

MAXINE: We're there for each other now. We take up the slack.

MAXINE: Plus I'll have enough space for my office . . . I'm a little emotional about buying the house. It's finally happening. I feel blessed.

I started the company in 1993 and named it the Divine Remodeling Company. I'm trying to stick with something that's spiritual. Divine to me means great, utmost, marvelous.

Ever since I was young I enjoyed construction. When we was growing up, I was always grabbing that paint and wanting to do something to my room. I'd always want to make something better, want to change it. There was a playhouse in the back and we cleaned it out, me and my brothers. But they stopped. I painted it white and purple and put up a door.

My dad and mom separated. There was nine children. My mother had a nervous breakdown and we was on public aid. We moved every year, like gypsies. There was a time when me and my two brothers had to share one can of Campbell's soup for lunch. That's how poor we were. One day my grammar school teacher asked me about my headaches and she started buying my lunch.

The year I turned eighteen, I graduated from high school and moved out of the Housing Authority where I'd been living with Mom. That's when I met the kids' dad. I was infatuated. He was a draftsman for the McDonald's Corporation and a licensed general contractor.

I learned about the construction business from him. Each place we moved into he'd always tear down a wall, or want to put up a closet, or take out a window. He'd always start and I'd have to finish. He'd mostly come up with the ideas, and I'd mainly do the labor.

We moved into the first apartment when Jamillah was a baby and I was carrying Keekee. We lived on the second floor and there was a third floor that was like an attic. The kids' dad wanted to make a living space upstairs, so we knocked out some walls. That's when it all started, from that apartment in 1974. The reason we had to move from that location was, the landlord, he didn't want the wall knocked out. He didn't want nobody living upstairs. My husband went and did it anyway.

Our first home was a two-flat that we made out to be a family dwelling. We did a lot of work on that. A lot. We cut a hole through the first floor so we could get to the basement. We dug down eight inches into the dirt and poured in a new foundation. We were living in a mess. It was cold. It was around Thanksgiving. He even took out the windows. And we're talking about windows six feet high and two feet wide. He wanted to "modernize" the windows, but he'd cut a hole, start to frame it, and I'd be the one who'd have to put some plastic up there because the window would be open.

The second floor was unlevel. It was on a slant. We talked about what to do, and when he came home one evening I'd leveled the floor. I couldn't believe it myself. It looked nice. I got me some two-by-fours, I got some plywood, I got a leveler, and drew a line on all four walls, so I could get a straight level. I put the two-by-fours down, cross braces, and laid my first subfloor. It was like fitting pieces to a puzzle. I was able to visualize the finished product, which looked a hell of a lot better. It was like I finally created something wonderful with my mind and hands.

Then the kids' father lost his job and just didn't give a damn. A gang shot out the front door. I just gave up and got heavy into drugs. I used that as a relief.

When I look back on it now, it gives me a lift when I run into problems. When I think I cannot accomplish certain things, I look back and see what I've come from.

After their daddy left, I had a minimum-wage job at a bubble gum factory. I ate a lot of bubble gum and ruined my teeth and I didn't make enough money. I went on public aid for about two years. That was enough. I wanted more out of life.

There was an article in the newspaper that Motorola was taking applications. I mean, the line was like two blocks long, okay? My brother and my sister were also out there, and her and I got hired but not our brother. I guess it was just God's will that I got a job. After about two years I got laid off due to lack of work.

It was easy to get a job at Northrop because they knew the people at Motorola are quality workers. I worked my way up to materials coordinator. I handled ordering materials for the B-2 bomber and the Stealth bomber. It was a military atmosphere. That was a real trial because you can't ask no questions, you've just got to do what they tell you to do. I was the lowest-paid person in my department, but I trained young white guys to be my boss, because they were ex-servicemen. I had no say-so. I hated that job, but I had to keep it because of the kids. After leaving the nine to five, I'd always fix or remodel something. That's what really pushed me to do my own thing.

JAMILLAH: Even when my mother had a professional job and she dressed up in the daytime, she'd always come home and say, "Okay, it's time to do the basement now." I'd hand her nails and stuff.

I'd signed up for the Marines my senior year in high school, but I found out I was pregnant the night before I was supposed to leave. (I was an employee at Church's Chicken and he was the boss. I think I was naive and gullible because he was much older.) After that I had my son, and they don't take single mothers with kids in any of the armed forces.

My mother and I went to Chicago Women in Trades together. We signed up for the carpenter's school.

MAXINE: The course at Chicago Women in Trades is a free twelve-week pre-apprenticeship program where they prepare you—your math had to be up to par—to get you into the union school to be a union carpenter.

The union school got me a job doing highway work. Bad experience. I was a carpenter's apprentice. We don't do the manual labor part. Only laborers do the labor part. We was forming concrete walls up on the highway. There was this black journeywoman—a journey is a man or woman who's been in the field more than four years—and this foreman had her and I doing labor work, carrying sixteen-foot two-by-fours. That's when I had my accident. We'd just poured a concrete slab and put plastic on top of it, and I was carrying three sixteen-foot two-by-fours, and I slipped and hurt my leg.

That accident was a sign, God saying that ain't the place

for me to be. It didn't give me a chance to be creative, and I wanted to do the rehabbing. I said, I'm doing my own thing.

I went out there like a handyman. I wouldn't even make no proposals or anything. I'd just go ahead and do it. (I didn't get my contractor's license until last year.) When I needed a licensed tradesperson, I'd get someone who was licensed and bonded, usually a male.

I've made blunders. I've learned the hard way. I've lost money. That's why I have Keekee managing, because I love doing what I'm doing. I'd do it for free. Now like the guy I'm doing the bathroom for, he wants me to do the ceramic tile. I told him I'd have to get back to him because I don't give out no prices. I let Keekee do my pricing.

KEEKEE: A lot of things my mama wants to do, I know a quicker way to do those things. It was too much for her to do the work and type the proposal, so I handle all the paperwork, the contracts, setting up all her appointments, calling to see if they're satisfied with the work. I make sure the funds are in. When people call the office, they talk to me. I handle my nieces and nephews. I go up to their schools, take care of their lunch, all that to keep Mama and Jamillah on track with work they have to do.

I always wanted to be a model when I was little, but having had the kids at an early age, that's really messed me. I didn't want anyone watching my son, so I left school when I was a junior to care for him. I've been on and off public aid for about five and a half years. I took a training course at the business college, and when I finished I got off public aid. I got my last check August 1996.

JAMILLAH: When we was in Chicago Women in Trades,

kids and was working for UPS at night, part-time. I was on public aid for four and a half years. They might cut your food stamps, but they allow you to work a certain amount of hours. I got my last check January 1996.

The job I'm most proud of was this house on Augusta Boulevard. Mama left me by myself and I was like, "Mom, are you leaving me with the saw? The electric saw?" I'd used the electric saw at Chicago Women in

I was pregnant with my second child. The following year I passed the test at the union school to become a carpenter's apprentice, but I lost my place on the list. I never got the letter in time. I cried and cried. Mama told me it wasn't to be, it wasn't my time. And it would have been quite a strain with my baby so young.

I ended up in the construction business because my mama needed help. At the time I was home with my two

Trades, but there was always someone watching me. I had to use it on two-by-fours. She showed me how, told me how to keep it straight. I think I messed up about two or three pieces.

MAXINE: She was more down on herself than anything else.

JAMILLAH: I enjoyed the work. A lot of times she had to send me home because I wanted to stay. I'd say, "Come on, Mama, let's finish." She'd say, "I've had it. We'll start again tomorrow."

I recently quit UPS, and I work as a furnace operator at Temple Steel at night, and I work part-time for my mother during the day. Construction work is slow in the winter, but I work at whatever she needs me the most . . . I'm always tired.

MAXINE: We're working toward a goal right now. That's why we're pushing.

JAMILLAH: I want to go to appentice school. I want to learn the basics from the beginning. After I get the license and I'm a union carpenter, that's when I'll work full-time for my mother.

MAXINE: Or I may be working for you!

JAMILLAH: I'm proud of our mother because she's been all the way rock bottom as far as drugs and things my father put her through. Now she has no way to go but up. She keeps her head on level and she's accomplishing what she wants to accomplish.

I'm a better role model for my son now. Like my son says, "Mama, are you goin' to work with Grandma now?" I want them to know I've got some get-up-and-go about myself. I want to be somebody.

KEEKEE: It's the same with me. It's like I have an office at home. They know not to bother me because I'm working. They know not to mess with my typewriter.

MAXINE: I see great things in the future. My minimum goal is to make $50,000 a year, that's net. It's not just me making the money. I want to help individuals live in a nice, decent home without paying extravagant prices.

Since my daughters are in the company, there's a lot of things I don't have to be concerned with. There was a time that I'd be so bogged down that if I didn't do it, it wasn't going to get done. I was so busy working I didn't have time to wash my own clothes. Jamillah works at night, and she came home one morning and took my clothes to the Laundromat. She hadn't even been to sleep. It's like we're there for each other now. We take up the slack.

The work is out there. I have people calling me. Like the guy who wants me to do his bathroom. I told him I'd have to fit him in. I've got this other guy with a seventeen-unit building and he wants me to rehab five apartments. I'm on the crust of success.

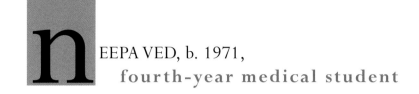

NEEPA VED, b. 1971, fourth-year medical student

Neepa was blessed with a rare, straight career trajectory: from the

age of two she knew with an unshakable certainty that she would be

a doctor. Her challenges have come from the personal side of her life.

An Indian woman married to a Mexican-American man, at twenty-

three she was almost derailed by depression and divorce.

Neepa

i have this belief that we're the sum of what we've been through. It's more of a Western philosophy in the sense that we control who we are by choices we make rather than a Hindu philosophy, where people have their own karma or destiny. I can't say I wish I'd never tried to kill myself because the suicide became a dividing line between *this* was what my life was before and *this* is what my life is going to be now.

I've wanted to be a doctor since I was two years old. I had this little doctor set, some plastic stuff, and I walked around the house with that, playing doctor. I honestly can't come up with a specific instance where this idea was born. It's something I've always felt. It's not even a desire. I'm going to be a doctor. It is my calling. But who called, and calls?

I'm going to be a doctor. It is my calling. But who called, and calls?

In medical school my first patient was a thirty-something black gentleman with a spinal cord injury. He told me he'd been on the way to his brother's funeral, was driving this van full of his family, and ended up crashing. His mother had died, another brother died, and his sister was hurt. He understood that this was the first time I'd interviewed a patient and gotten a history. He was incredibly open, probably one of the most open patients I've ever had. All I did was listen, but it made him happier. It made me feel I was definitely where I was supposed to be.

Miguel and I had started dating when I was a freshman and he was a senior in college. He went off to Michigan to do his MBA, and when we saw each other we made up for the lost time together. In the beginning he was supportive of me becoming a doctor. He'd say, "Of course, I'll cook sometimes. I'll carry my load in terms of cleaning up. I know you have to study." After we married, he'd watch TV and try to keep it low. But quickly it became frustrating for him. I think we would have had problems regardless of whether or not I went to medical school. I can't see myself being a housewife, and that's what he wanted. A smart housewife.

As a first-generation Indian woman in the U.S. I got a lot of mixed

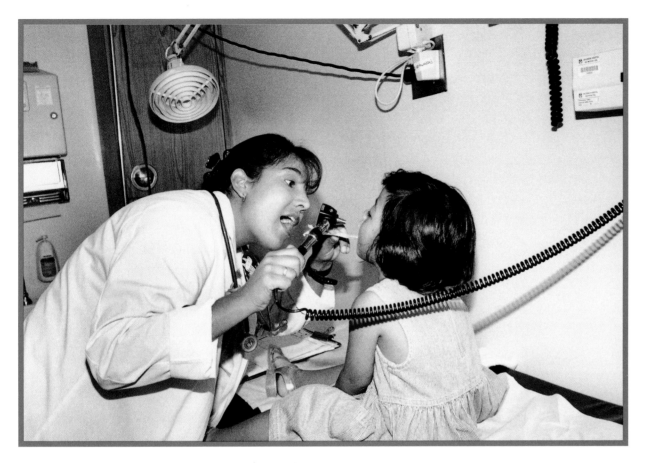

underserved community. It was a big step for me—getting the scholarship and knowing I was working toward my dream of helping people who really needed help. Miguel had a hard time with that and had discouraged me from applying. With the scholarship I could support myself through medical school, and that was difficult for him. Even though he was born here,

messages. Mom would praise me for being ambitious, but at the same time she felt the woman's role in a marriage was to take care of her husband domestically. I should always have dinner ready every night, warm and ready when he came home. So for me not to be able to be home when my husband got home, I felt very guilty.

In my second year in medical school I received a National Health Service Corps Scholarship. They would pay my tuition and I'd pay back by serving as a primary-care physician in an

Miguel is Mexican-American, and his family is traditional—the husband supports the wife. By January 1995, we'd been married a year and a half. That's when he said he wanted a divorce.

I'd been depressed before Miguel dropped the bomb, but afterward I really withdrew. When I went to school—*if* I went to classes—I didn't pay attention. I wouldn't talk to my friends. I wouldn't answer the phone. I'd lie in bed, staring up at the ceiling. I couldn't sleep. I didn't eat. I ask myself now, How come I didn't flunk out of medical school?

Maybe I was lucky to have known some of the material beforehand, or I could test well enough?

I started seeing a psychiatrist, and I think this shows Miguel still cared in that he insisted that I seek therapy. It's a different position to be in as a physician-to-be, to have studied depression, to know what disease you have and the ways to get around treatment, because you don't want to be treated. I went from thinking about suicide once a month, to thinking at least once a week, to thinking every day, to thinking all the time.

In March 1995, I tried to kill myself. I'd wanted to do it earlier, but I waited until spring break so people wouldn't be looking for me when I didn't show up for classes.

I studied the pharmacology text in terms of what I could use that was easily accessible. Because I have asthma, I react adversely to aspirin. I thought, Okay, let me start with aspirin. I bought a new scalpel blade that I knew would be sharp. I figured if I took aspirin my blood would be thin enough that it wouldn't clot so much. This was at a time when I was sleeping in the guest room and my husband was in the bedroom, and he tended to sleep pretty soundly.

I was found by Miguel in the morning. I stayed in the hospital only overnight—long enough for them to take care of the wounds on my neck and wrists. I was still thinking I could try again. Quite quickly it became evident that having to take medications and having to talk to my doctor did start making me feel better.

By my third year in medical school Miguel and I were separated. There were days when I thought, Is medicine really what I'm supposed to do? As much as I wanted to be a physician, I loved this person so much that I would have been will-ing to give it all up to have a chance at a solid marriage. I was in this abyss. I'd come home and no one was there. I had my cats, but I didn't want to pay attention to them.

Now I can say I've learned from my depression. I know what signs to look for in myself and in patients to catch this early on. At the time I thought, I can't be a healer if I can't heal myself. But looking at how I feel now, I have no doubt being a doctor is what I'm supposed to be. It's a combina-tion of a couple of things. The first is being in a position where I can say, *"I understand."* It could be something as simple as asthma. When a patient says, "You have no idea what it feels like not to be able to breathe," I know how scary it is.

I feel much better about my ability to be a good physi-cian. I don't think happy is the word, but exhilarated is how I feel. I've rediscovered the joy of being able to tell a patient, "This is your diagnosis. We can—*I can*—help you." On my obstetric and gynecology rotation, the joy of bring-ing a baby into the world was almost, for me, like a rebirth.

Part of the reason I feel better is the nourishment I get from working with patients. The kid who's been through so much, and I'm the first one to hear him talk again. These things may seem little, but they're huge. I live for those moments. It's an adrenaline rush, and it's a feeling I like to get over and over again.

I'm still in the process of getting to be a full doctor. But whatever interactions I have with patients feed my desire to continue—not just with the career but with life. The career is, at this point, my life. This is more than a job. This is really who I am. I can see myself doing this the rest of my life. I feel *home.*

mOLLY VANDEWATER, b. 1979,
high school senior

I'm a volunteer wildlife rehabilitator. Last season we took 1,200 animals into our house—exotic animals that were injured or orphaned. During baby bird season we had 150 animals we were caring for. Baby birds have to be fed every hour, and baby hummingbirds have to be fed every fifteen minutes. It's a lot of work. When I go to school, then my mom takes care of them.

My dad turned our garage into a bird room, and it's got banks of cages and incubators. The whole family's kind of involved, except my brother's not interested in the animals. He's into his music. Right now I have a redtail hawk (with infected feet), a barn owl (he's dehydrated), a possum, a squirrel, an American kestrel, six doves, about nine pigeons (one has eye problems), two seagulls (they have botulism), six crows, a raven, a finch, a goldfinch (wing injuries), two hummingbirds (both were cat-attacked), a wood-pecker, a whippoorwill that hit a window, three wild ducks, and a baby raccoon. A wild rabbit came in last night from the vet. He was car-hit.

Three of the parrots—Elvis, Dork, and Melbourne—come into the shower with me every morning. They run around the floor and take little baths while I shower. Elvis enjoys it best.

Molly

j

JUDY MULHAIR, b. 1944,
flight attendant/youth hostel owner

I come from the

After her divorce this ex-rodeo queen wasted away to 89 pounds.

Then Judy, a fighter and scrapper, seized on a plan to rescue her

property and herself. Her solution embraced an ironic blend of the

commercial and educational sides of the travel industry. To welcome

guests arriving at her hostel on Vashon Island, Washington, she

chain-saw carved a totem pole. She put a bear on top because it's

the Native American symbol of the dream state, and this hostel

represents her dream.

Judy

hard side of life. I've learned that maybe I'm not terribly smart, but I have a lot of horse sense.

I can plumb. I can wire. I can put a motor in a car, brakes in a truck, install a fireplace. I can build a log cabin from the Douglas firs on my property. I can carry on a conversation about politics. I'm not "dumb and stupid" like my eighth-grade teacher said I was. She also said that I probably couldn't graduate from college. Talk about setting a course for the rest of your life! I was out to prove that I wasn't stupid, that I could go to college and graduate. A lot of people aren't good at taking tests, but they're good at everything else.

I've learned that perseverance is much more important than intelligence. When I didn't have money, when I didn't have a man, I just kept putting one foot in front of the other. I told that to my nephew who was going to drop out of college because he couldn't get good grades. I said, "Hang in there. It's perseverance that they're looking for. They want to know that you have stick-to-it-tiveness." That's the one thing I've learned in my life—anyone can quit. It's those who stick with it who come out on top.

In college a counselor asked what I was interested in. I said, "I want to be a geologist." A copper mine had been in our family since my great-grandfather. It hadn't produced much, but I thought I could help Dad fulfill his dreams. My adviser said, "You can't be a geologist. You'd just be a lab rat. You can't be out in the field. You're a woman."

I followed my mother's career, which was accounting, and later changed to marketing and finance. It was a hard grind because there were so few women in the business school [Washington State University, 1966]. Maybe twenty-five women and two hundred men. And we were picked on. I was always the "little cheerleader," the "homecoming queen." They'd tease me, "What are you doing in our business class?"

After I graduated, I became a flight attendant. I'd never been on an airplane. Because I'd come from such a very tiny town [Waitsburg, Washington, pop. 1,000], I thought it would give me an opportunity to see the world, or, at least, go coast-to-coast. I joined United and have been with them thirty-one years.

At twenty-three, I married my childhood sweetheart. When I was thirty-five, he left me for another woman. I'd loved being married, and when I was pressed into this divorce situation, I felt fragile . . . frail . . . lost. I lost me in my marriage. For three years, I moaned, "He did this," "He did that." Finally a flight attendant friend on a layover said, "I'm so sick of hearing 'poor me.' Get a life!"

From that day forward everything that came out of my mouth had to be what I was going to do for me, not what had happened to me. I had to concentrate on things that didn't remind me of him, find things we hadn't done. We hadn't traveled that much and I wanted to show my boys,

who were five and ten, the world. I had no money, but I remembered about hostels. I called American Youth Hostels and asked, "Can an old lady use these if she has children with her?" I was thirty-five. I felt really old then.

My boys and I bicycled around Holland and stayed at hostels for two weeks. I was so sold on the friendship, the helpfulness, the long tables with people talking and trading stories. It felt like family. I thought, By gummy, this is what I'm going to do with my property.

You have to understand—in the divorce I didn't get any advantages. He left me with little money and a seventy-year-old, 3,200-square-foot, half-finished house on ten acres of land. He left a big mess and walked away from it. But I wanted my house so bad, even though it wasn't finished—the porches weren't done, a fireplace was half-finished, a bathroom wasn't done.

In my dreams I kept seeing huts all over the property, little round domes. After Holland, that vision made sense. My brother had a tour business on the Snake River and he was getting rid of some tepees. I wanted them. I also wanted covered wagons, the real ones that had come West. I chose the theme of Cowboys and Indians for my hostel.

By 1982 I was chartered with American Youth Hostels. My brother's big tepees became "dorms" shared by five or six people, and the smaller ones were family tepees sleeping two to four. The covered wagons held a single twin-size mattress. I turned the sun room in my house into a bunkhouse with eight beds. I charged $3.25 a night for a cot, pads and pillows, and breakfast. I thought, Gosh, if I could just get ten people a night.

Now we sleep upwards of forty a night, and with tents we sleep sixty. I have to laugh—one night recently we had ninety-four. Our whole first summer we served only eighty-three. Last year we served seven thousand at $9 a night.

A lot of people I'm flying with say, "How do you do

I dedicate my hostel to those who have the guts and the perseverance to make their dreams reality.

this?" Well, it is a mystery—how I fly for United and do this at the same time—but basically I haven't had a vacation in twelve years. You have to remember, the American Youth Hostel season runs from May 1 to October 31. It's a summer hostel. I would bid all my vacation time and I'd take June, July, and August off, so I'd be here for three solid months. In slower months, I'd get some staff, local people to help me. And I'd bid, like, three-day trips where I'd leave in the afternoon one day and be gone all the next day, and be back the afternoon of the third day. It's not like I was gone on a ten-day excursion with the airlines. I was always touching base.

118

I mean, I was exhausted. I'd fly in from London and come home and joke that I have a 747 in my backyard. But I'm a people person. And I've continued flying because I like the job, and I couldn't have developed the property without my income from flying. Also, the skills I use in the airplane are not all that different from what I do here. I've had situations on planes that are explosive, in the sense of people's personalities, fighting over the window seat, or whatever. Handling those situations and situations that arise in a hostel are similar. I like dealing with both—problem-solving.

It was extremely difficult being a single mom, flying out of the area and running the hostel. Dad had passed away and I said, "Mom, please come live with me." She took care of the kids when I was flying, was the bookkeeper for the hostel, and has been my main sidekick.

I have to step back a moment. I have to explain that when I wanted to build these facilities I was in a tight money crunch. I started using a lot of my business knowledge from college that I didn't think I'd ever use again. I bought an RV, and that was one thing that helped me get out of debt. The guy who sold it to me, he rented it out all summer, and with the rentals I could write the RV off. And at the end of three years, when it was totally depreciated, this guy bought it back for exactly what I paid for it. It helped me save tax dollars from my United income, and I took the money from the RV and started the log cabin.

I've used many, many hands to put this hostel together. Other people saw what I was doing and kicked in and helped. The first two covered wagons were put together by a German boy. British boys helped with the bathhouse. A guy from Massachusetts helped peel logs for the log cabin. People just pitch in because they like what's going on.

Some people lay their bodies down and protest the Trident missile coming into this area. I'm not the kind of person to go and demonstrate. But I believe in the hostel movement for world peace. I know how I felt in a foreign country. That hostel symbol—a triangle with a house and a tree—had this safe, friendly feeling. I thought, Oh, thank God, it's home. And then I thought, I can do this for the world, bring people together to get to know each other. I dedicate my hostel to those who have the guts and the perseverance to make their dreams reality.

My most unusual guests were an Arab and an Israeli. Two males, twenty and twenty-one, they had met in a New York hostel and had traveled six months together. This was the end of their journey. At dinner they had all of us in tears, talking about how the hostel network had changed their lives, how they didn't want to go back to the hatred they'd been taught and had used against each other. They'd found true friendship. It made me think that I was on the right path.

And that's just one story. I don't want to brag, but people love my place—the ambiance of what I've created. Not every day does someone say, "This is really neat," but it happens. I think it's because we're on this island and we're out of the hustle and bustle of the city. It makes me feel good—that something so simple is appreciated. I'm the facilitator. The people have to come and make the magic.

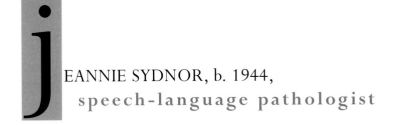

JEANNIE SYDNOR, b. 1944,
speech-language pathologist

Jeannie's job hunt took twenty-five years. From her graduate-student apartment in Alexandria, Virginia, a third-floor walk-up, she credits aptitude testing with finally helping her over the hump. Hers is an example of a woman who refused to settle, even though her persistence didn't pay off until she was forty-eight years old.

Jeannie

my career path has been a living hell of learning one negative lesson after another of what work should not be: watching the clock, living for weekends and vacations, doing a good job only so I could respect myself rather than because I enjoyed the work, being underpaid and exploited and learning this isn't only acceptable but to be expected. The good thing that came of all this was that I learned I was incapable of living and working like that forever. I kept searching for alternatives. Looking back, I think, How did I persevere? Thank God, I didn't know how long it would take.

I had a distinct moment of truth when I was nineteen years old. I come from a family of four daughters and one son in which it's very supported if, as one of these daughters, you're attractive and entertaining, clever, gracious, more like a hostess, or a smart geisha. When I was nineteen I was at a wedding reception for this quite wealthy couple in Greenwich, Connecticut. It was a summer evening and I was standing under a pink tent, talking to three men. I was the only woman, and I was laughing, having a good time, and it hit me: This is what I've been trained for, I'm doing a good job, I'm enjoying myself, and it's not enough. It's whipped cream, but not the main course. It's pleasant, but not something to arrange your life around.

> People had always said I was a good listener, but I thought that was like being told, "You have a nice smile."

I'd been raised with the expectation of getting married and having children. Since that moment of truth under the pink tent I've been obsessed by the question, "What am I going to do?" My dream was to earn a living doing what I like as I'm doing it. Not feeling satisfied I had done it, but being in the moment. I wanted to be revved by the activity.

It broke my heart when someone had a perfect fit. Once I attended the ordination of a friend who became an Episcopalian priest. While I shared a hymn book with Brother Seraphim, a monk, I thought, Jan's got his, where's mine? At the time I was working at a bank on Park Avenue, where I was one of the customer service people up at the front who open new accounts. I dreaded when someone in a social situation asked the inevitable question: "What do you do?" I was ashamed because the bank felt so wrong, like I was living someone else's life, wearing someone else's clothes. The discrepancy between how I spent my days and how I wanted to spend them was enormous. I felt, You should know by now. People know by twenty-five. Why can't I find the big It?

I had the feeling that the best I could do was coast along, and get some job to supply myself with an income so I could pay my bills, and when I was off, I went to the theater. In my late twenties I became involved with the Theater for the Forgotten, a group that put on plays in prisons. As a volunteer, I had an almost spooky identification with the prisoners, perhaps because I felt imprisoned in a world where I couldn't find a place for myself.

I kept a notebook, which grew to four very fat notebooks, about jobs. I jotted every idea in my notebooks— advertising, arts administration, personnel work. I'd have a conversation with someone who was enthusiastic about their work, and I'd jot that tidbit down, hoping it would trigger an interest in me. Since everything was a shot in the dark, any crumb counted. I thought eventually something would ring a bell with me.

Searching for The Answer, I took dozens of courses from "TV Commercial Production" to "The Nuts and Bolts of Screenwriting." I learned I liked movies, but the field was too competitive. I wouldn't be happy fighting for one of those jobs. As the years went by, the more discouraged I became, the harder it was to keep searching.

I have a sister, Gleaves, who was well aware that as I'd gone from job to job—fund-raiser, administrator in a real estate office, ten years at a second bank—I'd become numbed by the effort of trying to find what I should do. She found out about this company [the Johnson O'Connor Research Foundation] that did aptitude testing. She said, "Let's do it together." It was a huge amount of money, and she offered to pay for it.

Without even enough hope to try anymore, I was so reluctant that I actually hoped Gleaves would cancel. The testing lasted one and a half days, and I learned something surprising. My counselor said my strongest talent was listening, being able to pinpoint sound. I said, "Oh, no, I couldn't have done well on that." I told her that the test where we'd distinguished these high and low beeps had been at the end of the day. I hadn't been paying attention. I was exhausted. "That's aptitude for you," she said. "It doesn't matter if you're tired."

This was brand new to me. In all those notebooks I'd kept, listening skills had never jumped out at me. People had always said I was a good listener, but I thought that was like being told, "You have a nice smile." I didn't think it meant anything as far as my quest went.

After this was pointed out as a talent, slowly something clicked. There was a bull's-eye here. It wasn't that I'm such a good listener, but I know what I'm hearing as far as auditory accuracy is concerned. Because of the testing, something happened. It wasn't like a big bang, more like a little spark.

I continued taking courses with a vengeance, trying to understand how I could make a contribution. In 1991, I was in a "Shakespeare in Production" course when the teacher said, "Next week we'll have the voice coach." Something went through me. That was the first time I'd heard the term "voice coach." I said, "The *what?*"

When I heard the voice coach describe his profession, I realized all those years I'd been going to the theater I hadn't been paying attention to costumes or sets—the actors could be in blue jeans sitting on folding chairs. What I'd been doing was listening to how they used words, how they sounded. I decided that's what I'd shoot for: voice coach.

I applied to the only school in the U.S. that taught voice coaching. I was turned down because I didn't have acting experience. I couldn't get into the full program at the Central School of Speech and Drama in London, but I was accepted into their three-week summer course. To this day I think it was an accident I was accepted. This is the same school where Sir Laurence Olivier and Vanessa Redgrave studied. This was a refresher course for professionals who were already coaches. As the date approached, I felt, I've stepped way out of bounds here. I don't even understand Shakespeare, and these people speak of Cordelia as if she's their next-door neighbor.

The first day, there were twelve of us in class and we introduced the person next to us. Mine was a voice coach at Stratford-on-Avon, and I thought, Oh, God, what is she going to say about me? That I work in a bank? She said, "This is Jeannie from Ahhh-lex-zahn-dree-ahhh Vir-gin-ee-ahhhhh. Isn't that lovely?" This chill went through me, and I thought, I'm with the sound people. They hear sound. I'm with the right people.

I had all this energy. I'd go to classes during the day, the theater at night, and wake up the next day and still be just as interested. To have that feeling was such a luxury. This was what I'd always wanted.

There are four schools on the entire planet that teach voice coaching, and over the next eighteen months I applied to each of them. They all required acting experience. I was turned down by all four. I'd hit a wall. I contacted David Carey, the head of voice at the school in London. He recommended I take acting lessons so I'd be using my instrument, and that I get a master's degree in speech-language pathology. I did not want to hear that because I knew that was scientific—physiology, biology—and they work with pathology. People who stutter, who have throat cancer and have had part of their tongue removed. But David knew me, knew the huge gap between what I wanted to do and what I could do, and he said this is what I should do.

For three semesters I kept my day job at the bank and took speech-language pathology courses at night [University of the District of Columbia]. Frankly, after the first course, "The Anatomy and Physiology of the Speech and Hearing Mechanism," I was ready to quit. This is dry. This is not, How can I sound like Cordelia and make it come across to the second balcony?

But I was also learning that speech-language pathology is a field in which there is a huge need. These people don't have trouble getting jobs. They have choices—to work in a school system, a hospital clinic, in private consulting. I'd never earned more than $20,000 at the bank, and I'd be surprised if my first job as a speech clinician would pay less than $40,000.

son. I'd never sought how to apply banking principles. I knew what forms we used, took my paycheck, and went to another play. I began to think I'd made a huge mistake in choosing this profession.

I plunged into a depression that landed me in a shrink's office. I asked her, "Does this mean I have to start all over again searching for a new line of work?" My present search had taken twenty-five years. She said, "My job with you is to be a cheerleader, to urge you to stay in this profession you've found." She said

I was ecstatic to be leaving the bank, but it was excruciatingly hard being a student again at forty-eight. I said to myself, weekly, daily, "You can always quit." Still to this day when I'm buying books, I have doubts. "Am I going to go through with this?" It's a negative habit to think that I'm dabbling, that things aren't for keeps.

When I started the practicum, which is like an internship, I was awkward applying what I'd learned to a real per-

she'd seldom seen such a perfect match of personality with work: I, who for so many years had not found a way to express myself within society, was now helping others express themselves. I asked her if other women needed "cheerleaders." If a lot of people in her profession found themselves doing for other grown women what she was offering me: support and encouragement, so I wouldn't give up. She said, Definitely, yes.

During the practicum, one of my first clients was an attorney with such a soft voice the judge was always saying, "Speak up, Counselor." I worked on his volume. When he said something that rang out, the energy I felt was so exciting. I was loving what I was doing while I was doing it. *It* was happening.

Another early client was a five-year-old boy with an articulation problem. Jimmie was so impaired I had a terrible time understanding him. But the thing about Jimmie is he never quit. We'd go back and forth maybe eight times—repeating *bed* and *bet*—before he got it right. I was amazed how he stuck it out. Even though I was thinking, I'm not interested in articulation, I'm interested in voice, and I don't care if he pronounces this right, *It* was still occurring.

I'm not home free just yet. Every time I have a client I feel, What if I look into their eyes and don't have any ideas? I'm learning that the person I'm working with has the answers. They will tell me what they need, not the textbook.

Because I've found this interest in working with voice, I've developed other interests in my life. Before, I didn't have much outside of theater. I didn't have things like knitting and horseback riding. Now, like ripples expanding in a pond, I have secondary interests. To learn how my own voice works, I started taking singing lessons. Singing is nothing more than exaggerated talking. My teacher said it would be good if I could accompany myself, so I took up the piano. Now I have music in my life.

I feel alive. When I'm waiting at a traffic light, I'm thinking, What am I going to do with Jimmie? My God, I'm not even worrying about the light turning green.

P

EGGY O'BRIEN, b. 1963,

mother

"Society doesn't consider motherhood a profession, especially for an educated woman, but I do," says Peg. A self-described intellectual and a Truman Scholar, Peg's current place of employment is a modest two-bedroom, one-bath family home just north of San Francisco.

Peggy

i always knew I wanted to be a full-time mother. It was never a question. I wanted to make a home for my children. I didn't voice my true desire to anyone—except my dad—for fear it would look as if I wasn't ambitious.

I grew up during the throes of the women's movement, when there was a lot of emphasis on "you can do anything you want," which is wonderful and a terrific freedom. Yet there was always the subtle message that because you can do anything, you can do better than choosing the traditional role of staying at home and running a household. You can be a fireman or president of the U.S. or an astronaut.

Being a full-time "professional" mother is not respected by society. It's not considered an accomplishment. There's no prestige attached to it. It's seen as an interlude between "real" jobs. I'm often asked when I'm going back to work. I wish being a mom could be recognized as a valid goal for college-educated women.

If I'm at a social function, there can be a dismissive attitude when people ask, "What do you do?" Depending on the person, I might say, "I'm a full-time mom," or if I feel the need to impress them I might say, "I taught XYZ." Then the lights and bells go off and they'll want to talk about that.

Someone might get the impression, "Oh, she's like June Cleaver." Nothing wrong with June Cleaver, but Ward ran the house. I'm looking back to a richer historical tapestry when motherhood was a great ambition. As a child, I was well aware of Abigail Adams, Francis Dandridge (Martha Washington's mother), Sarah Bush Lincoln (Abraham Lincoln's stepmother). These were women who ran great households, and they were well-respected, dedicated mothers. That's what I'm looking back to. Not that I want my children to be Abraham Lincoln, but I think there's a huge value and importance in creating an environment for your children.

I'm constantly thinking about how I can do my job best, as you would in a

> ## I think that raising my children well is the most important public service I could ever do.

profession. As a teacher you think about the long-term objectives for your course, and I certainly do that with my children. I'm always teaching them, hopefully not in a pedantic, overbearing way. I'm always thinking, What's the best environment for them?

I think, for example, that the best environment is that we all have dinner together. It would be easier for me, sure, to feed the kids macaroni and cheese at five-thirty, and trundle them off to bed. Mac, their dad, leaves at six-thirty and doesn't get home until six-thirty, so maybe the first eleven hours go well, and that last hour can be pretty bleak. But I think it's better for them, for all of us, to sit down as a family. Even though Lindsay's only four and Benjamin's not quite two, we sit here at the dinner table, we light the candles, and we talk. It's a lovely routine. I must say I'm amazed that the kids will sit as long as they do.

My mother gave me mixed messages about being a mother. She's a wonderful woman but she had more children [five] than I have. She put more emphasis on running an efficient household than in, say, the joy of making a cake by hand. Often she considered the physical needs of the household or her own needs before the needs of the children. "Honey, I can talk to you now but only if you help me fold the laundry." Or, "I must escape to the mall by myself." I remember thinking that if I were to create a home I'd like to stop doing the laundry once in a while and realize that my job is the development of the children. It's maintaining a household as well, but my primary goal is to help with the spiritual, intellectual, emotional, and physical development of my children. That's my job.

My father's an extraordinary man. I think he perceived his role as the role of the mother. Interesting, his father died when he was quite young, which was sad for him, yet in some ways I felt it was a benefit for myself. He didn't have the traditional male role model that I saw with many of my grade-school friends, where the dad went off to work and wasn't a participant in raising the children.

My father certainly went off to work and worked hard, but he was intimately involved with the development of his kids. Every night at bedtime he'd read with each child and each child got a different book, which was lovely one-on-one time. He must have spent an hour and a half putting the kids to bed. As an adult, I think, Boy, it would have been a whole lot easier to put us all on the couch, read one book, and be off with it.

Now he lives between Florida and Maine, and I talk to him several times a week. He stayed with us over Christmas. Lindsay and I were reading Laura Ingalls Wilder. When Dad went home he went to the library and got Wilder's *On the Banks of Plum Creek*. I'll say, "Lindsay, let's call Dado. Do you want him to read to you?" She'll sit with the phone at the table with her book, and her grandfather will read to her.

I went to a liberal arts college and graduated magna cum laude. I won a Truman Scholarship. It's a wonderful thing, a living memorial to Harry Truman, and a huge honor. The scholarship pays for two years of college and two years of graduate school. It's given for academic excellence and commitment to public service. One interviewer said to me, "So, Margaret, do you really think you're going into public service?" He spoke in this voice that cast great doubt. It really struck to my core. I said, "I don't know what it's going to be. In fifteen years I might just be planting flowers in the town park, but that's public service." That sort of silenced them, as opposed to other applicants who, I'm sure, said they wanted to be a senator.

I think that raising my children well is the most important public service I could ever do. Lindsay and Benjamin will be part of this society, and they will be citizens, and they will echo the virtues our country was founded on, as well as my Catholic faith. I think that's a great public service. I don't have any doubt about that.

After my senior year, I deferred the last two years of my Truman Scholarship and looked for a job. I was interested in business. My father was a businessman, so it was common lingo at home. I knew I wouldn't always be in business—knew it wouldn't be totally fulfilling—yet I was intrigued with it. This was the '80s, and a lot of emphasis was put on it.

I got a job in a wonderful management training program at Sheraton. I spent a year working at a beautiful small hotel two blocks from the White House. I worked in every single department. The first day I was with Hazel Davis in housekeeping and I learned how to triple-sheet a bed. I worked concierge, operator, reservations. The idea was that you'd learn the field and at some point you'd become a manager. Everyone was given a mentor, and I was given the CEO. The CEO. The chairman of the board. You should have seen my face when I found out. I think that was because they knew I was bright and ambitious and had the capacity to not just be a manager but to manage the company.

After two years at Sheraton, it was, Okay, I enjoy business, but I don't have a sense of making society better. It was

that public service thing again. And I wanted to utilize the scholarship. I went back and got my graduate degree in art history. It was at that point that I knew I wanted to teach.

Right after graduate school I got married, and my husband and I had become interested in California. I was raised in New England—we were very provincial New Englanders, where we didn't know California existed. My husband ended up going to graduate school at UCLA, and I taught history at a fine all-girls high school. That was rewarding. I really enjoyed it. Like mothering, it used a lot of my capabilities. One of my fellow teachers told me something so wise. Twenty years my senior, she said, "What I like about teaching is that it's a job where you can love." She obviously loved her students and wasn't afraid to love them.

So, I'm teaching. I'm at a wonderful school—terrific staff, terrific faculty, great students—and I get pregnant. It was as if there was no decision. I knew I'd stay home with my child. I didn't want the stress of having to conform my child to my work schedule. I didn't want that sense of getting up early and taking her to day care. I wanted the joy of it.

What a joy to have this huge learning experience, because I'd never spent any time with babies. What a wonderful sort of awakening to walk down the street with a baby in a stroller, and everybody smiles at you.

We're fortunate in that my husband is in a management position, so he makes an above-average salary. But we live below our means. We drive the same car we drove across the country eight or nine years ago. My husband takes public transportation to work. We make all our own meals. I frequent the thrift shops. We rent, we don't own a house. It's a

choice we've made. If we had a huge mortgage, I might feel compelled to have to work.

I had to learn new job skills. Nursing a baby and taking care of a newborn are difficult skills. Learning how to nurse took a terrific amount of persistence, but I knew it was the right thing to do. It was one of the reasons I was staying at

What a wonderful sort of awakening to walk down the street with a baby in a stroller, and everybody smiles at you.

home. It took about seven weeks with Lindsay before I felt, Okay, this is natural.

I had a moment when I knew I was doing exactly what I was supposed to be doing. We lived in this apartment that had a terrific long hallway. Lindsay was sixteen months old, crawling down the hallway, dragging a favorite book as she crawled in search of me. She was saying, "Book, book," ask-

ing me to read to her. I was in the middle of some task. I went to her and sat in the hallway and read. It was lovely. It felt so right. Nothing else mattered except that my baby wanted to be read a book, and I had the luxury of time to sit down and read, and I didn't have to hurry.

I feel that luxury of being able to work on my child's time schedule, not mine, very much now that I have two children. I think that my life, in many ways, is about walking my children to school. It's three blocks away. For an adult it would take six minutes. It takes us forty minutes. First off, Lindsay's in preschool, so she doesn't have to get there at a specific time. I'll hold Lindsay's hand and she'll hold Benjamin's hand. There are things they like to look at on the way, a particular rock they like to sit on, a tree they like to play with. I don't have to push them and say, "Come on, come on, get out of the car, get in the car." Because this is the important thing—the walk.

I have time to sit in Lindsay's preschool, and Benjamin feels part of it. We'll be there for fifteen minutes talking to the moms, the teachers. I know all the children's names. And then I walk home with Benjamin, and that can take forty-five minutes. I'm home here for an hour and a half, and we have another forty-five-minute walk back to school. If it's a rainy day, it can take us two hours to walk back home because the children want to splash in the puddles and look at the ducks. It's a micro-exploration, a time of soaking up information about their environment, a time of observation. It's also a small moral play: You can walk on the grass here, but you can't walk on the grass there. A lot of values are being learned.

runny nose most of the time. Everyone said, "It's because she's two. Kids always have runny noses." It was interesting, because once I stopped working, she didn't have a runny nose anymore. So, I felt like maybe that wasn't the best option for her.

I view this as a vocation, as opposed to a job—that it's a "coming home." I don't have any reservations about what I'm doing. There are days and moments of frustration, but, ultimately, it's the right thing. I have a sense that it must be like when one knows a calling, when one decides to be a priest or a nun, and then you know this is what you were meant to do. I feel the same way. That this is what God meant me to do—to be a mother. I think that's why I'm so happy. Because I'm not fighting anything anymore.

When Lindsay was little a school I'd taught at asked me to come back for a semester. I was a working mother for five months. The timing in our life was good in that Lindsay was almost two and was more in need of a social setting, and I had her in a nice small day care. And also I was pregnant with my second, and it helped make the pregnancy pass quicker. I taught a couple of American history courses and that was wonderful.

On a small note, when Lindsay was in day care she had a

Misty

mISTY COPELAND, b. 1982,
high school sophomore

Misty comes from a family of six children who live with their mom in a single motel room. She's been dancing for less than a year, yet as Patrick Bradley, her instructor at the San Pedro City Ballet, says, "Seasoned ballerinas do pirouettes en pointe after a year on point. Misty did them after a month. She's born to do what she's doing right now."

I never took dance lessons because I always wanted to follow my sister, and she was in drill team. I wanted to be in drill team like her—until I saw ballet.

I got my first pair of ballet shoes this year. I started late—I was fourteen—so I have to work faster and harder to catch up.

I want to be in the American Ballet Theatre. One of the girls I dance with told me that there are so many people out there that have talent like me, and I might not even get a chance at it. I don't know why she told me that.

My toes are ugly. They have blisters on them. I use lambswool pads, but once the toes bled through my tights. It made me feel like I was a real dancer.

CASS PETERSON, b. 1949,
farmer

A morning sun rising over a rolling green Pennsylvania farm-

stead finds Cass, a former Washington Post *reporter, perched*

on a crate, cleaning garlic. She stops every now and then to

smoke a cigarette. Small-scale farming, in which a three-week

drought or a three-minute hailstorm can wipe out profits for a

whole year, is truly living on the edge. Cass says she doesn't

need to go bungee jumping for adventure.

Cass

Ward and I had some friends who have a farm about six miles from here. He's an editorial writer who worked with us at the *Washington Post*. She's a lawyer for the Justice Department. We'd go out and visit them from time to time. Ward [Sinclair] was covering agriculture at the time, and I was covering environmental issues. We both liked gardening, had a backyard garden, and here are these people that had this beautiful farm, all this lovely land, an endless supply of cow manure because they had a local dairy farmer using the barns, and they put in a tennis court and no garden. We used to give them a lot of grief.

Ward and I were in New Hampshire on a political trip—it was an election year. They called us and said, "There's a farm going up for sale in Fulton County [Pennsylvania], and you're going to buy it." It was a public auction. We didn't buy that one, but we bid on another one. It was total spur-of-the-moment. We'd never thought about buying a farm, a piece of land, or anything. We had a lot of theories about how small-scale agriculture ought to work and how farmers weren't growing the right crops, all the sorts of things you talk about when you cover these things. But we'd never seriously thought about buying a piece of land and doing this. When the idea came up, we both said, Why not?

We weren't in the category of our friends who could afford a little weekend retreat. The farm had to pay its way. We were going to run it as a part-time enterprise. We made an arrangement with the *Post* whereby we took our vacation off one day at a time during the summer months. After working a four-day week, we had Friday, Saturday, Sunday out here throughout the growing season. We had a little Five-Year Plan. We decided if we could double the gross income from the farm every year, by the end of the fifth year the farm would be paying for itself—in other words, the mortgage payments, the seeds, the plants. It wouldn't be providing any income to

> I still think, I'm so tired I don't know if I can get up and go to market tomorrow. But I do.

us, but it would be paying for itself. Then we'd quit our jobs under the assumption that if we were here to work the farm full-time, it would also pay an income to us. That's what we did in '88, after we'd had the farm for five years.

Flickerville Mountain Farm and Groundhog Ranch was really Ward's idea. He had a few things he wanted to prove. He believed that by growing high-value crops intended for the consumer—asparagus, blueberries, things people want—you could still make a living in small-scale farming, which, of course, all the experts said you couldn't do. I didn't wrestle with this decision and say, "Oh, my God, do I really want to do this?" I wasn't bored at the *Post,* but after ten years I was ready for a different challenge.

We have sixty-six acres—thirty acres tillable land, fourteen acres actively tilled, twelve acres woods, ten acres pasture. I can remember when it was just Ward and I, and we were doing it all by hand. The only thing I was concerned about was, Can I handle the physical demands? One early spring day the wind was blowing like crazy and I was trying to lay a strip of black plastic for mulch. It was four feet wide by eighty-five feet long. First, I created two little ditches with this old-fashioned push-plow, which made furrows on either side of this four-foot row. On my hands and knees, I had to push the dirt over the plastic, while trying to hold it down with my body. Before I could run to the other side of the furrow and tuck the loose ends of the plastic down, the wind would catch it and whip it up. I was so frustrated, so physically tired, that I just sat on the ground and cried, "I can't do this! This is too hard!" But then the wind died down, and I said, "Okay, let's try again."

The first planting stock we ordered was blueberries—concentrated picking period, high value. We thought, We'll pick blueberries for three weeks and take our vacation. Man, we were naive. UPS delivered boxes upon boxes of three hundred huge blueberry plants, which we stacked on my sundeck in Alexandria, Virginia. We had to leave in the middle of the week to plant them, otherwise they'd croak. We finished by flashlight at ten o'clock at night, and both of us felt, What have we gotten ourselves into? If it was going to be this hard, we didn't know if we could do it. And because we were too ignorant and didn't realize blueberries are shallow-rooted and have to be watered, we killed all those plants.

There were lots of moments like that. There still are. I still think, I'm so tired I don't know if I can get up and go to market tomorrow. But I do.

My strong work ethic probably has something to do with my rural upbringing. I grew up in a farming community [Weskan, Kansas, pop. 85]. It was a place where children are introduced to work at an early age because they have to share the load. Your parents would choose tasks you were old enough to do—washing the dishes, combing the dog, whatever. This was never "playtime," it was "worktime." My parents ran the Weskan Motor Court, a service station/truck stop in western Kansas, way out on the Colorado line. I stood on a wooden crate at the double stainless-steel sinks when I was about eight, washing dishes in the café. I cleaned and rented out motel rooms when I was ten. When I was in college, I was a terrific bartender. I studied every manual and could mix an Angel's Tip, a Godfather, or any weird

ried two brothers and they were the neatest people. I mean, full of life. They could do anything. Aunt Eleanor used to make pies for the café, could make eighty cream pies at a time, could stir a pot of cream filling for the pies with one hand, swat one of her five kids with the other, and go over and churn the butter with a third hand. They were enormously skilled, efficient women. Maybe because nobody told them they were just homemakers and therefore shouldn't feel they had fulfilled themselves. Boy, they filled their lives with every conceivable activity and filled their kids' lives with every conceivable activity, and were good at all of it. They worked their little tails off, had a great time, drank martinis, and spoke their own minds. What more do you want out of life than that?

Through trial and error, Ward and I tailored our crops to satisfy our customers. We did heirloom tomatoes—black tomatoes, yellow tomatoes, sausage-shaped tomatoes, striped tomatoes, pink tomatoes. People loved them. They have fabulous flavor and they're interesting to look at. We grew seventy different kinds of vegetables, from asparagus to zucchini, and weird ones like petit pois and radicchio. We figured out how to grow these things, the right stage to pick them, and we were on top of the world! Our customers at the markets were ethnic people who knew what these things were supposed to look like, and they were ecstatic, and the restaurants were ecstatic. It was so satisfying. We'd made ourselves into experts.

Our friends in the city asked us constantly, "Don't you miss the city? Don't you feel isolated out here? Don't you miss the *Washington Post*?" Well, no.

drink the customer could think of. Customers liked that.

My role models were my mother and my aunts. My two aunts, German ladies, married my uncles. Two sisters mar-

Lots of people can go to journalism school, get out and get a job at a newspaper, and, if they apply themselves, can get pretty good at that. It takes ten years to learn how to grow a good garlic. The first year you don't get it quite right, and, unlike a newspaper story where you can run another one the very next day, it takes another whole year before you can bring a garlic crop to fruition. This is the best garlic we've ever grown. [She stops peeling the skin from a plump, glistening, silver-white garlic and holds it up for admiration.] It's a twelve-year investment in learning how to grow garlic. I happen to think that's probably worth money, that kind of skill.

In October 1994 Ward started feeling punk, energy-less. His doctor said it was irritable bowel syndrome, due to stress. Ward thought that made sense because farming's real stressful. You're always worried about something—can I get the snapdragons picked before the hurricane blows through? Ward got worse in the winter and the doctor said, "Learn to live with it. It's a chronic condition." On February 8, he went into Johns Hopkins for a CAT scan. On February 23, two weeks after he was diagnosed with advanced pancreatic cancer, he was dead.

The morning after he died, I got behind the wheel, and my friend who was going home with me said, "You okay to drive?" I said, "I can drive. It's fine." The closer I got to the farm, the more eager I was to get there. I needed to get back to the farm. There is healing in this earth. There really is. To come here and put my hands in this dirt, touch that tree we planted, there's such strength in this land. Maybe that's something to do with a rural upbringing, too. You get such an attachment to the land that you don't get in the city.

Last fall when Ward wasn't feeling well, we took shadow walks at the end of the day. It was late enough that we didn't want to start another job, and a beautiful slant of sun would be turning everything golden. We'd check things out, see if the onions wanted to be hoed the next day. He had his favorite spot on the top of the hill where he could look at the whole panorama of the farm. Standing up there we'd remember the first time we tilled that piece, the crop we put in over there, and what a struggle it had been to get the rocks out of that field. Looking at what we'd accomplished over the course of the years, we had this fullness in our hearts. The kind of feeling you have if you go to a national park and see some incredibly beautiful scene with the mist

It takes ten years to learn how to grow a good garlic.

rising just right and you get this sense of awe, gratitude, and love all wrapped up into one. It's a very emotional kind of thing. I still get that when I look at this farm. Ward used to get so carried away. He'd be out in the woods and shriek at the top of his lungs, "Love this farm!" And he did. I don't do that, but I know his feeling. It's not me living his feeling. It's mine, too.

I got the most beautiful letters from customers at the Farmer's Market. Maybe I only knew their first name or what kind of beets they liked, but they said the most beautiful things about Ward, the food, the farm, the little life salon we're running here. It showed that we'd accomplished what we wanted to do, which was to make that connection directly with the people who are eating our food. It's part of the psychic reward of what we're doing.

Ward's death was so fast that my first thought was, Man, I'm not sure what I want to do. I had no choice, at least for the first year. It was February and I had responsibilities. I had a farm to run. I had to throw all my attention into getting the onions in the ground, the tomatoes seeded in the small greenhouses.

Ward and I had helped Brian, who'd been an intern here and wants to be a small-scale farmer, start his own operation on rented land nearby. Our deal was that we'd be his advisers, help him find markets for his produce, help him figure out how to grow things. Under the circumstances, there was no way I was going to help. My hands were full. But I had a responsibility to him. The best option seemed to be to throw the two farms together and operate them as one. That way Brian could help me and I could still help him.

Ward and I hadn't made any business decisions separately, and one of my first decisions was a rather large one: to build an expensive greenhouse that cost $35,000. (This is a farm that can't afford a new pickup.) There's no greenhouse of any consequence in this end of the county, and a lot of weekenders are moving in who want to buy shrubs, roses, bedding plants like marigolds and impatiens, and perennials.

It was pretty clear that the farm's income that had been sufficient for Ward and me was not going to provide the income necessary to keep me and Brian and his family alive. I figured the greenhouse could provide an early cash flow to get us over the crunch all farms have in the spring when you have nothing to sell and lots of bills to pay. I was concerned

My career path has consisted of doing the best I could with whatever job I've had.

with what Ward would think. He was frugal, a Scotsman, who knew that to make a living on a small farm you don't throw money around.

Living on an isolated farm, Ward and I were each other's life. That was it. In the evening last winter, drinking my two glasses of wine, I realized I couldn't build a life with three cats I adore. I needed time to be with other people. The greenhouse played into that. It's labor-intensive over a shorter period of time, potentially more lucrative, and certainly less risky than growing crops in an open field where deer can eat them up and groundhogs can ravage them. It meant I could spend more time with my family—my mother, brothers, and sister.

I still do a little writing, freelancing, basically on gardening, horticulture, and farming topics. I do "Cuttings"—it's a monthly column for the *New York Times*. A number of writers rotate on that column, and I'm one of them. And I write a column for *Pennsylvania Farmer Magazine* on direct market gardening.

I like writing, and I manage to squeeze it into the schedule. I'm an early riser. I get up about 4:30 and this time of year the sun isn't up till six, so I have an hour and a half to put in at the computer. Well, you know, when you move into a new career you don't automatically unlearn all the skills you had from the previous career. If you can still make use of them, why not?

My career path has consisted of doing the best I could with whatever job I've had. I never took a job I didn't expect to spend the rest of my life doing. I expected to retire at the *Kansas City Star*. Circumstances intervened. I expected to retire at the *Washington Post*. Circumstances intervened. I expect to retire from a farming and greenhouse business in Fulton County, Pennsylvania, but I know better than to second-guess circumstances.

What's a career path? It's an urban phrase. Most of the women in this part of the world don't have a career option. My full-time greenhouse worker, Alice, worked for twelve years in the nearby London Fog factory, sewing epaulets on raincoats, until London Fog moved its operations to Mexico. Alice has a high school education, a three-year-old daughter, and a lot of home responsibilities. But she will, in the course of a few years, be a first-class plantswoman. Being in the right place at the right time, or maybe just making the best of whatever place I'm in. That's been my career path.

n
ANCY EVANS, b. 1950,
media executive

Nancy's path has been stratospheric: while she was still in her

thirties she ran two great American companies: Book-of-the-

Month Club and Doubleday. The living room in her town house

on the Upper West Side of Manhattan is furnished with plump

chintz furniture, her daughter's artwork, and books. New books

are stacked everywhere—a testament to Nancy's belief in the

power of the printed word to change people's lives.

I grew up in a time and a

Nancy

town where the women, no matter how smart they were, were housewives and the men all commuted to New York and had jobs. It wasn't a culture that bred ambition for women, or men for that matter.

What I do remember is that from the get-go, from nursery school and kindergarten, I was the leader. Being the leader in the classroom, or the most popular, or the smartest, can put you in a vulnerable spot. It can mean that you make others jealous. I was always aware of that, and I didn't want people to not like me. Sometimes I downplayed my accomplishments. That's probably a girl thing. I tried to not talk about what I got on my report card or on a test. Success was more scary to me than failure.

When I was in graduate school, studying for my doctorate in English literature, what I deep down wanted to do—and when I say deep down, to me that's the thing that if you were to admit it you might feel embarrassed and you might even blush because you think this is beyond your reach to attain—what I thought was beyond my reach to attain was that I could work at a national magazine.

I was very attracted to writing and editing, both of which I'd been doing in college and in the summers. Here I was, somebody who on the face of it should have had all the confidence in the world, and yet I didn't think I could do a lot of the things I wanted to do. Recognizing that I didn't have the confidence I needed, I started a self-education course. This was when I was in graduate school, so I'd be studying the seventeenth century and then I'd turn to working on myself. I dedicated a big part of my time to studying—success, failure, reading books, keeping a journal, really analyzing myself. I did it in the old Yankee tradition of self-help. I didn't see it as a problem for therapy as much as a cultural problem of which I was a victim.

Ken Heyman was a photographer for *Life* magazine. Very famous. He came and was photographing students who were living at the International House, which is this kind of UN of students at Columbia [University]. While he was photographing me, he was looking through his lens, and photographers do have an eye, and he said, "You want to be working in journalism, don't you?" This was just by looking at me. I said, "Yes." He said, "Then why are you here studying seventeenth-century literature?" I said, "Because I do love literature, I'd love to teach, and I'm too afraid that, I mean, who would give me a job at a magazine?" He said, "I'm here to tell you that you would get a job. Do you want me to put you in touch with people?" I said, "Thank you, but no."

I thought that using contacts was like cheating. I'm over that, and I tell every young person if anyone offers you a lead, please follow it. Because he'd said that to me, as this kind of angel from the real world who had entered my life, I thought, Maybe I really can get a job.

Joseph Campbell in *The Power of Myth* talks about finding your bliss. He makes this wonderful point that when you're aware you are searching, then when that elder tribesman or guide comes into your life, you recognize it there in front of you and say, "That's a Bingo! moment." But you need to be self-aware to recognize those moments. Being awake to the Bingo! moments is half the ballgame. I think these things happen to women, in particular, and they don't recognize them. Some of these things don't come boldface. They can be just an aside in a conversation, a compliment that can be taken as a reinforcement of your dream. But if you're aware of it, that aside can become a real opening. You can take it and use it to go to the next stage. That's why I'm constantly going around to people saying, "Did you see that?" "Did you hear that?" Because I think these moments are often missed.

After I met Ken Heyman, I stayed up all night in my little dorm room and created a résumé and wrote this impassioned cover letter saying why I wanted to work at *Harper's*. It was the magazine I most loved at the time. I was very interested in taking the lessons of the intellectual life and applying them to real life, to some good cause or effect. I felt that in the very best of magazines, that's what you were doing—carrying on a discourse that could change people's lives. To put this in context, this was at a time when the women's movement was at the forefront of political and cultural thought, and was oftentimes on the front cover of a magazine like *Harper's*.

I sent out résumés to *Harper's* and almost every other magazine, from *The New Yorker* to *Vogue,* and got interviews. What happened was—and I think this is great to hear, too—that I got job offers from almost everybody, but I did

> I thought that using contacts was like cheating. I'm over that, and I tell every young person if anyone offers you a lead, please follow it.

not hear back from *Harper's*. I wrote them another impassioned letter about why they should hire me. I don't possess a lot of chutzpah. I'm not assertive about saying, *"I'm the one you need for this job,"* so it was unusual for me to go back again into this void to keep trying to interest them. It seemed to me not a polite thing to be doing.

About six months later when *Harper's* did hire me, I learned that the editor-in-chief had kept my letter on his desk all that time but they hadn't had an opening. What happened was that *Harper's* revived *Harper's Weekly,* so when they launched that I came on board as one of seven editors.

Harper's Weekly was reader-written, which meant that we were asking people all over the country to write about what they cared about. I was also dealing with famous writers who to me were like gods, like Norman Mailer and Kurt Vonnegut. I was finding out that they, too, had bad days, that they couldn't spell, or they handed something in that didn't work and you'd have to go, "Well, we'll just have to try this one more time, won't we?" That was sort of wonderful to learn early—that even gods are human.

There I am editing, right? At the same time I still want to be a writer and go off and live in Maine. I was tortured by how many things I wanted to do. An editor at *Harper's* took me for a walk and he said, "Listen, God willing, you'll have a long life, so you might think about it this way. Be an editor now. Then you can go be a writer, and then if you still want to go do this farm up in Maine, kind of drop out, you can do that. And if you want to go be a teacher, you can do that later. You can probably do a whole lot of these things over the course of your life." He called it "serial living." Why this should have been so momentous . . . but it was at the time. I'd felt I had to do all these things now, or they wouldn't always be there.

He was taking the shortsighted perspective of a young person and extending it into the long-term perspective of a grown-up. I was twenty-three years old, and that change of perspective put me at peace.

The other thing is that seeing your life as "serial living" makes you less fearful. When one era of your life ends, not necessarily by your choice, you may feel scared, you may feel sad, you may feel anxious, but there's some underpinning of faith from that long view that something will happen next.

Harper's Weekly folded after two years. When a magazine folds, this is not a happy thing. You're out of work. But what happened was that the managing editor had an idea to do a book, *How to Get Happily Published.* In the course of editing *Harper's Weekly,* we'd seen how many people didn't get published. We wanted to teach people the etiquette of getting published.

The larger theme here is that for the next seven years—while I was co-writing the book, writing for magazines, and doing book reviews—I was freelancing. To be able to make my own money without being dependent on a paycheck from one company was a huge lesson, a huge piece of learning.

About one of the only advantages of being in New York City is that things happen to you. While I was freelancing, a TV show about books was starting up at PBS. I auditioned along with a list of other people who knew about books and who might be somewhat telegenic. The offer to co-host the show did sort of drop out of the sky. I certainly hadn't been thinking, Boy, do I want to be a TV person. But it did match my love of books.

The show was underwritten by Book-of-the-Month Club. The chairman of Book-of-the-Month Club saw me reviewing books and talking to authors. Talk about a leap of faith—during the first season he asked if I'd be interested in becoming editor-in-chief of Book-of-the-Month Club. At that point my executive experience was being president of the Jolly Rogers Club, a neighborhood club, when I was in the fifth grade. I wasn't even sure I wanted the job, but I so love mail order, which has always been a passion of mine, and Book-of-the-Month Club is a mail-order vehicle. I study every catalog. What makes one work and another not? I'd just intuitively been studying the field for a long time.

It did not compute that my editorial work segued into my work as an executive, and it caused a whole ruckus in the industry. I don't know that it was because I was so young. I think more of the shock was that I was coming out of thin air, rather than having worked in the company and moved my way up.

I had to learn the language of a whole new industry, like "back end" and "response rates," all kinds of terms that came with the territory of a direct-response business. I mean, I'd be in meetings, and not even know. It was Greek, the language. I kept a notebook. That, to me, was more the steep learning curve than the people. I didn't go in there thinking I knew everything, because I didn't.

When you're head of Book-of-the-Month Club, you obviously meet book publishers, a lot. I'd been there about two years when the head of Bantam approached me about the job of president and publisher of Doubleday. (They had just acquired Doubleday.) I loved my job at Book-of-the-Month Club, but when it was time to make the decision, I felt that I couldn't say "no" then, and think something like that would come up again in my lifetime.

Doubleday was a great American publishing house but at that point it had fallen on some—its reputation wasn't as illustrious as it once had been. I was definitely moved by the challenge to make it a great publishing house again. The reason I was a good fit was that Book-of-the-Month Club was known for having a quality reputation, and they wanted to have that for Doubleday, to be a blue-chip publisher. We'd started an award at Book-of-the-Month Club for books that made a difference. That was what I was about, trying to publish books that made a difference, whether it was in the culture or one person's life, but books that mattered.

I was in my mid-thirties and I was president and publisher of Doubleday. For the first three to four months, I was doing both jobs—running back and forth across the street between Book-of-the-Month and Doubleday, which was sort of crazy.

A lot of what had to be done at Doubleday in the beginning was cleaning house, which meant firing. I'd done a little of that at Book-of-the-Month, but never to the degree that I had to do at Doubleday. Most people don't end up firing as many people as I had to fire—it was a lot, it was substantial. With all the experience in the world, it never gets any easier to fire someone. Never. Ever. Each time the top of my head would be about to fly off.

I'd been there about three years when the head of the company, who'd brought me in, left for another publishing house, and I knew with him gone, my days were numbered. Then I was fired. By nature of the fact that I was in the media, and the media gets written about, it was public. It's hard enough for anybody getting fired, but when you're

involved in my life, think or write. With the television show, I'd already gone through having things said about me in the press. The *Wall Street Journal* wrote about me, basically, How could someone who looks like that have a brain?

When this firing happened I had a wonderful friend in Jackie Onassis. At Doubleday all the editors were on the same floor, so she was down the hall from me. She was great. When I first got to Doubleday she ran down the hall and said, "Nancy, thank goodness you're here. We can finally do real books." Because they kept making her do these coffee-table books. They just saw that side of her. In fact, she was the one—we did *The Power of Myth* together. She came to me and said, "Do you know who Joseph Campbell is?" and I said, "Of course I do," and she said, "Well, nobody else here does."

If there's anyone to give you perspective on dealing with publicity, it's Jackie, who was a real mentor during that time. She'd come over to the house after work and give me lessons on how to deal with the publicity of it all. Jackie never read anything written about her. She said, "Who cares what they think? You know what matters and what doesn't." Her other advice was, "Get up and get dressed and go on to the next chapter."

Getting fired upset the applecart, it upturned my worldview. After I left, I had to think through what I was going to do next. Back to my "serial living" scenario. I decided I would never work for another company again. I did not want to be in that situation again. I'd rather be in control of my fate, own the business, and to the extent that one can be in control, control the business. That was another huge piece of learning.

fired and it's getting written about—that was hard.

I've always tried to operate by caring about the people I care about, and caring about the job in front of me, but trying not to care about what others, who aren't directly

Also, I had my daughter during this time. I'd postponed getting married until my mid-thirties and I had Samantha when I was thirty-nine. It was the '80s, when we thought we were Superwomen and could do it all. I was with her to some degree, but not what I'd want. But one of the best things about having a child is that they make more manifest what's truly important. And with that thought, and not to mention that I'm a great magazine reader, I wasn't finding in magazines the reality of my own family life, nor the reality of many of my friends. That's when I started to create what was to become *Family Life*. I created the magazine in my house, and my daughter learned to write on the computer keyboard as she sat on my lap.

That was a huge step for me—becoming an entrepreneur. I was creating the business I'd be running rather than running someone else's business.

In early 1995, one day my husband was in our living room with Candice Carpenter and me. Candice had been president of Time-Life video and had started up Q2, the shopping channel, for Barry Diller. My husband said, "One of these days you two should start something together." We both looked at him and each other and just noted it. At that juncture Candice was still at Q2 and I was still with *Family Life,* but I knew we were going to sell it. That's probably why my husband said what he said.

A while later Candice came to me and said, "Take a look at this on-line world." She'd been mulling over this idea of what would become iVillage, and the summer of '95 we started putting it together.

There's a natural segue from *Family Life* to iVillage—I called *Family Life* a national kitchen table for parents. I wanted parents to come together and talk about how to raise kids nowadays, which is a different ballgame from our parents. What I saw in this new interactive medium was the true ability to create an interactive kitchen table where people could meet immediately and collectively. I found that, and I still do, an immensely powerful medium.

We came up with the idea of iVillage, where we'd create

I'm big on visualization, holding on to your dream.

virtual villages—parentsoup, aboutwork, vicesandvirtues— for grown-ups on the Internet. Candice and I were going into something neither of us had ever done before, and we had to raise twelve million dollars. It was quite huge. You need a door-opener, and we couldn't have done it without hiring this CFO [chief financial officer] and her contacts in the venture capital world.

When you run your own business, it needs to be said, you're working like crazy, so it's not like you have more time on your hands. But what you have is a feeling of being integrated. When one of our senior V.P.s needs to go to a parent-teacher conference, we get it. We know what our lives are like. There's no questions, no looks.

I'm big on visualization, holding on to your dream, and I've always done life planning, which I started years ago in graduate school. It's almost like they're two steps. I do the visualization first, the raw thinking of what I'd like to have happen. Then the life planning is when I take pencil to yellow pad and figure out the steps necessary to make it happen.

In graduate school I did it alone because I was too scared to admit to anybody else what I wanted to do. Since then I've always done it with a friend and for my friends. The main purpose of being with someone close enough that they can knock you around a little bit is to make you 'fess up to what you really, *really* want to do. These life-planning tools add up to self-awareness.

I do this personally, as well, every New Year's Eve with the man I'm married to. My husband and I have this big leatherbound book and we write down the highlights of the year and what we hope to accomplish the next year. It can range from "Finally fix up bathroom" to "Write book." My daughter, who is now nine years old, has her own leather book, and we do ours together. First, we read over her previous years. Hers are like "Learn ABCs," "Jump horse." There's a power in looking back over previous years and knowing you made a lot of those dreams come true.

gWYNN MURRILL, b. 1942, **sculptor**

Some people think if only they were an artist, if only they could paint or draw, then they would automatically know what they were supposed to do. Gwynn's story of the birth of a sculptor shows that the path for even a talented artist can be just as confusing and circuitous as for the rest of us. As Gwynn describes her journey she's in her studio, located in an industrial area of Los Angeles, and we're surrounded by her work—life-size animal sculptures cast in bronze.

I'm absolutely surprised.

Gwynn

Nobody is more surprised than I am that I'm a sculptor. If you'd asked me when I was a kid what I wanted to be when I grew up, this would have been nothing I would have thought of in my wildest dreams.

The first time that I remember somebody saying that I was a good artist was a teacher telling my mother, "She's so good, she painted the mountains so well. They look just like the Borego Mountains," which are the mountains east of San Diego where we used to go a lot. I was six years old. I guess it doesn't take much to encourage somebody. She could have said that to anybody as a teacher, and she probably did a million times, but it was something I really heard.

The thing that discouraged me in high school was that my mother, who is very practical, said, "You have to be really, really dedicated if you want to be an artist." As a sixteen-year-old I wasn't thinking about devoting all my time to anything except boys and clothes. And I didn't know anybody who was an artist, had never met an artist, had never seen the work of real artists. So I didn't have much to go on.

The first thing I wanted to do when I went to college was be an interior decorator. It was something my mother had always liked doing around the house, and she used to let me do my room. I loved to see the transition my bedroom made when it was one color and then I made it another color. But I didn't get along with the interior design teacher, so I dropped the whole idea and took painting classes and ceramics, the regular fine arts program, and got more interested in that.

Before I finished my degree I had a chance to travel in Europe for nine months with my mother and brother. In Florence I saw Donatello's *David*. It was almost painful. (It's funny, it wasn't Michelangelo's *David* that intrigued me so much, it was Donatello's.) You know, when you see something that you think is so beautiful that you just don't even know how to describe it? I felt that way when I saw that. It didn't make me want be a sculptor. It just made me see that sculpture could do that, could really be as moving as any painting, or maybe more moving because you can walk around it, and from each position it was moving in a different way. It was heart-wrenching. That was probably the first moment that I realized that I like things in three-dimension.

When we returned, I thought about going back to San Diego State and finishing my B.A. and then going on to graduate school, but I needed a way to support myself, and the only real job I could get was with the telephone company. My mother, who'd always wanted to go to this really nice secretarial school back East called Katherine Gibbs, suggested

that. I liked the idea because I'd get to go to a new city, Boston, and afterward I could live anywhere in the U.S. and get a job any place, supposedly.

I'd always had a very difficult time getting jobs because I had this little girl's voice. I'm fifty-five and I still have the same tiny voice. Now my determination overpowers that voice, but when I was young that voice, it was deadly. Nobody would take me seriously, so I could never get a job.

Before I went I told myself that I was not going to fight with them, because I was putting myself in a situation where people were really into rules, and I've always had a problem with rules. It was kind of fun, like typing to music and learning shorthand. You had to dress in high heels like you were working in an office. But it wasn't bad. While I was going there, I started taking art classes at Harvard night school. It was like I couldn't help myself—I was taking secretarial classes during the day and life drawing and art history at night.

I still had a hard time getting a job afterward. I moved to L.A., and nobody had ever heard of Katherine Gibbs out here. They'd heard of it, but they didn't know it was that great. I finally got a job with TRW, which was probably a good thing because it made me want to get out of the secretarial business real fast. I worked for twenty aerospace engineers, and if you know anything about engineers, they don't communicate very well with people.

I started taking art classes one night a week at UCLA Extension. I had this intuition the first night when I met Tony Berlant, the instructor, that this guy was going to be real important to me. And he was. He encouraged me to go back to school, which was what I wanted to do.

A girl I met in class was a bathing suit designer, and they needed a fit model for her company. I quit TRW and worked there for about six months. You just stand around with your clothes on, but when they want you to try on a bathing suit, then you put it on and they pin it. I wanted to go back to school full-time, so I was working as hard as I could to get enough money, but I was getting skinnier and skinnier and sicker and sicker with colitis.

I think it was my confusion about being twenty-three, and all the things I thought were supposed to be happening weren't happening. I was very confused by, What am I supposed to do with my life? I hadn't been happy working as a secretary, and I didn't think I'd be happy as a mother and a wife with any of the guys I knew. I thought about going into regular modeling because a few people said I photographed well. I could do catalogs, like J.C. Penney. I probably would have made an okay living, but it wasn't going to be *me* doing that. It would have just been a job. So, what do I do now? The future looked kind of bleak and black.

I decided in order to survive in this world I had to go back into art. Some people think artists have it easier, but a lot of artists don't know we have that kind of talent right off the bat. It's something that you still have to discover. It's not so automatic. It's just as hard to discover that as any other path in life.

During my evening art classes, Tony Berlant said to me, "You should be going to graduate school." I said, "Really? Do you think I could get in?" He said, "Sure, easily."

There are people that all it takes is one person telling

you to do it, giving you permission—and then you're off. I suppose if nobody had ever said I was a good artist, and I didn't have the opportunities, I wouldn't have done it. But you also need a second level of encouragement—of being in the right place at the right time, having the right environment, for what you're doing.

To get my M.F.A. in painting I had to take a sculpture class. I decided to make a rocking horse out of wood because I thought if I ended up with it afterward, I could actually use it as a piece of furniture and sit on it. I decided on a rocking animal because I was making these long things, these legs, and I didn't know how to support them.

I didn't know anything about wood. It took me three quarters, nine months, for me to finish that sculpture. I decided that I wanted to make a second piece. I asked the head of the sculpture department, and he said I could as long as I worked outside because I made too much noise and mess.

I guess I must really like to get dirty because the way I worked when I started off, I was just sanding wood and making sawdust everywhere. I had to be covered up with all this equipment—hat, mask, gloves, goggles, an extra shirt. It's still the way I work to this day. I think, How can I like doing this? It's such a horrible messy job, and I'm always dirty, and I'm always having to change my clothes and everything's so disgusting. How come I like doing this?

I think I must like the tools. I like handling the tools. I like the noise they make, even though I do wear earplugs. I can't hear anybody. I can't do anything except focus on that form.

My first tool was a Milwaukee Grinder, which weighs about ten pounds and has a big sanding disk. It gets really, really heavy when you hold it for any period of time. I hold on with two hands and lean the sander onto the piece and move it back and forth. I have to do it over and over again. It's very repetitive. People always talk about meditation and all that stuff. This is how I'm able to live in this world without feeling like I'm just going to go nuts. I have a tremendous amount of energy, and doing the same movement over and over again focuses that energy on something.

What I like to do is take the animal form and use that as a vehicle for making what I consider abstract sculpture, even though I'm using a realistic form. My animals are actually so realistic that animals recognize them as a threat—dogs will bark at my dog standing. So there's a certain realism in my work, though I don't put faces on them, I don't put hair or eyes. I'm trying to capture a power in the form—a power that has nothing to do with being syrupy and sentimental.

There wasn't any point where I decided I was turning from being a painter into a sculptor. But by the time I finished my M.F.A. in painting, I had enough sculpture for an exhibition. I didn't sell anything, but it isn't always sales that encourage you. I was encouraged because I was making something.

For the next ten, twelve years, I was working pretty hard for other people, helping them in their studios, and doing a lot of little jobs—painting houses, working as a receptionist for Rustic Canyon Arts and Recreation. I was able to make only one sculpture a year because that was all the time I had on my own.

My mother, who was in real estate, had helped me buy a house. I met my husband during this time because I was having a deck put on the house, and he came as an architectural consultant. David was much younger than I was, so I never thought of him as someone I'd ever go out with. He'd come over a little bit more than he needed to, or stay after—something like that. One time he asked me out and I said, "I can't go out with you. You're just a kid." I was thirty-six and he was twenty-two. After he left, I thought to myself, That was dumb. So I called him up and told him I wanted to go out after all. From then on we started dating. His background's in construction and engineering and he likes to work with his hands, so he's been very helpful and encouraging to me in my work.

The biggest encouragement I got was in 1979 when I got to go to Italy to the American Academy. I was thirty-seven when I won the Prix de Rome. It was the first time in my life that anybody had ever given me money just to be an artist.

I got another boost when I got an NEA [National Endowment for the Arts] grant. That money enabled me to make my first pieces in bronze. All of a sudden instead of just making one or two pieces a year, I could make an edition. And all of a sudden people bought my work. They never bought the wood. I couldn't sell it if I tried. Like one piece every three to four years.

I don't work in wood anymore. Instead I've been working in bronze. I carve and sand polyurethane foam similarly to the way I did the wood. Then I make a mold from the foam piece, and wax is poured into this mold. It's a long process involving many steps to turn the wax form into the final bronze sculpture.

In 1996, I got a gallery in New York to represent me. I was absolutely thrilled to have that representation in New York, not that a lot has happened. But it's still the number-one art marketplace and it's like, she must be okay if there's a gallery in New York representing her. It could be a gallery with more prestige, I suppose. The more prestige a gallery

A lot of artists don't know we have that talent right off the bat.

has, the more people think it's okay, but it's a good, well-respected gallery. It's small, but actually I was thrilled to death.

David and I were getting dressed for the opening of my first one-person show in New York and I felt this thing in my breast. It felt huge to me. Isn't that funny how that happens? I was thinking, Are they trying to ruin my good time? It was my first show in New York. I wasn't too concerned, just slightly concerned.

Later this doctor looked at my X-ray, and he said, "Yeah, that's it." I said, "What do you mean—it?" He said, "A tumor." "Cancer?" I said. He said, "Yeah." I started to cry. It's very shocking when you've never had too much wrong with you, and they say you have to have it taken out, and if you don't, you're going to die.

My biggest fear was that I might have problems with my arm. I had a friend who had breast cancer in the early '80s, and she had her lymph nodes removed, and she was never able to raise her arm completely.

A couple of days before the operation I made an appointment with the doctor and I took my catalog in. It was just a general catalog of my work. I said to him, "Here, this is what I do. I want you to do whatever you can not to hurt my arm." He was really impressed with the sculpture. It was like all of a sudden we had a certain connection because before I was just a crying breast. (They're looking at your breast and you're crying, so I say, "a crying breast.")

Luckily, it was a small lump that didn't involve any of the lymph nodes. But the thing is, I never stopped working. I never had any problem with my arm, not even the first two weeks. And in fact, the pieces that are in my studio right now are what I call my therapy pieces, because while I was going through radiation I couldn't go anywhere, so I'd just go to radiation, go to the studio and work, and go back to radiation.

As soon as the radiation was over, I got this commission to do an eagle for the American Embassy in Singapore. That was April, and they wanted it by July. It would take me a certain amount of time to make it, and then it needed six weeks in the foundry, but I decided, Okay, I can do this. So I had to get right back to work in a real physical way.

It's funny, I sold more artwork this year than ever. Isn't that weird? My gallery dealer says, "Gwynn had to get cancer to have the best year she's ever had."

Cancer is such a scary word, and it just terrifies the bejesus out of you. Once I was facing the possibility of dying, I thought to myself, Would I want to change my life? How would I want my life to be different? And then I thought, No, this is exactly what I want to be doing—making sculpture.

When Sunday June was growing up in Philadelphia, her family was so

poor that sometimes she didn't attend school because the soles of her

shoes were worn out. Sunday June still lives in the inner city, but now

home is a restored thirty-room Victorian in the 'hood in Baltimore, and

her closet is crammed with hundreds of pairs of shoes. Since becoming a

doctor, Sunday June has risen fast: she's the only female, and the only

African American of either sex, who is a national physician vice presi-

dent at Green Spring Health Services, a managed-care organization.

Sunday June

When I was a little girl I wanted to do two things. I wanted to be an actress and a doctor. However, in my family I wasn't the best looking, so I wasn't going to be an actress, and my brother, who is truly far more brilliant than I am, was considered to be a potential candidate for medical school. The focus in the family was more toward males being the super-achievers. My mother said, "You ought to plan on being a teacher. You're going to have to work hard, so prepare yourself."

I did know that my two great-aunts were nurses. Their best friend was a black female physician named Dr. Kimbrough. Dr. Kimbrough told me that I didn't have to limit my options to being a nurse, if you want to call that limiting, that I could be a physician. Now I noticed that she'd given up her entire life for it, never married, and had an extremely difficult time.

I was afraid if I tried to be something like that, I'd be such an outcast that I couldn't have a family, I wouldn't get married. I'd just be a stand-alone person, and that's all I'd have in life. I did want more than that. I also have this dread of trying to do something and being the laughingstock. "Oh, she tried that and look what happened. It's a terrible thing, she was such a failure." I didn't want to be in that position ever. I was mulling these things over, and not having an ounce of courage to break with what I was scripted for, I decided to go with what I thought I could accomplish.

> The idea of giving people what they need at odd hours of the night, being there for them, is so important to me.

I went ahead and graduated from college in secondary education. I taught reading in junior high and high school. I've always been lucky somehow with kids. Those that were already very gifted were reading grades ahead, and we'd talk. They were such young kids, but we could talk on such a high intellectual level. I found it very satisfying.

Because some of the kids had problems that weren't just reading problems, they were emotional problems, I thought I might like to be a counselor. I got a master's in counseling education and worked for the government in

Washington, D.C. in 1972. The goal was to take women who were on welfare, give them regular government jobs, and support them totally with a whole force of teachers and counselors to get them up to speed.

In working there I was impressed by some of the psychiatrists. Well, with all of them. Some of them were so gifted, so aware of things that I never would have thought of in terms of what a person's problems might be. I wanted to have that level of insight. Some of the psychiatrists may have had a degree, but I thought they were what I call shallow, thick and slow. Like stupid. I thought, God, if that person can be a psychiatrist surely *I* can be a psychiatrist. Whether they were brilliant or vacant as a lot, they were all, in my estimation, making a lot of money. They could kind of breeze in and pontificate about this, that, and the other, and kind of breeze out. I'd like to be able to do that.

My actual decision to become a physician, the final motivating factor that propelled me to medical school, was the result of an incident in my life that was so devastating and so deeply personal that I can't relate it. The impact had enormous consequences—some negative, and some powerful enough to propel me forward. After my pain gave way to rage, I erupted and said, "This is total bullshit! This is crazy! I've done things I didn't want to do. I want to be a doctor." I'd always wanted to be a doctor but felt I wasn't good enough, I wasn't smart enough, I wasn't whatever it was. Right then I felt very foolish and decided that I should go for what I'd wanted to be.

At the same time I also changed my name legally from Paula to Sunday June, the name I'd always wanted. My papa called me Sunny or his Sunday June. It was his impression that I had a sunny, happy personality, and I was born on a Sunday in June. Just as I was taking the control to do what I wanted, starting over, getting ready to go to medical school, changing my name legally helped identify me to the world as I wanted to be presented. My brother always tells the joke, Thank God, they didn't call him Tuesday April. He says it just doesn't have the same appeal.

It took me two years to prepare, take the exams, and get admitted. I was thirty-two when I started medical school. My brother and I have always been close, and one of my concerns was that he'd resent me for stepping ahead of him. In my family it was, Let the men take the lead and do the real spectacular thing. If you were to talk to him right now (he's fifty-six), he'd tell you in a year or so he's probably going to apply to medical school. He says that even now.

It was my intention from day one to go into psychiatry. I can remember going with Mama to her psychiatrist. That was the other thing about being a doctor. I think now in terms of what her diagnosis really was. I think she was manic-depressive with psychotic features. She was called schizophrenic by her psychiatrist.

Mama really had problems. There was a two-year period where she never went out in public. She stayed in the apartment, spoke in "thees" and "thous"—thou will come to supper now, thee will do this. Really hyper-religious. Then she had these eight-day candles that she insisted had to be blessed by a priest, and we weren't even Catholic. My brother and I'd accompany her. My father clearly should have taken her to a doctor. I think he was ashamed of her

haven't opened them." He said, "Any blessing that can't go through paper isn't worth it." My brother and I were on the floor. We said, "This is a guy we want to see again!" We were sick of wrapping up these damn candles and opening them up to be blessed for God knows what reason.

Mama had problems. That's absolutely what attracted me to psychiatry. I had this dreadful fear that I would become psychotic. If it happened to my mother, it would probably happen to me. Perhaps I'd luck out and be able to heal her. If not, I'd better figure out some way to keep from falling off the edge myself.

When I finished my residency I began my clinical career in the state mental health system. I was the ward psychiatrist—I directly cared for patients—in the largest state hospital in Maryland. There were people in there who had been born on the grounds, and I loved working with that population. It was so exciting to be working with schizophrenics and to have the very latest research advances in science available to us. Later I became a clinical director at a private for-profit hospital, and as a private contractor I provided health services for the inmate population of the Baltimore City Jail.

In 1990 I got into managed care through the back door. I started doing it ten hours a week, so I'd understand it better. Today one of the hats I wear is medical director of the on-call service. More than fifty percent of all the admissions that are reviewed by Green Spring occur at night, weekends, and holidays. The idea of giving people what they need at odd hours of the night, being there for them, supervising the process that never sleeps, is so important to me. It's speaking to what people go through at night when they need ser-

and didn't know what to do. You buy these candles, wrap them in paper and string, and there would be a great ceremony of unwrapping and opening up the candles. Once this very busy priest came in and blessed them. Mama said, "You vices, when they need somebody to talk to, when physicians have problems with patients and they need help getting someone admitted, evaluated, and somebody is there for them. Often it's me, because I'm up at night.

From the time I was a child I was constantly getting into trouble for staying up at night. Mother would come in and feel the warm lightbulb under the covers because I couldn't sleep. After years of battling with this, I realized, Hey, this can be an advantage. I'm an insomniac and only need four hours of sleep. I used to think it was odd, but as I've gotten older I realize I have extra time to get things done. What happens to other people when they can't sleep? We know that most suicides occur between two A.M. and six A.M., when people can't sleep and they're troubled.

The way I got the chance to do this is that I spoke to the person who later became president and CEO of the company. He used to do all the on-call service. I said, "Henry, why don't you let me help you with that?" At first, he let me do one week a month, and he'd do three weeks. Then gradually it was half and half. When he became president and didn't have time for it, I said, "Let me! Let me! I want to do this." For almost two years I did it by myself. Now we have a full corps of twenty-five physicians and to varying degrees, they like it. I'm the one who loves it. I'm the medical director now, and I don't have to do this. Yet when all these case managers call, they say to me, "I knew you'd be awake."

The weekend is when I see private patients at the house, because I'm not traveling for Green Spring as much as before. The people I see in this cluttered office are my own patients. I have some people I see for $5 an hour because that's what they can afford and that's what I'm willing to accept. When I'm conducting reviews, like when I'm directly on-call, I think I'm very sensitive to what a person's going through because I myself still have patients and I know what it is to have somebody in crisis.

On Saturdays I also have neighborhood children who come to the house. I call it Operation Open House. It's my own casual program that I started when I graduated from medical school. Many of the kids come as a result of coming by to ask for a job. Then they bring their friends and that's how the whole thing has grown. We do tutoring in subjects they have in school, talk about things they may not be studying but I think should be of interest to them, like Black history, or negotiating in our social system, applying for a job, getting in a club. And we go to restaurants. One of the things my mother felt was very important in my upbringing was that I knew how to go to a restaurant and order.

I like to work. I consider it my salvation, being occupied, having something to do. I have my greatest difficulty in times of trouble if I'm not really occupied. It seems like I'm prone to feel a lot worse than if I have lots to do, deadlines to meet, obligations to keep. Then I'm not focusing on my father's dying or my mother's stroke. The fact that I have so much to do, and can't dwell on that, keeps me going.

Considering the circuitous route I've followed, it's hard for me to think of a path. I think of it in terms of following a light, some flicker, something I was seeking. And I found it. I'm out here where I can breathe and see and do the kinds of things I want.

Doreen walked away from graduate school before finishing, and then

lost herself for a decade in dead-end jobs. What's most striking about

Doreen's path is how fast her career skyrocketed once she found her

niche. After less than three years in business, she was voted one of the

top head-shot photographers in Los Angeles.

Mine is a story of illness.

Doreen

My mother's had multiple sclerosis since I was nine years old. My father died eight years ago of a rare disease, scleroderma.

My forty-two-year-old sister has lupus, is down to eighty-five pounds, and is following in our parents' footsteps.

In my family the only time you got attention was when you were sick. Then Mom would feed me little spoonfuls of 7Up. After going to the doctor, we'd stop at this store where I'd get to pick out something special, like star-shaped stickers, or cutout paper dolls, or a box of new crayons.

We took a one-week vacation every year. We'd always go to the same place, San Diego. My mother would bring the medicine chest, literally. She'd have a separate suitcase filled with medicines. My sister and I always got sick. Always. We could never go away like a regular family, where it was okay and fun and normal.

In my last year of high school I talked to Mom about going to the Fashion Institute of Design and Merchandising [in Los Angeles]. I went for an interview and afterward she said, "You better be sure this is what you want, because it's expensive." Of course, when you're seventeen years old, how do you know? So I let myself be talked out of it.

We always had help during the week for Mother, but before I left for college, there was a time when we didn't have weekend help. My grandmother and I would switch every other weekend, taking care of my mother for twenty-four hours a day all weekend long. I'd wanted to go away to college up north. My grandmother, she's ninety-two going on forty—she's amazing, don't get me wrong, but she's a ball-buster—she said to me, "You cannot do it. You need to stay close enough that if your mother needs you, you're near. You can go to San Diego."

My grandmother has had such a major impact on this family. I don't know if I can describe it in exact words, but there was such incredible guilt around ever having, wanting, to do, to be anything for yourself when Mother was so sick. My grandmother still, to this day, bombards me with this crap. That's why—all the success I have right now?—there was a time when I had a fear that this would all be taken away. Because why should I, of all the family, be so successful? Why me? Why am I not bedridden? Why am I not anorexic? Why do I have great friends? It didn't make sense to me.

I went to San Diego, where I studied special education and worked with autistic children. That's what I knew: illness. It never occurred to me to be a teacher of normal, healthy children. As if trying to "fix" my entire family, I decided to get a master's in vocational rehabilitation.

In my second year of graduate school, I took a class where each week a different doctor discussed a disease. I was sitting in that classroom with twenty other students,

listening to this cancer specialist, and suddenly I thought, If I hear one more thing about illness, I'm gonna go crazy. At the recess I walked out. I was twenty-two years old, and I

felt a little scared walking down those stairs, but there was a sense of excitement and freedom. I didn't know—obviously, I didn't know what I was going to do—but as soon as I started down those stairs I knew I'd made the right decision. I kept getting calls from the guidance counselor, "Where are you?"

For the next ten years—as Mom deteriorated from cane, to walker, to wheelchair, to bed—I did secretarial work, mostly temping at $10 an hour. She was deteriorating, and I was numb. I don't necessarily want to say that they were wasted years, but I didn't know where I was. I was living, but barely. I had a very sick mother and a very sick father, and nobody in the family talked, so I couldn't describe how I was feeling to anybody.

To a small extent the temping was good for me, just the fact of having a routine in my life was good. At least I had something. Although I was miserable. I hated it—hated the repetitiveness of the same tasks, filing, filing, filing, the tediousness of typing letters, making coffee, making copies, answering the phone. I kept thinking, When is this going to end? I felt tired all the time and lost. I consoled myself that temping was temporary, but it was dragging on for years.

On weekends I escaped by taking pictures. I would explore some of the sleaziest, scariest areas in downtown L.A. and capture life in the faces of strangers—a homeless woman, a Mexican family at their daughter's confirmation, a transient passed out on a bench at a bus stop. When I was fourteen I'd gotten my first Instamatic, and I used to pose my little five-year-old brother. I'd say, "Pretend you're walking down the street and you're really sad."

Those were appropriate instructions in my family.

While I was temping, my interest in photography resurfaced as a hobby, but a pretty major hobby. I'd temp nine to five, and the second I got off work I'd rush to the darkroom at Everywoman's Village [a community center]. It's sort of interesting that it was a dark room, that I was in the dark. There was such a sense of—I could not wait to get in that door and work there—there was such a sense of freedom that nobody could say anything to me, not my grandmother, not my mother.

About five years ago at a party, I met Nan, a woman who manages actors. We ended up becoming friends, and she loved my work. (Now when I look at those photos, they seem so amateurish.) She asked if I'd be interested in taking pictures of her clients. I'll never forget the first shoot I did for her. She had this modeling class of girls from seven to fifteen years old at a community college. Having no clue about studio lighting, I dragged in one huge flood—it could have lit a football field. I said to the girls, "Pretend you're a fashion model on the runway! Give me a sneaky smile!" The chemistry that happens between a photographer and her subject clicked in, and I was working.

A very dear friend let me put my first decent camera on her credit card. The head shots I did for the actors Nan represented started coming out really, really good. Except for the ones that didn't—like the time I was clueless how to light a shoot in the middle of the street, or the time I forgot to set the strobe in sync with the shutter and ended up with half images on the film.

I'm definitely self-taught. I could never afford to go to the big schools—the Otis Art Institute, the Art Center, the Brooks Institute—so I took a basic class at Valley Occupational Center. It cost $34 and it was a twenty-week intensive, every Saturday, six hours. I learned so much from that teacher, I can't even tell you. It was a wealth of information.

I'd started working at a company that was opening up one-hour photo stores. I worked in the corporate end, doing secretarial. The reason I worked there was they said they'd pay for photography classes I wanted to take. They allowed me to go to this photography seminar, and I met this guy whose whole philosophy was about capturing the eyes. The eyes were everything. I asked if he'd consider having an intern, which he'd never done before. I did that for six months.

I'd never thought about doing head shots—the eight-by-ten black-and-white photographs that serve as an actor's calling card. When I'd thought about photography it had always been as a hobby, maybe "photojournalism" or "travel photography." It never occurred to me to do it for money. I fell into doing this and found I have a gift for shooting faces and for working with people. People are horrified most of the time to have their picture taken, and I seem to bring a comfort to them.

When I was a kid I was always the family clown. I was always trying to make them laugh. Always. I think it's kind of interesting how I do that now in photography. I have to get these actors in a place that's comfortable and fun. You can almost feel the tension in a person, and I have to work through that. In my family I was always trying to make this person feel happy, that person feel happy. It never worked in my family.

At first, I worked out of my small, one-bedroom apartment. We're talking makeup and hair done on the kitchen counter, tripod and camera set up in the kitchen, the actor standing against a backdrop in the living room. I never advertised and I started getting busier and busier. Finally, I got a call from a Japanese client who was doing a catalog on wigs. When he heard I was working out of my apartment, he didn't even want to see my portfolio.

I knew I needed to make a transition. As scared as I was and as limited as my money was, I didn't care. Even if it took two jobs, I was going to have a studio. Just then I was interviewing for a job to take school pictures. You know the kind—flat, ugly-looking, boring photos of the ballet class, the soccer team. I turned down the job, but the office manager said he was looking for a third person in his studio.

For three years I shared the space with two photographers. Soon I was using it more than the other two guys—I was booked six weeks in advance and my business was flourishing. January 1, 1995, the lease on the studio was mine.

When I walk in here, I go "Hi, studio!" I love being here. I just painted the walls and they're buttered rum, crushed violet, and lime ice. The floors are olive. The black-and-white pictures against the crushed violet—they look great. Sometimes now, as I'm getting ready for a client, I just look around—at all my equipment, at the portfolios of my work—and I think, This is all mine.

Gosh, for someone who started working outdoors because I didn't know about lights, and then worked in her little apartment, this space—studio, dressing room, makeup area—feels big. Trust me, in my wildest dreams, I never dreamed I could do this and get paid for it. I charge $125 a roll, makeup and hair separate. Yesterday I shot eight rolls. My reputation is that I get it in the first roll, so actors don't have to spend a lot before they get something. Now I'm booking four months—*four months!*—in advance. It's pretty crazy.

Being raised with such illness, I've had to struggle with

People are horrified most of the time to have their picture taken, and I seem to bring a comfort to them.

being successful. By that I mean the guilt of, Oh, my God, Mom's lying there in bed, and my sister's reduced to eighty-five pounds, and I just bought my first brand-new car—a black Altima with a sun roof. I always thought I'd have to have a man do that for me.

Of the children, I'm the closest to Mom, and four years ago I moved back home to live with her. It was easier for me because if her caretaker needed me to pick up medications, I was going to be there anyway. But when I look at her, I feel such sadness. She's in bed, can't walk, can't swallow. She cries all the time, and her cries are so heart-wrenching and so primitive, like when a small child wants their mother and their little tongue goes all the way to the back of their throat. I've been in therapy for eight years, and work hard on trying to understand these things. Her cries are still so painful for me that when I'm home I go into the bathroom and turn on the water so I can't hear them.

I'm thirty-nine years old, and I've been feeling that I need to have my own place because it's so hard to go home. It's almost like I live two different lives. I have such an incredible life outside of that house. I will always be close to my mom, we'll always share a bond that no one else in the family has. You see what goes on here in the studio—we have fun, we gossip, we talk, we play. I go home and walk into my mother's room to say hello, and she immediately starts crying. Then I have to pull inside of me to try and change that for her. I'll say, "I'm going to tickle you if you don't stop crying." I try to fill her in on my day, a crazy client, whatever. It's hard. I found a place, a beautiful four-bedroom house. I'm only moving one mile away.

It's hard to describe in words how far I've come. I grew up middle-class, and money was always a major issue. Now I do about eighty head shots a month, and the money and the independence it brings are one thing, but the excitement and appreciation I feel go deeper than that: It's the sense of, Oh, my God, I'm finally *living life*.

SARAH KASAI, b. 1989, third-grader

When I grow up I want to study about fish—sharks mostly, and jellyfish, dolphins, giant clams, sea stars, squid, octupuses. I like to swim, but I can't swim that well. I just like to look at the sea animals.

I want to be a scientist, actually. Like a marine biologist—that kind of scientist. I want to go down under, on an adventure, looking at other things down there, exploring. My parents said okay. They take me to the ocean to see the tide pools.

I have a little sister. She's six. I think she wants to be an actress or a doctor. She can't make up her mind.

Sarah

aLEXANDRA LEBENTHAL, b. 1964,
financial services executive

Alex followed in her grandmother's and father's footsteps. She's

the third-generation Lebenthal to run the seventy-one-year-old

family business, Lebenthal & Co., a Wall Street brokerage firm

specializing in municipal bonds. In the dining room of Alex's

co-op on the Upper East Side of Manhattan, four-month-old

Charlotte bounces on her mother's lap, grabs at the microphone,

and tugs on her pearl necklace, while two-year-old Ben throws

cookies on the floor. Alex, whose firm oversees $3.5 billion worth

of assets, describes a career path that starts and ends with family.

Alexandra

my grandmother Sayra founded the business with my grandfather, and when he died in the early fifties she took over. The work was completely her life. She used to say she felt old only on legal holidays and weekends. She worked until 1993, when she was ninety-three and a half.

When my sister and I were very little, I was probably three or four, Dad would take us down to the office. My grandmother would motion for us to come in with her finger, a very gnarled old-lady hand, and she'd say, "Dear, your Nana loves you very much and I'm going to put you to work." She put us to work for twenty-five cents a day, putting reinforcements on her client books.

I think as a young girl, going in and seeing my grandmother at work had a very strong effect on me. At an early age it started me thinking that it's completely natural for a woman to work, for a grandmother to work, for a mother to work.

Today I sit at her desk. It's a semi-circular desk made out of cherry, I think. Underneath the desk I have the footstool she used and I rest my feet on it. She was four foot ten, very tiny. I'm five foot two and three-quarters (I'd die to be five foot four). When I sit at that desk I really feel the family. I feel the sense of honor and history, and I feel the incredible woman she had to have been to have succeeded on Wall Street, and that drives me as well.

Municipal bonds are a sophisticated concept for a kid to get. I didn't understand what Lebenthal did, what the product was, until I was twelve or so. I credit my father with making it understandable. We'd be crossing a toll bridge and one of us would say, "Daddy, does the toll man get to keep the money?" and he'd explain, "No, it goes to pay the debt service. The bridge was built by bonds." There was constant conversation about it.

I learned everything in life is touched by a municipal bond. You can't get up in the morning and turn on the shower, turn the light on, or even take a

> I've certainly found the "lyrics" to the song I'm supposed to be singing. My work, the family business, feels like a natural extension of me.

drive on the road without a bond touching your life. So, I knew the concept of bonds building roads and tunnels and schools. The financial, or economic, aspect I didn't learn until later, when I was in college.

A couple of years ago I spoke at a Columbia Business School class on entrepreneurship. Afterward the professor had the students write comments, and he sent me copies. I was so surprised at how many people got the impression that I'd planned out every single step in my life, because I really hadn't. I can look back now and say, Yes, this all fits together. But while I was doing it, while I was a history major at Princeton, while I was deciding that I didn't want to be an actress, I was not aware of each step as a calculated move toward an ultimate goal.

There was one thing that happened which was somewhat fateful. The summer after my freshman year at Princeton I was supposed to go to Williamstown, Massachusetts, to the summer stock theater and be an apprentice. I was studying acting and they have a wonderful program. However, I hurt my knee, and about a week before I was supposed to leave, I knew I'd need therapy on my knee. It wasn't an epiphany, but at the same time I think it was somewhat fateful that I didn't go. I ended up working that summer at Lebenthal.

I spent several summer vacations and Christmas and Easter working at Lebenthal. One of the things I enjoyed most was the history of dealing with people. We have loose-leaf binders with a page for every client. (Some of the accounts that were my grandmother's have forty pages.) Every trade the customer does is posted, and every time you call and they say their husband's sick, or whatever, it's jotted down, and you see the history of that person's life with us. When I was very young, working with my grandmother, I'd just learned to read, and I'd read all the names. (I remember there were ten Greenbergs, twelve Smiths.) It's interesting, when I took over her accounts, I recognized my handwriting from the various summers and vacations I'd helped out.

It's hard for me to describe graduating from an Ivy League university in the 1980s. But if you could add and subtract, and you wanted to make money, you went to Wall Street. That was where the majority of people went, that was where all the recruiters came from.

Wall Street beckoned me, but I did not want to go to the family firm. I will admit at the time I had somewhat of a snobbish view toward our business, which essentially deals with individual investors. Although I talk glowingly of the history of dealing with people, there were times when people would come in and they had their bonds in a shopping bag and they were elderly people, and it was not 1980s, not glamorous. All of my friends were gravitating toward big jobs, where you work in big firms and take limos all the time.

It's scary to be twenty-two and looking for somebody to give you a break. Nobody would give me a job because they thought I'd leave and go to Lebenthal. It took me about four or five months. In the meantime I started running. I hadn't been a particularly good runner before, but I did a half-marathon. That was something I achieved that I never thought I could. I'd run eight or ten miles and experience the runner's high you hear about, and have a wonderful sense of achievement. That kept me going when the job search got a little bit tough.

I went to Kidder, Peabody, an investment bank. I was hired to work in the institutional bond department. I did well and was promoted to another desk. Within two weeks I made a stupid error that cost about $20,000. I left the office

in tears, and every day for the next couple of weeks I felt I was never going to get this, and I was going to be fired. It was a very fast-paced job, dealing with the tough, mean side of Wall Street, where money is the only thing that matters.

I began to realize that what I'd turned my nose up at, which was the retail side of the business, had greater appeal. It was more about dealing with people and not just numbers. Maybe I had to go through two years of what I thought was the glamorous side to come to that realization.

It just so happened that the person who'd hired me at Kidder was then president at Lebenthal. I called him up and said, "Let's talk." I wanted to talk about managing career issues, how to keep my head above water, how to come to terms with not being happy at work. I just wanted some advice. He ended up offering me a job selling, and I ended up accepting. I'd been reluctant to fall into the family business because it was family, so being hired by somebody who was not a family member was very important for me.

He went into my dad's office and said, "I just hired a new salesperson and her name is Alexandra Lebenthal." Dad, who is the chairman, was completely floored. There had never been any pressure for me to join the business or even be in the industry.

The first day I was very nervous. I was twenty-four years old, but there were people there who remembered when I was a four-year-old toddler in my grandmother's office. They were friendly, but I had this hang-up that they were thinking, Oh, there's Little A, which is my nickname.

I was a salesperson, a broker, like everybody else for a year and two months. Then I went to my grandmother's office and took over her accounts, so we worked side-by-side when she was ninety-one and I was twenty-six. Emotionally, it was a very interesting time to have had the experience when I was a tiny child and then to come full circle years later. I was chosen because as Grandmother deteriorated, my father, as chairman, and the president had felt it wasn't correct to have just any person go in and take over her accounts. Her accounts were used to dealing with a Lebenthal and the owner of the firm.

The more she deteriorated, the more she hung on to try and keep control. We had moments when we were really at each other's throats. There were times when she'd say to someone, "I'll turn you over to my secretary," and I'd just go crazy because when I first started in her office I'd said to my dad, "I want it clear, I am not her secretary."

She'd ask me about trade problems that had long been resolved. If I'd get testy with her, we'd have this yelling thing where I'd storm out of the office in tears. She was hard of hearing, so I had to speak to her in a loud tone of voice. I was yelling all day long and it was physically exhausting. I was also at this tiny little desk, just shoved into this corner of her office. I was miserable, couldn't breathe, couldn't get enough air. It was really only when I was asleep that I could breathe. That lasted nine months, and, psychologically, I couldn't have taken much more than that. Also, I'd met my then-boyfriend (now husband) at Princeton, and we'd been dating all through my working career. At the time I was working for my grandmother, he was in business school at UCLA, and we had a long-distance relationship, which probably contributed to my stress.

Over my first seven years at Lebenthal, I did about five or six different things: I worked on the development of a new product, a savings bond for small investors; I went back to sales; I ran our mutual fund department. I think Dad was watching me, but I don't think he was necessarily grooming. I think he saw a desire in me that he knew he didn't have, so he had a great sense of relief—"Thank God, here's someone to take over." I have a passion about the day-to-day details of

In any family business you hope your children will want to carry on.

running a business. He really cares more about the creative side, the theatrical side of the business—the advertising, the marketing—and doesn't want to get involved in the who, what, where, why, and when of what's going to make this business work.

Spring 1995, Dad invited me to lunch at the City Midday Club. It's across the street from our office, on the fiftieth floor, so you have a view of the whole city and uptown and the harbor. He brought up the possibility of my becoming president and said, "What do you think?" I was thrilled. He said, "I want you to know that I'm not doing this because you're my daughter. I'm doing this because you deserve it, because you've made an incredible success in a short period of time, and because of how the salespeople respond to you." It made me the youngest female president of a brokerage firm on Wall Street. I was thirty-one years old.

On the other hand it was bittersweet. My grandmother hadn't lived to see the day when the third generation took over the management of the firm. She'd died six months earlier at ninety-five and a half.

My father prepared an announcement ad, "Meet the Next Lebenthal." It was quite a splash. There was a photo of me done by Mary Ellen Mark. I was standing with my arms folded, just looking at the camera with this little half-smile on my face with Wall Street behind me. I love the picture because it's what I love about being a young woman on Wall Street, which is just, Hey, you know what, I'm here and it's not about being a stodgy old man. It's about having fun and being yourself and being outspoken and taking life as it comes.

I'd gotten married while I'd been working on that savings bond for small investors. I was pregnant when I ran the mutual fund department. This just goes back to the thing about having that picture taken. I think, Hey, you know what, life's changed. Women work, women get pregnant. I like being someone who people think, Hmm, how's she doing that?

There are some days when it's a crazy mess. I actually like it being crazy. Charlotte's four months, Ben's two, almost three. They have a full-time nanny. I generally work from eight to six. I used to do a lot of things after work, charity work. Now I don't have the time. I don't put pressure on myself to do anything more than just deal with the kids. No matter how important the mother's job is, I think the woman automatically is the one who figures out how the home's going to work. My husband's great and he's very helpful, but I'm the one who runs the house as well as the company.

When I was pregnant with Charlotte—I was president then—I took the subway home at 5:00 and went to the playground with Ben. Without going into graphic details, my water was breaking, but very slowly. Since my due date wasn't for seven days, I wasn't sure what was happening. I was having contractions, but I'd been having them—a general tightening in the uterus—for several weeks, so I didn't really think anything of it. That night at 11:00 I went to the hospital, and I gave birth the next morning. This is something women do, especially when they're pregnant in higher power jobs. You don't want to be perceived as weak in any way, so you go to extra lengths not to appear any different. So of course, I'd take the subway, and of course, I'd work the normal hours, because if a man were in the same position he wouldn't be pregnant and he wouldn't have to take it easy.

As president my sleepless nights are over salespeople leaving us, investors leaving us. One of our salespeople doing something dishonest that hurts the reputation of the firm. And then the final big thing I fear is the ultimate failure of the business under my watch. There are a lot of statistics on family businesses, and most of them don't make it past two generations. If they make it past two, getting past three is a big deal. Now it's on my shoulders, and it's a very frightening idea of potentially screwing up and destroying seventy-one years of blood, sweat, and tears. I don't ever let myself get complacent.

Six weeks after I became president I made a decision that strayed from the way I normally deal with people. I angered a lot of people, and a woman ended up leaving us. It was kind of like after six weeks of publicity about me being president and everything being great, there was this big pop in the balloon.

I had a lot of moments of doubt and feeling, Oh, my God, was I crazy to think I could do this? I went and got myself an executive coach. She was marvelous because the first thing she told me after she did all this testing was, "You're really smart." Now whenever I have a situation where I think, I can't do this, I think, You know what, my coach thinks I'm really smart. That gives me such an incredible feeling of confidence, to know I have that raw talent. Now after I make a mistake, I write down what the problem was, what the action I took was, what the results were, and what the lesson I learned was, so every mistake is a building block for me.

I still feel I have yet to make my mark on the company, because that would be to make the company grow a great deal. Until I'm farther along in my goals, it's hard to imagine the next generation being there. Especially with Ben, I can't picture him, except making his way through life the way he is now. He's adorable, but he's a whirling dervish. But in any family business, you hope your children will want to carry on. I've certainly found the "lyrics" to the song I'm supposed to be singing. My work, the family business, feels like a natural extension of me.

JOANN MATYAS, b. 1954,
designer

I grew up in a family

When I learned that JoAnn designs fountains—famous ones like

the fountain at Universal Studios / Citywalk in Los Angeles and the

one at Disney Village Marketplace in Orlando—I was fascinated. I

had to know what had led her to such an extraordinary line of work.

While a small fountain tinkles outside the kitchen window of her

Hollywood apartment, JoAnn describes the ripples and riptides in a

path that's still flowing.

JoAnn

where both parents were self-sufficient.

My father never hired anybody to help him with the electrical or plumbing when he built his house. He did everything himself. We never took an appliance anywhere to be fixed by anybody else. My mother taught me to sew. There was always this feeling of working with your hands and making things.

I was the middle child in a family of seven children, and it was a pretty egalitarian family in the sense that the girls were expected to help out as much as the boys. I used to help my father mix cement. I took a lot of pleasure in working with him and seeing things being made, whether it was a brick wall or a sidewalk. He could also be critical and sort of unforgiving, like you didn't dare hand him the wrong tool.

My high school counselor tried to encourage me to open up a little bit because my parents didn't talk to me about any of this, as far as how you decided what to do in life. He said, "The most important thing, as far as your career, is to look for the thing that gives you a sense of intense fulfillment, of all your talents coming together. Whenever you find fulfillment and contentment—go for that." I decided that for me that sense of pleasure came from working with my hands and making things.

I had the sense from my parents that once I was through high school, I was on my own. I did start working immediately, but I quickly learned that on a minimum wage I couldn't even afford my own apartment. I was just dying to be out on my own, dying for independence—and I didn't have that opportunity without going to college.

In college I declared myself an art major, but I could never see my way clear to what an art degree would do for me. It didn't feel right. It didn't seem like anything practical.

I had a real desire to travel and see the world, to experience things beyond my home in San Diego. My boyfriend was a high school teacher, and he had an opportunity to go to Australia and teach for a year. I'd been working full-time as an assistant manager in Robinson's linen department (which sounds really grand, but I was earning maybe twenty cents more than minimum wage) and plowing slowly through school part-time. I took off and went with him to Australia.

I decided that it was a matter of taking on another type of salesgirl position or going to school to learn a more marketable skill. When my older brother got out of the military, my mother encouraged him to take drafting. As a child I used to sneak into his room and see the wonderful drawings on his table that looked so complicated and yet so organized and neat. In Australia, I thought that would be a wonderful skill for me to learn to get a better paying job.

The only drafting course that was offered was part of a two-year mechanical engineering degree from Sydney Technical College. My first reaction was, "No way!" It didn't seem like something I could do, yet I couldn't forget about it either.

I began to realize that design was more what I wanted to get into rather than pure art. And rather than just knowing how to design things that looked nice, if I studied mechanical engineering, I'd be able to get beneath the surface and understand how things worked.

I can still remember calling from this wonderful old English-style red telephone booth with the little capped roof and having this man say, "Honey, are you sure you're not calling about the home economics course instead of engineering?"

I surprised myself at how much I enjoyed school except for this one class, machine shop. My boyfriend used to call them Black Tuesdays because I was so worried about going to that class. The lathes seemed ten feet long and were computer-controlled, and I was scared to death of them. I'd clamp a part into this lathe and the drill bits would be whirring at thousands of rpm. I had the sense that if I didn't

There's something magical about a fountain at night.

fasten the parts down properly, they'd fly off and kill somebody. It helped a lot that the guys in my class were comfortable with these machines and were tolerant of my saying, "Please, come here and make sure I'm not going to maim myself when I turn this thing on."

I completed only one year of the program while I was in Australia. I was near the top of my class, I'd even survived the Black Tuesdays, and I was intellectually challenged by all the things I was finding out about the world. That gave me the impetus when I came back to the States to go for a full-out engineering degree.

When I was in the San Diego library researching engineering schools, I came across the product design program at Stanford University. This program was described as a merging of the art and mechanical engineering departments and is the only program in the U.S. that encourages art for engineers. It clicked into place that that was the direction I wanted to go in. Even though I knew it was unattainable at the time—I didn't have a 4.0 grade-point average and I didn't have the money—I still allowed myself to dream about it.

Just going to school at Cal Poly [California State Polytechnic] Pomona was a huge step for me, at least in my family. My sophomore year, I got married at Christmas. It was hard because I was living in Pomona and going to school but going home to San Diego on the weekends to be with my husband. I was torn between the two lifestyles. I'd spend the weekends cleaning the house and buying groceries and enjoying being with him and not doing my studies. As anybody who's been in college full-time knows, you can't afford to ignore it.

It was widely known that your junior year in the mechanical engineering program at Cal Poly is the worst. I told my husband that I wouldn't be able to come home every weekend, or even every other weekend, so just bear with me. I did pretty well that first quarter of my junior year, focusing on thermodynamics, heat transfer, statics, but by Christmas the marriage had started to fall apart.

My husband admitted to me later that on one hand he'd

encouraged me, but he hadn't expected that I'd do as well as I had, that I'd really take off and fly with it. He'd studied industrial arts in college (that's what he taught in high school), and he told me that he'd always wanted to be an engineer, but he hadn't been able to handle the math and science part. My succeeding in those areas kicked up some problems for him as far as his own feelings of regret or inadequacy.

The last six months of school everyone was caught up in this interviewing frenzy. I knew IBM had a good reputation, and there was the sense of a stable career and a stable future, and I could learn a lot there.

I thought I'd be at IBM two years, but they kept offering me jobs that grabbed my attention. I was always happy as long as I was on a steep learning curve, but at the end of seven years I was at the point where none of the opportunities interested me anymore.

The hardest thing was to consider leaving the security of IBM, because it felt like a frivolous thing to do—to even talk about going back to school. In my family, where I'd been the only one to graduate from college, my educational status was already a major accomplishment. But I realized that when I got to the end of my life, I'd regret not having at least tried the Stanford product design program. I'd kept that dream in the back of my head all those years.

At Stanford the program was all about designing things. How do we design a hammer. Or can openers. Or chairs. Or hat racks. Those were the more practical things from the engineering school. The art side of the program—that was about designing wooden bowls, or a flag, or fabric.

There was a group of five men, five professors, and their form of teaching was to tell you what you were doing wrong. As a student, these critiques felt like personal put-downs. Sara Little Turnbull had started lecturing in the program. It gave me a lot of perspective when she, after a few months, quit coming to the critiques and told me she couldn't take it anymore. Here was this woman in her seventies, who'd had a wonderful career in the design field, and she had a lot of spunk and spirit and had done a lot of remarkable things— she was instrumental in creating Corning Cookware—and here she was saying that she had a hard time with it. Once when I felt so demoralized, she said to me, "The only problem you have is you're listening too much to these guys." She said, "I know you can do it, and you need to know you can do it."

I think I've always been more sensitive to criticism than the average person and more intent on not showing how much it bothers me. And that, again, is thanks to my father, who could be very good at putting people down. I was just back in San Diego, we'd opened a fountain there, and after the ceremonies I had to return to make some adjustments. My father said, "What? Didn't you get it right the first time?" When I was about eight years old I stood in front of him one Saturday, the day all of us children lined up to get our weekly allowance and our assigned chores, and I made some small request. When I heard his words of criticism, right then I made the decision not to ever break down in front of him. At Stanford, I relied on the stiff upper lip I'd acquired as a child. Engineers don't cry.

While I was still at Stanford, wrapping up my degree, one of my professors took us on a field trip to WET Design.

WET stands for Water Entertainment Technology, a company that produces fountains they call "water features" to distinguish them from traditional fountains. WET hired me to do some pattern work for a project in Saudi Arabia. I designed some grates that water would fall through.

Then they asked me to help out in their engineering department. It's rare to find a company that does this kind of creative merging of art and engineering, and it seemed like a perfect fit for my skills and interests.

For the first three or four years the job was extremely demanding, and I gave 150 percent to it. It wasn't all that uncommon for me to be in the office until ten or eleven at night, night after night. When I wasn't in there, I was traveling overseas to work on projects—it could be a fountain in Tokyo, Manila, Singapore, the Netherlands.

I didn't have much of a social life and I was happy to just throw myself into the company. But it wore me down a lot and got to the point where I felt I needed a little more balance. (I went for seven years without even having a boyfriend.) In 1994, I left WET as a full-time employee, and I've been freelancing as a consultant for them. It's allowed a bit more of a personal life to evolve, which has been wonderful.

When I'm working on fountains, I especially enjoy the animation process, which occurs at the end when the fountain has been constructed and is finally up and running. This process in animation could be likened to choreography. You have all these little dancers in front of you that just happen to be water spouts, and how do you choreograph their movements?

When I'm animating a fountain, usually I have a computer on my lap with cables connected to the equipment room. (The equipment room is below the plaza surface, hidden from public view.) A control panel in the equipment room operates the water nozzles through electrical signals. My computer has cables that connect it to that control panel, so when I'm animating the fountain I take over the control of the nozzles. That's how I'm able to sit on the plaza (usually in an uncomfortable chair) and send jets of water shooting into the air. There's such a love, for me, of that part of the process—of seeing the fountain come alive.

Since it's amazingly difficult to see a computer screen outdoors in the daytime, often I design at night, bundled in heavy clothes, with a security guard nearby. It's usually quieter, and the environments I work in, public plazas and malls, tend to be less populated at night. Then I'm throwing these big jets of water into the air—the super shooter goes up to 150 feet—and illuminated by submerged lighting, the water sparkles and falls back down like diamonds in the night sky. There's something magical about a fountain at night. The illuminated water is like a chandelier glowing from within.

More than once, while working on a plaza surrounded by huge office towers, I've become aware of having spent many years in cubicles, dressed for work at IBM. I'm aware of how glad I am that I'm sitting down on the plaza, choreographing the fountain, instead of working in one of those cubicles. I feel so fortunate to have found my way into this kind of work.

I've always fantasized about having my own business. That fantasy has evolved over the years, and more and more

I think I won't be happy until I have my own design studio. Of course, the ideal fantasy is to have a partner, a boyfriend, or a husband who wants to do the same thing. My ideal has always been something like the Ray and Charles Eames partnership. My mind's flowing a mile a minute, thinking about

The hardest thing was to consider leaving the security of IBM, because it felt like a frivolous thing to do.

the studio and all the wonderful, fun things that could evolve out of that.

I always wanted work that was part of my life, not just an eight-to-five job, like my father had. But work that merged with my life, that became part of who I was. Being a designer is not so much what I do as who I am.

SABRINA NICKERSON, b. 1956,
tow-truck driver

Way outside the Tucson city limits, at the farthest end of an

unpaved road, one runs into the headquarters of All Ways Towing.

The tools of Sabrina's trade sprawl across her front yard: a twin-

boom GMC (yellow cab, pink pinstriping), a twenty-one-foot

flatbed (the moneymaker), and a one-ton hook-and-sling.

Martha, Sabrina's aunt and dispatcher, works the phones from

a brown plaid sofa in their living room. With a wad of keys

dangling from her rear hip pocket, Sabrina describes how a

pre-law student, copper miner, and long-haul truck driver has

ended up as the only woman tow-truck driver in western Arizona.

Sabrina

way, that my goal in life would be to catch a man. I guess that's why I didn't think about how I was going to earn a living.

I was encouraged to dress up, wear makeup, don't cuss, and don't eat a lot in front of him. All those really corny things.

All of a sudden I was out of high school and I was out there, and what was I going to do? I got scared and ended up working a lot of odd jobs while I went to college. I worked at a 7-Eleven nights and went to school days, studying pre-law. It was probably an eighty-hour week, and on top of that on weekends I interviewed prisoners for the court.

I got burned out from working full-time and going to school full-time. I'm aware that probably a lot of students do that, but for me it was too much. It wasn't a traumatic decision. I thought I'd take a break for a year and return. As I look back, I don't think I would have been happy being a lawyer, sitting in a library.

I worked for public housing for a while. We interviewed people for public assistance, Section 8. I also had a job as a secretary for an air-conditioning company. Both of those jobs required you to wear a dress, the whole bit. It wasn't my cup of tea. I didn't do well. The work took me longer than it should have. I had to stay after hours to finish. I wasn't happy.

At that time [1979] the economy of Arizona was based mostly on copper and cattle, and the copper mines were just opening up to women. San Manuel Copper mine, where I went to work, is one of the largest in Arizona. They blast the ore underground, send it by train to the crusher, and then to the mill where it's floated and separated. I worked surface in the filter plant. I was really happy with that job. Every day was something different. It was physical work, it was challenging, and I got $13 an hour plus good benefits.

The mine worked seven days, twenty-four hours. We never shut down. Toward the end of my third year the price of copper started dropping, and the company felt it in their profit margin. I'd worked my way up from laborer to operator. Being an operator is a lot of responsibility as it is, and they were laying off people, so you were expected to do two or three jobs, and it wasn't safe.

I got hurt. I'd climbed up to the top of a huge steel sump tank and was trying to unplug the drain with an air hose. The ladder was flimsy and slipped, and I fell about thirty feet to the concrete floor. I bounced once and broke my leg, and bounced again and broke my jaw and busted all my teeth.

It took a year to heal. While I was recuperating, I married this guy I'd been dating for two years. The very next day he changed into someone so angry I didn't even know him. I divorced him. I won't tolerate that.

At the mine, management was good to me. They appreciated that I worked hard, and they said I'd be foreman one day. They were more than fair with me. But I didn't feel I was doing a good job anymore. I had a plate in my leg and couldn't get around fast enough. They never said anything, but, you know, when you're doing something, you want to be good at it.

I quit the mines and went to truck-driving school. Most of it you do by correspondence, but the last week you go to this class where you drive a truck, a semi, tractor-trailer. They call her an eighteen-wheeler. It's eighty thousand pounds loaded, fifty-five feet long. When you pull doubles, it's eighty feet long.

Eventually the gentleman that hired me, we formed a partnership and bought our own truck. We hauled L.A. to New York. I liked the truck and the driving. It's beautiful in the morning when the sun's coming up. There's a feeling of independence. There's none of the responsibilities that you have when you're home. There's no mail. You don't have to clean house. You don't have to fix your car. It's an independent type of freedom.

After three years my co-driver almost killed us twice. The first time, I'd driven my shift and we'd just switched. I'd eaten my dinner in the sleeper and was getting ready to lay down in the upper bunk. I decided to get up for a minute. I don't know why. I opened the leather curtain between the sleeper and the cab. We were on a state route in California, heading west, and he was going about seventy-five miles an hour. We were pulling doubles, so it takes a mile to stop. There was a train coming alongside us, and I could see the point of intersection ahead where the railroad track crossed the road. He was not slowing down and a train was coming. I realized he was not going to stop. I screamed and he hit the brakes. He pumped the air brake and hit the switch to engage the jake brake. If I hadn't screamed, I'm sure we would have been dead. He stopped at the very last second, just inches from the track. He claimed he never saw the train. I don't know how you could not see it.

He was getting more and more unhappy. Neither of us wanted to get a different partner because it's hard to find someone you can live that close with, and we had worked well together.

When you're pulling doubles you have to be particularly careful about ice and snow. They call it black ice. It's dangerous, and you don't see it. When you're pulling doubles it's worse, because that back trailer will come around and take you wherever it wants to go.

In Oregon he was heading up the mountain, and it started getting cold. There was enough warning, I think, that he should have seen it coming and pulled over and stopped. That was our procedure, especially in the mountains. He kept going and got us to the point where we were slipping on the ice and the back trailer was starting to come around beside us. Very calm, he woke me up. He said, "Sabrina, get your clothes on and grab your dog. Get ready to bail, because we're gonna go over the mountain." I kept saying, "Can't you just hit the brakes? Can't you just stop!" It was happening slowly. The back trailer was coming around a little bit, a little more, until it would get to the point of no return.

It was snowy, dark, and we were both really scared.

We'd come up the mountain and we were about to start down, and that's when you lose it. He yelled for me to get on the radio and warn the other drivers we were coming

down sideways and to clear out, so we didn't take anybody else with us. An old-timer came over the radio, and as calm as could be, he told him to hit his trolley brakes. He told him to use the most gentle touch and go back and forth between the front brake and the trolley brake. What you're trying to do is stop that back trailer until your cab can get up front again. He did it and I'll be damned if he didn't pull out, which is real rare. Once you get to that point, you almost never straighten out. That's the scaredest I've ever been.

Those two incidents were real close. I told him he was on the verge of a nervous breakdown. I wanted him to sell me his half interest in the truck. He didn't want to do that. I said, "Okay, you take a break and I'll keep working until you're ready to come back." He didn't want to do either one, so we terminated.

It took me a long time to get over that. I was happy to be home. I'd been real homesick. But I didn't know what I was going to do. You're a little scared when you don't know how you're going to earn your living.

One Sunday afternoon my aunt Martha, a friend, Mark, and I were sitting at the dining room table, talking about how the money I had left from truck driving was running out, and what should I do.

My aunt and I have always wanted our own business. She's my father's sister. When things got so bad with my stepmother, I left. One morning I was supposed to get on the school bus and I didn't. I was about fifteen, and Martha took me in. We've been best friends ever since.

Mark had owned a tow truck for years. He said, "You can always put bread on the table with a tow truck."

It seemed like I had a background to do that, which I thought would increase my chances of success. My aunt thought it was a good idea, too. She had a job with civil service, so I was going to start the business and she was going to keep working there.

I took whatever money I had, she put in a couple thousand, and we bought a hook-and-sling truck, which nowadays most people don't want because it drags their car.

At first, I was a joke. The shops would call me just to see a woman tow-truck driver, a five-foot-tall, woman tow-truck driver. Maybe I was a little sensitive, but I'd get there and all the mechanics and the shop guys would stand at their bays and watch while I hooked up or unloaded, waiting to see if I was going to screw up. Everything would go fine but they wouldn't call me back. I was just something they wanted to see that one time.

I learned by trial and error. I knew a guy who owned a salvage yard. The cars are already wrecked. It's the most work for the least amount of pay. You get about $15 a car, and you're expected to move ten or fifteen of them a day. Once in July I was out in the middle of the desert, it was probably 120 degrees, so hot I couldn't touch anything, and I spent four, maybe five hours getting one car loaded. It was wrecked so bad it wouldn't move. By the end of the day I was so tired, I just wanted to cool off and go to bed. Those are the hard times, when you're not making any money, when you start questioning what you're doing.

For all the trouble and all the mistakes, I don't want to brag, but I was a natural at it. I had a reputation of never coming back empty.

I started getting calls for jobs nobody else was willing to do. If the wheels are bent so they'll roll against the frame and start a fire, or the car's wedged in so bad you can't get it out, a lot of guys won't do it. My competitor has very, very, very fancy trucks. So fancy that he picks and chooses the jobs he takes, so his trucks don't get scratched.

> They say every tow-truck driver loses a vehicle off the hook. I've never lost one, and I've been driving eight years.

As far as I know, I'm the only female tow-truck driver in this area. There are advantages to being a woman in this profession. Women tend to be more gentle, more meticulous, pay more attention to detail. They say every tow-truck driver loses a vehicle off the hook. I've never lost one, and I've been driving eight years.

I allow my customers to make their own decisions. I don't take advantage of them financially and I'm careful with their cars. Often I'll get them to a shop and then get them squared away in a motel. It's a kind of caretaking, because when people are broke down they're real vulnerable, they're real insecure.

I get most of my work because I'm on rotation with the Police Department in Marana. It took me five years to get on the rotation list. I like accident recovery the best. There was a gentleman not too long ago that went into the irrigation ditch, and he had cerebral palsy. He was fine and his little girl was fine, but he was devastated because that was his only truck. He was so happy when I was able to flip it over and get it out of the ditch without doing any damage so he could drive it home. I love when that happens. He kept saying how good I was.

Also, when you're on rotation for accidents the police have got to know they can count on you. Every time I've tried to conduct a relationship it's gotten to the point where it's a choice between the relationship and the business. I'm on twenty-four-hour call with the police, and the guys I meet want me to turn my beeper off and not answer the phone for a night. They also think they've got to protect me. I resent that. I carry an ATM .38, an automatic, to protect myself.

I don't want to do this just good enough to survive. I want it to grow. I envision a thriving fleet of tow trucks coupled with a thriving workforce. I'd have both men and women because we should all be working together as partners. To me succeeding means not just dollars and cents but being good at what you do, like in the old days. The old-timers had a skill, and they passed it on to their children. It was their lifeblood. When those young people went out into the world it helped them have a sense of security, because they knew they had a skill they were trained at, that their forefathers had done. They went out into the world with a sense of well-being. We don't do that anymore.

k

KIM SU TRAN LA, b. 1941,
restaurateur

"Mama La" and her family escaped from Vietnam and were left to die on an Indonesian island. In 1980 she arrived in Houston with her family, the clothes on her back, and the recipes of her homeland. Now her dynasty has nine Kim Sỏn restaurants. On the second floor of the mothership—a 22,000-square-foot, red-and-gold banquet facility—she finds us a quiet corner table that looks out on the skyline of downtown Houston. As we sip endless cups of jasmine tea, she tells the story of her family, who pledged to live together and die together.

Mama La

Kim Su Tran La speaks no English. This interview was translated by Alice Y Huynh, Vietnamese interpreter.

during my childhood, there was a revolution called "Viêt-Miñh." I was on the run until I was eleven and the family was evacuated to Viñh-Long province. I was young and ignorant. I was also very *nhà quê* (country hick) and, actually, there was no one in the province where I lived who became *ông này, ông kia* (big shot). My family was in the wholesale fabric business and I helped out, moving the bolts around, selling fabric. I had a normal dream to be in *buôn-bán* (business). I did not know to expect to be a big professional person.

I got married when I was twenty-one. In Vietnam when you get married you have to go where the husband goes and live where the husband lives. I had to serve my husband's family, and I had to live with my mother-in-law. It's kind of cruel, but you're no longer part of your own family except to go home and say "hi" and "bye."

My mother-in-law was preparing food for the cafeteria at the police headquarters in Saigon. That's how I came to know my cooking techniques. When I was living with my own mother I didn't even know how to make a pot of rice. My mother-in-law prepared *lửởn* (eel), *ếch* (frog), and *cá lốc hấp* (steamed fish). Also, she was fixing *đồ nhậu* (drink snacks) that men like to eat when they get together and have beer, like *cua rang muối* (fried salted crab) and *lửởn nửởng* (charcoal-grilled eel mixed with salad). It seemed like she could do almost everything.

In 1967 another general took over and they kicked us out of police headquarters. At that time to do business in Saigon, you must have strong *phe-đảng* (powerful friends). We went back to Viñh-Long, and my mother-in-law opened Kim Sởn in 1968, the same year as the Tết offensive.

The *nhà hàng* (restaurant business) was really, really tough and a lot of hard work. My husband was bookkeeper, cashier. I was cook. It was real hard on me because I had to get up at five o'clock in the morning to open the restaurant, and I worked all the way up until nine or ten o'clock at

Escaping by sea was a dangerous gamble. We could either win or lose.

night. Then I had to clean up, so I wouldn't be through until eleven or twelve. I sent my children home to my own mother to take care of them.

It was my mother-in-law's business, and even if I wanted to have my own business, I could not. In a family with the only son, you could never get away from the family.

The Communists took over [1975] and confiscated the restaurant. I was really relieved and happy when I quit the restaurant business because there was no more hardship, hard work. But I was also concerned about our future. I had to resort to another way of making a living. When the Communists took over the south, they controlled the jewelry business, and all the gold stores were closed down. People who had money, who wanted to escape, had to buy gold. But they could not carry gold on the escape trip, so they must buy diamonds to trade later. (Diamonds are easier to hide, not only from the Communist government but from robbers on the sea.) I was *buôn lậu* (smuggling) diamonds on the black market. I was scared. If I got caught, I'd be put in jail. Thanks to that income we got the money to escape.

When I made money in Saigon at the police cafeteria, I invested in real estate. I was thinking that when my children grew up, I would give each of them a house. But it was all confiscated by the Communists. My husband and I decided to escape, because our oldest boys were sixteen and seventeen and it wasn't possible for them to continue their education there. They would be accused of being "capitalistic" and they could be drafted and sent to Cambodia to fight. Because of that, I had to find a way to escape.

Altogether, both sides—my family and my husband's family—we were thirty-seven. When we left [June 16, 1979], all seven of our children were with us. My mother-in-law said, *"Nếu sống, chúng ta cũng sống, nếu chết, chúng ta cũng chết."* ("If we die, we all die together. If we live, we all live together.") Escaping by sea was a dangerous gamble. We could either win or lose.

We boarded the boat in Bặc-Liêu very late in the evening. The boat was about twenty meters long, four meters wide, and did not have enough space for the four hundred people. The water was really rough, and we were seasick and threw up a lot. We were on the boat for thirty-six hours when we stopped in Malaysia to refuel.

In the afternoon a huge military ship from the Malaysian navy pulled up alongside us. The *tài-công* (captain) on that ship sent his servicemen to our boat, and they robbed us really good. We couldn't resist. We would be killed. They were pointing guns at us. That was the most terrifying feeling.

They sent all of us up to the deck and searched through our bodies and our wallets. I myself had a gold chain on my neck. They took the chain off and my children, each of them, had a little bit of chain, too. The diamonds were hidden in blouse hems, hems of slacks, and even in the waist of our clothes. They didn't get those.

Because the refugee camps were overloaded in Malaysia, they towed our boat away. Their ship was a big military ship made out of steel. Our boat was made out of wood. They were going so fast that our boat was tipping back and forth, and it could have flipped over and all of us would have fallen into the ocean. During the time we were towed, the wood of the boat was making a cracking noise like it was about to break into pieces. They were towing us so fast and so forcefully, the rope kept breaking. Finally, they got tired of reconnecting the rope, so they let us go. They said, "There's an island, go there and don't you return." The island [Kuku Island, Indonesia] was still a blur in the distance. It took us one more night to drift there.

About two thousand pioneers [earlier escapees from Vietnam] had arrived at Kuku Island already. There was no refugee camp. The camp we stayed in, we made ourselves. When we left Vietnam, each of us had two or three axes and plastic covers. The plastic was to cover the frame and the walls of the house.

The United Nations had not been there yet, and people who had left Vietnam without any kind of preparation were starving to death. When we left, we had two bags of rice. The boat people allowed us to do that. Actually, they loved to have the rice on the boat because that weight kept the boat stable, so it didn't shake. We would not dare to eat the rice as *cơm* (steamed rice), because there wouldn't be enough. We made *cháo* (rice soup), so there would be a lot more. We'd brought pots with us. I even brought those pots over here to America for memory. I still have them at home.

Food was very expensive on the island. For one ounce of gold you could buy six kilos [thirteen pounds] of meat. We sold all our diamonds to feed ourselves. I traded diamonds for gold, right on Kuku Island. The escapees, the ones who had previously arrived there, would do the exchange.

I get a little emotional talking about this; it makes me cry today. People dying every day at the camp . . . I was afraid I would lose somebody to illness. My husband got really sick with *sot rét* (yellow fever), and he was about to die. It came from the mosquitoes on that island. People died, about four or five people a day. I was really frightened.

What I was scared of most is that the children would get sick. If you got sick, especially something affecting your lungs, you would never be able to leave the island. Therefore, I sold all my diamonds in exchange for twelve bars of gold, and I bought a little place to sell coffee. (Someone had owned the coffee shop and they sold it to me.) I made the business in order to make money to feed the kids well, so they could survive the island in order to leave.

The rumor was passing around that everyone should go to America. That America is a better place to live. The reason my immediate family got to go was because of my mother-in-law. She'd been on a list with my older sister whose husband had served in the military, so he had priority to come to America. My mother-in-law left the island first, two months earlier, and she sponsored us. Month after month people got to leave. We lived on the island for fourteen months. My husband and I and our children were the last to leave. . . . Leaving that island was an indescribable feeling, as if I was going to *thiên-đàng* (heaven).

The United Nations High Commissioner arranged our travel plans and took us off the island to the airport. A U.S. charity lent us money for the flight from Singapore. (We paid it back month by month for two years.) When we arrived in the U.S. [August 1980] the UN had given each of us a sweater, so that's what we had with us.

In Houston we lived in a four-plex with other family members. My husband and my family—six sons, one

and my husband got a driver's license, we started working.

I found a job at a little Vietnamese restaurant as a cook. I had to work the night shift, from three in the afternoon to six in the morning, and they paid me twenty dollars a day. They did not know my experience, they did not know whether I knew how to cook or not. After two months I proved myself, and I got thirty dollars a day.

The goal was that I wanted my children to further their education. The second thing I wanted was to have our own business. When I was working for that restaurant as a cook, I learned that the restaurant owners here in the U.S., the Vietnamese ones, had no experience of cooking in a restaurant. They were making very simple dishes like *bún bò huế* (beef noodles from the central area) or *phở* (beef noodles from the north). I knew how to make special dishes for *đồ nhậu* (drink snacks). Therefore, I knew deep down in my

daughter, mother-in-law—we had ten people in a run-down, two-bedroom apartment. Each of us received $250 from a Catholic Charities refugee program, and government assistance gave us food stamps for the first eight months, so we could eat. After we took care of the Social Security cards heart that I could make it. I was just waiting for the time when I got enough money, and I'd open my own business.

Everybody worked and saved. In two years, the family saved $18,000. Having the business was basically my determination and my husband's. I was confident about my abilities, but I felt it was a gamble. I'd started out with nothing,

I'm holding the ultimate power in this family just as my mother-in-law used to.

so if it failed and I ended up with nothing, that's what I started out with.

The other reason I had to start my own business is that my husband is really a *thật-thà* (too nice, too naive) kind of man, and then he didn't understand English, either. He helped run a U-Tote'em convenience store for the owner. We were just about to take another U-Tote'em, but there were so many shootings, robbings in the convenience store. And if the robbers told my husband to stay still, he wouldn't understand. So we were scared for his life.

We named the restaurant Kim Sởn, after my mother-in-law's restaurant in Viñh-Long. I was the cook and I was working sixteen, seventeen hours a day. My mother-in-law made *chè,* the Vietnamese dessert. My children and my husband helped me out, also. After I cooked, he had to clean up because I did not dare hire anyone else. On the weekends we closed the business at three o'clock in the morning, and we cleaned up until five o'clock. At eight o'clock we had to reopen for business. We didn't have time to go home. I put chairs together to make a bed out of it, and my husband and I slept there. Those were the rough days. We hadn't quite let go of the U-Tote'em. We were worried, so we were doing two things at one time.

The first year we had hardly any American customers. We had only a Vietnamese menu, and our customers were Vietnamese who knew our restaurant in Viñh-Long. We were a success because no one received any salaries. All the money we made went back into it. That's how we built.

We moved to another location in 1983, and that's when we started serving menus in English and business started booming. The next Kim Sởn opened in 1985. The big one [22,000 square feet] opened in 1995.

It was not my idea to expand. The young generation, my two sons, were thinking that this is the golden opportunity that comes only once, and we have to grasp it. I don't want to expand anymore. I feel that way because Vietnamese cooking is very delicate. I can't just pass you a recipe and tell you, "Go ahead and make it." In the Vietnamese restaurant, for example, in *gà xào xả ớt* (chicken cooked with lemon grass and chili pepper), when you mix the *nước mắm* (fish sauce) and *xả* (lemon grass), it has to be cooked for five minutes for it to taste really good. If you cook it four and a half minutes, it doesn't taste right.

My job now is going to each restaurant to train the employees and to make sure that the seasoning is the way I'd do it myself. The specialty of this restaurant is *đồ ướp* (the marinade). I still have to do that myself, and when I'm not here my two younger sisters come in and do exactly what I do in the warehouse.

My legs have been bothering me a lot lately. Doctors say it's overexertion. Just walking in the kitchen, it's so large, is tiring. I stayed home one Sunday and that was it. I went back to work. I have to work. Even when I'm old and wrinkled and in a wheelchair, push me into the restaurant and leave me there. Also, I'm afraid of *thất-bại* (failure), so I want to come in. I'm afraid that my children will not do the job as good as I would.

In the restaurant it's not all roses. I don't want to fight in front of the customers, in front of the employees. I wait it out until no one's around. We have quite a few locations now, so the only time we can sit down and iron things out is when everything's closed. Sometimes at one or two or three in the morning, that's the quiet time because no one has anything else to do, except go home and sleep. That's conference time.

The *bí-quyết* (secret) of my business is family. I don't know how American families are, but in Vietnamese families, normally, the wife's side and the husband's side always fight. Very fortunately, it doesn't happen in my family. Both families help me.

On Monday the restaurant business is slow, so Monday is the night for family, when the children come to my house for dinner. Sometimes we eat steak, or *mắm* (fermented fish), or *bún* (noodles). We eat whatever the restaurants don't sell. Monday night is very important night to us, to me. Because I want to see all my children together.

I have two children who are dentists. One is a petroleum engineer. Two are in the restaurant business. One daughter-in-law is going to law school, one is in pharmacy school. My daughter, Tina, is in business school. She does payroll for the company. If she wants to have a career in the restaurant business, that would be perfect. But if not, I'm accepting it. Everybody has a career. That's my happiness.

We are still very close, and we maintain certain traditions like the Vietnamese New Year's Eve and Tết (Chinese New Year's Eve). When the whole family gets together at my house, there are over sixty of us. We eat, we celebrate, and then we *mừng tuổi* (pay respect) to *ong bà* (the ancestor altar). That is a tradition that is maintained.

The tradition of matriarchy is maintained, too. I'm holding the ultimate power in this family just as my mother-in-law used to. But I am different from my mother-in-law. She was supposed to be always right, whatever she said was right, whatever she did was right. I am not that way today.

Today when I'm sleeping, I still dream about the past, the time after the Communists took over, when I was so poor in Vietnam and did not have anything. That still comes back to me in my dreams. I could never imagine that I would be so successful. There are times when I can't believe I've done it. I can't believe that this is all a part of me.

eMILY BEATTY, b. 1990,
third-grader

"Gymnastics is a demanding sport. It doesn't take much of a lapse to produce a big injury out there. I require that they focus, concentrate, and pay attention—all the time. That's a tough thing for a little kid to learn, but it sure puts them in a good spot when it comes to school and their homework."

Joanne Bockian, *coach*

I want to be an athlete. A gymnast. I might go to the Olympics. My best event is the beam. Back walkovers, cartwheels—I always make 'em. One time I did my back walkover and my leg hit the side of the beam. I didn't cry. Because I'm tough.

When I do sports it's serious, not playtime.

Emily

ELLEN PANEOK, b. 1959,
bush pilot

A poor student who never finished school, a rebellious girl who was shuffled among seven foster homes, Ellen's wobbly beginnings didn't promise much in the way of a soaring future. But, as she says, "I bamboozled them." Following her bliss, she pursued what seemed to be a most unlikely field: a career in aviation. An Arctic breeze ruffles the wolf fur on her parka as she returns from ferrying a crew of gold miners and a load of dynamite into the Alaskan bush.

Ellen

i'm a romantic flyer. It's amazing the beauty you can see in the stark Arctic landscape, just by looking at different designs in the snow from where the wind pushes it around. And the colors—such a pristine shocking blue of the water melting over the sea ice. And the mountains around Anchorage are totally out of this world. It's like you're flying through a mountain pass, and each time you come around a corner there's this brand-new vista that opens up.

I like off-airport work—landing on sandbars, beaches, tundra, mountaintops, riverbeds, anywhere you can land that's not an airport.

I'm like a raven. I love to play in the wind. When it gets really windy ravens go to the lee side of a building and do flips and rolls and play with the wind. That happens up here all the time. To me the epitome of flying is to make an airplane sing, and to do that you've got to make it do something besides flying straight and level. So whenever it's windy, to me, that's when you're really the master. That's when you can make an airplane sing in the wind. It's like you're jockeying with the wind, and you're part of it.

My parents got divorced, and my mom couldn't cope with three kids on her own. Before we got put into foster homes we were living on Salvation Army and welfare. I got hand-me-down clothes and started to feel the difference. The kids in school made me feel I was way lower class. The white girls would call me these racist names, and pretty soon the black girls, too. I'm Eskimo, and they'd be calling me "Egimo" and "Skimoe" and trash like that. You know how kids pick on one kid in the whole school? I was that kid. I started skipping school, stealing things. One time I went into this grocery store and filled the shopping cart full of food and walked out. I went all the way home, driving this cart full of food, and nobody caught me. I was still living with my mom in a disgustingly slummy apartment in Anchorage.

Mom couldn't afford to take care of us, so she let us go as wards of the state. At thirteen I was on my own. My two other sisters and I were separated from each other throughout the course of going through all these foster homes. Several foster homes were a blur, and then there was one where they treated me like I was their pet Eskimo. While they were nurturing the growth of their own two kids, I was made to do the housecleaning.

At age fourteen I was put in a girls' group home where you're under lock and key. It was a home for rebellious kids. There were some shelves where they had magazines and books, and I picked up a flying magazine. I can't tell you any kind of rhyme or reason, it just happened to be fate that made me pick up that magazine. It was an issue on aviation careers. I was thumbing through it. They had crop-dusting planes, an airline pilot, a mechanic, careers like that. I thought to myself, Hey, I can do this. Right then and there in my head, it clicked. I knew flying was going to save my life.

It got to the point where I did nothing but eat, sleep, and drink airplanes, and draw them, paint them, write about them—even though I'd never been in an airplane. (I wouldn't even get to sit in a small airplane until two years later.) The people at the group home were very negative about it. They said, "Where in the world would you come up with the money for it?" I was becoming so obsessed that they sent me to a psychiatrist. I went a couple of times to talk about why I wouldn't talk about anything but airplanes.

My last foster parents saw that I had a propensity to do artwork. I'd been doing portraits for kids at school, ten bucks a pop. Everybody was prodding me to take art as a career. My aunt (I call her my aunt) made an arrangement through the Bureau of Indian Affairs—I'm part Cherokee— to send me down to Santa Fe, New Mexico, to this summer art school. I thought, This is so cool. I'll just be an artist. Then I turned around and bamboozled them.

There was an airport about a mile from the school. I said, "This is it. I'm going to fly." I looked up the flight school in the Yellow Pages and made arrangements for a demo flight, which was only $20. I walked to the airport. I was shocked that the guy let me fly the airplane. It was a Cessna 150, a two-seat trainer.

The sensation of taking off into the air and actually having my hands on the controls of an airplane was just mindbog- gling. Of course, he was right there helping. We were flying over high desert, and it was a gorgeous hot sunny day with white puffy clouds. That's where the turbulence was coming from. It was frightening, yet still way fun. The plane was bumping around and, of course, having never been in or flown a small airplane, there were times when the wing would tip over and I'd tell the instructor, "It's going to go all the way around, upside down!" He said, "The airplane will fly just as easy by itself if you let go of the wheel." It did. I thought that was the neatest thing I'd ever seen in my life. I was on cloud nine, not a care in the world. I was hooked.

About the same time I got interested in flying, I learned scrimshaw carving. My grandfather used to carve whale bone and scrimshaw tusks. He didn't exactly show me. I just saw it and kind of figured out what tools to use. It's legal for an Alaskan native to carve on white ivory. I started going downtown to the gift shops and selling there. Everything's interweaved between the art and the flying: the ivory bought me most of my flight training and six airplanes. I still carve on my days off. I do it to supplement my income. Other art stuff I do for my pleasure, like painting and stained glass.

I got a $1,500 dividend check from ANSCA, the Alaska Native Settlement Act. The next day I skipped school, cashed the check, and took the bus to Merrill Field in Anchorage. I was seventeen and said, "I want to fly."

Even though I was starting to take flying lessons, I still wasn't taking things too seriously. I know that the instructor was frustrated with me because I wouldn't study. (To begin with, I didn't have any study skills.) At first, I was scared of the stalls. Of course, that's a normal fear for a brand-new student, because it feels like the airplane's going to fall out of the sky. It's not awful to me anymore, but it was then.

I guess you could call that a transition period. It was getting close to the point where I was going to be on my own. After you turn eighteen, you're booted out of the foster home. It would still take me a while to get out of that rebellious mode and start kicking into high gear and getting off my butt.

I started working in the flight school as a receptionist, answering the phones, and trading that for the rental of airplanes. While I was still a student, gaining flight time, I was ferrying this Piper Tri-Pacer—us pilots up here call that a butt-ugly airplane—and the engine quit. The pilot in command was frantically looking for a place to land, and there was nowhere but trees and swamps (this was during the summer). It ended up in the trees—twisting on its nose with the tail up in the air and the wings broken off. I ended up spending ten months in bed with a broken back. It didn't faze me at all. To me it was just like you get into a car accident, but you still drive around.

Once I recovered from that crash, I went bananas. That was a major banner year [1983]. I went absolutely nuts. I got my flight instructor's rating, got my commercial rating, my instrument rating, my float rating. (A float is an airplane that can land on water with the use of pontoons. There are bunches of lakes in Alaska.) I didn't have one iota of trouble, absolutely none, getting a job as a girl pilot.

I like to fly in the bush. I like off-airport work—landing on sandbars, beaches, tundra, mountaintops, riverbeds, anywhere you can land that's not an airport. The risks are obviously much higher than regular airport flying, and I get paid accordingly. But I do it because it's fun. It's ultimate flying.

My first off-airport landing was on the Knik River sandbars. I didn't have a clue. I just landed and then started testing my mettle with the countryside. I landed in every imaginable place you could think of where, actually, most people probably wouldn't think of landing. I found this one place—it was so neat—I landed on this four-wheeler trail, and it was like a natural amphitheater with mountains all around. I went home and got my boom box and flew back and put on the "1812 Overture."

It's like living in a Third World country out there in the bush. A lot of the villages still don't have running water. I know some pilots up here use flying in the bush to gain flying time and get multi-engine time. They use it as a stepping-stone to fly for the airlines. For me airline flying's too boring. It's like being a glorified bus driver. You go up, you go down, you look at the instruments, play with the computers, and that's about all you do. You don't interface with the people that much, and when you do it's always just numbers of passengers. I worked for Mark Air and they wanted me to fly the jets. I said, "No way. I'm too much of a bush rat."

When I'm flying here, specializing in off-airport work, it's more like a pilot-client type thing. You make friends that way. Like when I was flying freight and passengers into Wainwright—it's an Eskimo village roughly three hundred miles north of the Arctic Circle—I felt like I was a viable member of the community. They knew my signature when I was coming in to land. I'd fly low over the ice next to the

bluff where the village is, wave my wings, and then pull up, turn, and land. They knew it was me.

I went back to Wainwright for the first time after a year and a half's absence. I go in there and land with this load of mail, and there was one lonely truck on the ramp. The guy gets out and he's like, "Wow! You're back!" We were just bantering back and forth and I flew out to pick up another load of freight. When I returned to Wainwright I saw the most trucks— prob-

ably about twelve to fifteen trucks and about seventy-five people— I'd ever seen on the ramp. I thought, Gee whiz, why are they all there? People got out of their trucks, came over to hug me, to welcome me back. It was so cool. I felt like a politician, shaking everybody's hand, hugging babies. I wanted to cry right there.

I still love, live, and breathe aviation. Even after twenty years of flying, if I hear the deep throaty roar of a round engine aircraft take off, I have to jump up and watch it.

Judith

JUDITH LARSON, b. 1968,
assistant volunteer coordinator

Judith left Tepoztlán, Mexico, in 1990 and immigrated to the U.S.

as a twenty-two-year-old bride. We met in her tidy but very hot

converted garage apartment in Los Angeles. After staying with

relatives, she says, "This is a dream to me. It's our own space, even

if it's small." Judith's story, told in a heavy Spanish accent, is about

a young woman who married, fell asleep, and then woke up to ask

the most basic question: What am I going to do with my life?

My first job when I

was a child, about four or five years old, was selling my paintings and drawings for one peso each.

Every Sunday morning I sat in the park in my town doing watercolors. I earned about sixty to eighty pesos per month. My mother paid sixty pesos per month in rent, which came from the money I earned. She told me this when I grew up. At the time I did not realize how important this money was to my family.

My mom had a place in the *mercado* where she sells natural foods, granola and yogurt. So I want to sell something, too. My mom has a blanket and a little grill where she makes soya meat tacos. I have my own blanket where I sit with my watercolors. It start like a game because I really enjoy it. People would say, "So cute, little girl selling paintings," and then buy from me. My mother said I had commerce in my blood. "*Una vendedora nata.*" (A natural seller.)

When I started elementary school I decided to make tacos, and I sell it to my teachers. My teachers save some money to buy lunch from me, so I make one peso, two pesos. I sell my own bread, cookies. My mother teach me how to make yogurt, and when she doesn't want to sell it anymore, I still selling.

My father was born in Boston, Massachusetts, and went to the University of Mexico. He met my mom in the '60s. He wasn't a Mexican, so it was hard for him to find a regular job. My father doesn't have a regular job, even now. He makes jewelry from silver.

When you almost done high school, they talk to you about different careers. The teacher explain us about the Montessori system. When I found out I would really enjoy to be a Montessori teacher, I started looking for places to have training. I found one in Cuernavaca-Morelos and got a half scholarship. I worked eight months at a Montessori school there. I loved the atmosphere.

When I start the other teachers say, "I don't know how we're gonna work with Gerardo." He was a three-year-old boy and real mad. When we tried to touch him, he kicked us. I start talking with him. I found out he needs something to do. I give him duties, responsibilities. The thing with him, he gets bored very easily because he is so smart. He start smiling. I fell in love with him and he fell in love with me. He always carry a toy around in the pockets of his shorts. A plastic teddy bear. Sometimes when he nervous, he squeeze it. The end of the year, he gave me his best toy.

I'm teaching in the Montessori school, and I fall in love with my boyfriend. (Now he's my husband.) We came to the United States because we wanted to be far from our families for a while. In Mexico, families get real involved with marriage. I don't want his mom telling me how to cook.

For two years I was asleep. I was a wife, just a Mexican

wife. I wake up early or late, however I feel that day. I go to the market and prepare lunch or dinner. I take a shower and get pretty because my husband is coming back from work. He's QC [quality control] for a burrito company.

If I'm all day in the home, when my husband come home, I am real mad. "Take me out, just to walk or whatever," I say. "Honey, I'm so tired. I want to lay down on our bed," he says.

Always I have a little weight on me but not that much, not like now. I was one hundred and forty pounds when I came here. It make me feel bad when I found stretch marks on my legs, my arms. I weighed two hundred and four pounds. *Gorda!* [Fat.] Real *gorda!* Mexican mens don't care about weight. Because they know you're pretty but they don't want anyone else to see it. Some of them want you to be *gordas*. So only your husband knows you're pretty.

One day my husband came home from work and I was crying. I told him, "I just wake up. I don't want my life to be like this. I need to do something." I told him, "When you first met me, we was in the middle of something important in my town."

He say, "You're not used to hard work. Here in the U.S. you have to go to a factory, and I don't think you can handle that. What do you want to do?"

"At least, I go to school and learn English. If we here in America, the first step for me is to learn English." My husband said I was right, so the next day we enrolled ourselves in night classes in English.

One day I was taking a shower, and my husband tell me about an announcement on TV. He told me, "Hey, Gorda,

there's a place you might want to go. Because you really like kids and you're an artistic person." He gave me a phone number of Free Arts, this volunteer organization at the courthouse.

I never thought volunteering would work into a paid job.

I explain to Annie Buckley, the volunteer coordinator, about my life, how I'm a kindergarten Montessori teacher in Mexico, and I'm an artist because I like to paint sometimes. She says, "I think you'd be a real experienced volunteer." I made an appointment for an interview.

It took me two buses, one hour and twenty minutes, to get there. On the way I thought, It's gonna be hard for me because I'm not speaking the English, and there is a courthouse and everybody's going to be dressed up, and what do I do to be a volunteer?

But when I get there it was wonderful. Some of the volunteers are from schools, but some are like me, because the heart want to be there. They are people who cares about human beings and kids.

The kids are waiting at the courthouse until their case is heard about sex abuse, neglect, abandoned. The volunteers are there because Free Arts believes art heals. The volunteers go to the tables and work with the kids. Whether they make a puppet, or whatever, makes a difference in the kid's life, really. Because they know someone cares about them, someone in the world loves them for that moment.

To me that day was real, real important. I fell in love with Annie, the volunteer coordinator. She's a real sweetie, and she speaks Spanish fluently. For me, that day, she was an angel. The angel God send me to give me that big chance to say, "You're alive. You were sleeping but now you're alive."

I start going to the courthouse every day. I wear my apron and choose my art project. I start at nine and leave at one. It makes me feel good. I talk about it to everyone and to my husband. "I prefer if you volunteer," he says. "I don't want you to work in a factory."

One day we're making puppets, an easy thing to do when you're a new volunteer. A little girl told me, "I feel sad today. I'm sad because my mommy's in jail because she killed my daddy." I was in shock. "I have to take care of my brothers because my grandmother doesn't have the patience." She started crying. "I just want to be with my mom, even if she's in jail."

That was my first big experience, and I didn't know what to do. There are other kids at the table, but she pull her chair real close to me. She was Mexican and spoke to me in Spanish, so I say, "They need Spanish-speaking people here."

I'd been there about three months when the coordinator went on an urgent errand and left me in charge. When she left, I felt like, Uh-oh, I don't know if I can handle. I gave out the assignments to the volunteers, brought out the sup-

plies. When the phone rang I talked to the person who wants to be a volunteer. And I thought, I can do this!

After a year of volunteering, Annie encouraged me to get an education. I went to an occupational center and got training to be a teacher's aide.

There was a time when Annie left, and we don't have a volunteer coordinator. The supervisor asked me, "Judith, will you like to be the coordinator while we look for new person? This is a temporary job, but we need you." I never thought volunteering would work into a paid job. She told me I'd be paid $10 an hour. That's good, real good.

I told my husband but he can't believe me. He say, "I hope it's forever and not only three weeks. We're gonna pray for that."

I did a good job, but I need my English. The coordinator needs to go to special events, talk to people, and I'm not ready for that yet. But they offered me a paid job as assistant of the program, recruiting volunteers and doing all the Spanish-speaking programs.

Now I'm a more brave person. I'm in my first semester of college, taking twelve units in child development. I love it. I have to be honest, it's tough for me. But it's also great for me because I'm doing okay. I have my first A. I'm happy for that, believe me.

eRIN CLINE, b. 1977,

music student

The transcontinental highway ends near Homer, Alaska. One can go no farther. At nineteen Erin's leaving this end-of-the-road place to start her music career in Nashville, Tennessee. In Erin's story one hears the clear soprano voice of an unusually focused young woman who is poised at the very beginning of her career.

Erin

i feel blessed to know my lifetime calling so young. I have friends that still don't know what they're going to do, what the one thing that they're good at is. They always turn to me and go, "You're so lucky because you know exactly what it is that you're supposed to be doing." I'm going to Belmont University in Nashville, Music City, U.S.A., to major in commercial music.

I've been performing since I was two. My parents never pushed anything on me, but both my parents are musical and my mom teaches music. My mom jokes that I came out screaming on pitch when I was born.

Some people babysat for me that were next-door neighbors. I went to their house, and the wife played the guitar and I sang. I loved to sing. A friend asked my mom if I'd sing at a women's brunch at the Elks Lodge in our town. There I was, two years old, and my babysitter accompanied me on the guitar. I sang "Playmate." My memories are pretty limited, but I do remember standing up there, my babysitter right behind me, looking at all the people smiling at me, and having a really good time. I wasn't afraid at all. I thought it was so neat.

I started piano lessons when I was six, and it just grew from there. When I was eight, the McLain Family Band, a bluegrass band from Kentucky, came up to tour Alaska and stayed with us. My parents knew them because they'd performed when my parents had taught out in the villages in Alaska. I saw the lady, Ruth, on the stage playing the big stand-up double bass. I was drawn to that bass and to the music. It reached something deep down inside me. Something connected.

After they left, I listened to their tapes every day and made a fake cardboard bass, so I could pretend I was playing bass while I sang. Then my parents borrowed one from the high school because it's a very, very expensive instrument. At eight I was real small, obviously, and the stand-up bass—

> One of the hardest things is waiting. What I want to be doing right now is performing for people every night of my life.

Fatigue and Immune Dysfunction Syndrome. CFIDS. He was bedridden. With that illness it's even difficult to get up and walk across the hall. For nine years he didn't go to school.

Here's the thing about CFIDS. They haven't had any people die from it, but a lot of patients commit suicide because you're bedridden, so it's like you lose your life. My brother's in remission now, but looking back, it's amazing how music was my outlet, my refuge. I started singing sad songs, real tearjerkers like "Grandpa Tell Me About the Good Old Days." I'd see people around me that were going through struggles, and even though we weren't going through the exact same thing, we could cry about it, sing about it, and express that hurt.

Homer's a very small town, about twelve thousand people. I'd say it's typical of small-town America. I was born and raised here. I've lived here all my life. I know about everybody, and there were lots of opportunities to perform. Two major performances with my bass stand out in my mind. The first one was a Jubilee, a talent show at the high school. I got onstage and sang "Bubblegum Baby." It was the first time I'd performed on a big stage in a major auditorium with my bass. There were about five hundred people, and I was amazed at the audience's response. It was so neat. They were excited and screaming and clapping.

Have you heard of Tom Bodett? He did a show up here and asked me to perform. That's when I was ten. We had a little skit where he pretended to play my bass. I walked out onstage and said, "I think I can play that thing better than you." That's when I started going for the country image. I was dressed up like a cowgirl—braids, cowboy hat, jeans,

it's six foot three inches tall—was much bigger than me. I was playing and singing along with the McLains' music. That's how I got into doing the kind of music I do now.

The McLains came just after my brother had gotten sick. We were starting the roughest times we'd ever had as a family, because we lost my older brother for nine years. We're four years apart, which is a lot for kids, but we were really close. And all of a sudden he was sick with Chronic cowboy boots. I sang "I Want to Be a Cowboy's Sweetheart."

I feel very much that music's my ministry. It's where God has called me to be. It's my way of connecting with people. When I was younger I saw that with songs like "Bubblegum Baby" I could make people laugh. With other songs I could make people cry. I like being able to communicate with people that way. Also, just getting to know people, getting to visit with them after shows, I can encourage them. People need to be encouraged to follow their dreams. That's one of my core beliefs, encouragement. There's so much discouragement in the world today.

I feel very strongly that I need to leave Homer to pursue my career. I see a lot of people that just stay and don't follow their dreams. I'm a driven person and I'm going to go wherever I need to follow that dream. In Nashville I'll be right on the scene. There are three music industries that work out of Nashville—the country music industry, the country-Christian industry, and the contemporary Christian industry.

Belmont University is one of a few universities that offer a commercial music major and a music business major. They're known for putting students right into internships on Music Row.

My dream is to be at the top of the country music industry. I want my stage show to be one of the top stage shows anywhere—very exciting, lots of special effects. I want to be involved in producing my own albums. Ideally, I'd like to have my own management company and help other artists.

The first step is to get a recording contract with a major successful country music label. To do that you have to be seen, and Nashville is the place to be. Nashville's a pretty small town, and word travels that you're there if you're good. So it's a matter of being in the right place at the right time. There are certain places, like the Bluebird Café, where singers and songwriters go to share their music and perform. Industry people frequent those places. Again, it's a matter of being in the right place at the right time.

You read stories in magazines and see them on TV about people who haven't made it, and that there's no way anybody can really make it. That's very discouraging to someone like me. My biggest concern isn't whether I have the gift, but will I be lucky enough or blessed enough or have enough of God's providence to be in the right place at the right time?

One of the hardest things is waiting. Because what I want to be doing right now is performing for people every night of my life. I want to be out there on the road. I want to be recording albums right now. It's hard to wait. My biggest hope is that I can get in there and get that recording contract and get to be doing what I feel so strongly I'm supposed to be doing as soon as possible.

S HELLY LAZARUS, b. 1947,
advertising executive

Shelly has worked in advertising for twenty-five years, and now it feels as if all roads always led here: the CEO's office at Ogilvy & Mather Worldwide's headquarters in midtown Manhattan. As CEO, she oversees an organization that operates in eighty-two countries with 312 offices and more than 10,000 employees. Married twenty-seven years and the mother of three children, Shelly gave her husband-to-be a stuffed frog on the first anniversary of their engagement. George gave her a frog back. Now the most powerful woman in the advertising world gets frogs from people all over the world. "I get two or three frogs a week," she says.

Shelly

this morning I just came back from gymkhana. I don't even know what that means, what language it comes from. Every year my son's school does this gym demonstration, and I think of all the things we have in life, there's not much that's as unimportant to me as physical education. But, anyway, it was important to him—he's nine—that I be there.

One of the things I've discovered, after having three children, is that when I live in Manhattan and work here, it takes me seven minutes by car to get to his school. The event is forty-five minutes. I'm back in another seven minutes. And so for an hour I can sort of be the kind of mother I want to be, which is to be present whenever my kids think it's important. It makes life more interesting, too.

I've found that if you're honest about what your own values are from the beginning, instead of making up excuses, then people respect you for that. If you say, "I'm not going to this meeting because my daughter's starring in a play. It's the most important thing in her life this year, and therefore I have to be there," I've never found a client who had the guts to say, "I have a problem with that." Because it's not politically correct and it's humanly incorrect.

I believe it would be a benefit to my children and an enjoyment to me if I could be home from three-thirty to four o'clock every afternoon. Now, I'm smart enough to know that's only three-thirty to four. At four they go off and do other stuff. But there is that half hour that I think is crucial. Am I going to trade off a whole other part of my life to be home then? No. But I do know that being home then would be better in terms of my being a mother.

My mother has not been insignificant in giving me the emotional backup, particularly with my kids, that I need. Whenever I can't go to one of their school events because I'm in London or China, I know my mother will go. She loves it. And my kids love having their grandmother there. That's been an enormous help to me emotionally. I don't fret on the plane that I'm missing an event, because I know she'll be there.

I'll take a great idea anywhere I can get it.

One of the reasons that I've been able to balance my work life and my home life and my role as a mother is the fact that I have a husband who is not only wonderfully supportive of me, but is a fabulous father. The fact that he's a pediatrician makes it even better.

Everything's been an accident. When I was a senior at Smith and my now-husband was in medical school at Columbia, I got a ride down to New York with a woman who happened to be driving to a career conference sponsored by the Advertising Women of New York. She said, "Why don't you come with me? It might be interesting." So I went by accident, and I was mesmerized by it. Maybe because I'd never thought about it, dreamed about it, paid attention to it. I heard people talk about selling strategy, and how you could create television and print ads that would cleverly tap into what you discovered to be the motivating idea in presenting a product or service to someone. The conference went on for five hours. I could have stayed another day.

Smith was a wonderful academic experience, an intellectual experience, but I didn't come out with any career goals. What I did come out with was someone with whom I was in love. He was in medical school, and if we wanted to get married, which we did, someone had to earn a living. At that point I realized everything I came upon seemed to require typing. I did not want to type.

Someone said, hypothetically, "I think if you got an M.B.A. they couldn't make you type." That's why I went to Columbia Business School, so I could work and not type. I didn't have a big-business career goal.

My original plan was to go straight through and get my M.B.A. in sixteen months. After three semesters I needed a break, and I got a job as a marketing intern. I was the first female to be employed as a professional in the Maxwell House division of General Foods. Ogilvy was their advertising agency. That was my first exposure to them, and I thought they were brilliant. Again, looking back, it was probably because instead of giving you the objective for the project on a little eight-and-a-half-by-eleven piece of paper, they blew it up on a big poster board with a visual. It was the theater of it. It captured people's imagination. I'd never seen that done before. I actually remember a presentation Ogilvy did where they wanted Maxwell House to sponsor Neil Armstrong's walk on the moon. Instead of just saying that to the Maxwell people, they had these huge poster boards of a man literally standing on a moonscape. Everyone at Maxwell said, "God, yeah, I want to do that!"

Four months after I got my M.B.A., I got married and started working at Clairol as an assistant product manager. It was 1970, and it was actually a very interesting time. It was still legal in this country to say things like, "I'm sorry, we don't have women in the training program. We can't waste a space on a woman." I mean, people said this to me. So, my choices were a little more limited.

One of the reasons I went to Clairol is that they had a woman there. She was a product manager. I thought she was spectacular. That was the first time I'd had sort of a role model. She was beautiful and smart and funny, and she actually said to me, "Please, come here and be with me, because it's so lonely." That was so compelling to me, for whatever reason, at that time. I went there and I loved my first job. I think to love your first job is terribly important.

I'd been at Clairol for a year and got a call from a head-hunter about a job at Ogilvy. I had no intention of leaving, because I loved it. But I got seduced, because the truth is that at Clairol, all the energy, the bubbling and electricity in the hall was when the advertising agency came in. That to me was the time when you talked about ideas, positioning ideas, and how are we actually going to present this to consumers. You'd look at this advertising and think, My God, this could really be successful.

When you're interested in marketing, you can either work in the marketing department of a company or you can work for an advertising agency. I hadn't realized how intrigued I was by the agency side of the business until I had the opportunity to have an agency job.

One of the great discoveries for me about advertising was that I thought you had to be creative to be in it. I thought you had to draw, which I couldn't do at all, or write. I could write news articles, but I couldn't write creatively. I discovered you didn't have to do that. There's this whole other world within an advertising agency called account management. The account managers—they're called the suits—are responsible for developing all the marketing for the brands for which the agency is given responsibility. The creative side writes the words and does the pictures.

I came to work at Ogilvy as an account executive on Lever Brothers. It's so silly why I actually got the job. Lever Brothers had a product that they had taken national, a new shampoo called Twice as Nice. It had done brilliantly in test

market, but it had not done anything near as well when it went national. Lever was convinced that Ogilvy wasn't doing as good a job on Twice as Nice as they might because they didn't have anybody with hair experience. I had something they needed: my experience with hair-care products at Clairol. Therefore, they could say to Lever, "Great news. We've found a person with hair experience. She's a woman, but that's fine."

I was successful. Clients liked me. I got good work for them. There was a great moment in my life where someone had given me a project, which was to figure out how to sample Twice as Nice shampoo. Because when people tried it, they liked it. I'd cooked up, with one of the product managers, a program where we were going to do the center spread in *TV Guide*, and we'd offer small packages for free. This whole idea was about to go to the president of Lever Brothers. Now, I was only an account executive. I wasn't supposed to deal with the president, but I didn't ask. I just went and did it. It was my project. I'd gotten it done. I walked from the advertising agency on Forty-eighth Street and Fifth to Lever Brothers, which is on Fifty-third and Park. I was going up Madison Avenue when the man who was in charge of the account and the number-two guy on the account overtook me and literally ripped the materials out of my hands. They said, "You don't go to see the president of Lever Brothers. We do." They did. They went on to the meeting, and I didn't.

But there were enough instances where I could get things done—having the ideas wasn't enough, but I could drive them to happen—that people thought I deserved the next title, which was account supervisor. They'd never had a woman account supervisor before, and the thing that's surprising is that when they promoted me I happened to be five months pregnant.

I'd be in a meeting and shift in my chair and all these men would go, "Is it time? Do we have to go to the hospital now?" My boss actually did a run up to Columbia Presbyterian to make sure he knew the route, so that in case he needed to take me in the middle of the day, he was ready. It was so sweet.

The other thing—and I think this says more about Ogilvy, frankly, as a culture, and why I've stayed for twenty-five years—is what happened when I had trouble with my first pregnancy. The doctors told me I needed to stay in bed or I could lose the baby. I couldn't do it. I was twenty-five. Women would call me up and say, "You don't know it now, but children are more important than going to work." I'd say, "I feel fine. I'm going out of my mind here." So I went back to work.

The day I got back the president of the agency called me. I knew him, sort of, and he said, "I'm very upset with the decision you made. I think it's wrong." Now, first of all, the fact that he knew, and, secondly, that he cared—it blew me away. He said, "I accept the fact that you feel the need to come back if you choose to. But I don't want you to take the subway to work. I'm going to make my car available to pick you up and take you home every day." Which again, how could you have more support than that?

At the time of Vietnam there was a doctors' draft. My husband had to go into the Air Force, and we were sent to Dayton, Ohio. I took a military leave from Ogilvy. I decided that as long as I had this natural break and a four-month-old

baby, I'd stay home. But I hated it. I just hated it. And again, life is a series of accidents. If I'd been in New York with my friends and with all the intellectual stimulation that New York offers, I might have been perfectly happy staying home.

But living in Dayton, Ohio, I just went crazy.

The good thing was I found I was madly in love with my child, which I never knew was going to happen. It was almost because of that that I felt comfortable saying, I can love him just as much and do something during the day rather than sit at the pool.

I got this entry-level job in retailing at Rike's, a Federated department store. I was an assistant buyer and then I was a department manager. I'd never had a point of comparison before, but I started to realize that I actually did love advertising—the art and science of it. Because as fun as it was to work in retailing, it didn't, to me, have people who were intellectually as stimulating as I'd found the people in advertising to be. You have to get out to gain perspective. People hated working at Rike's. They couldn't wait to get out because it was unsupportive, it was uncaring, it was a stopover on your way to somewhere else. After the military leave, I came right back to Ogilvy as an account supervisor.

I never had career goals, ever. The reason I've wanted to advance, and I haven't actually thought about this until just a little while ago, is that I find it stimulating when you're thrown in at the next level and you don't know how to do your job. I think part of being at Ogilvy for twenty-five years is that I was always promoted before I was ready, so it kept me interested.

The low point in my career was in November 1991, and it made me question the whole advertising agency role and the basic industry I was in. American Express had been Ogilvy's largest client for years. I'd been the head of the account and we'd done great advertising for them—this great "Do you know me?" campaign. For the first time in their history American Express started to falter a little bit in their own business growth. At that point our relationship with them was fragile, and they put us into review and called two other agencies in. There was a capriciousness about it that after all those years and all this fabulous work, a client could just say, "You're finished."

If you say, "I'm not going to this meeting because my daughter's starring in a play," I've never found a client who had the guts to say, "I have a problem with that."

One of the great satisfactions of my life, at a moment that was extremely difficult for me, was that the industry was outraged. The industry ran this big double-truck spread in *AdWeek*, which is one of the trade papers. There was a big headline and it said "Fired for This?" Those two pages had all the work we'd done for American Express over the years, which was glorious.

It was personally difficult for me because I thought, Do I want to continue in an industry where so much rests on something that's so intangible? In the end, all things considered, I accept that that's the way it is and I'll just carry on. Because the other things it offers me—just the sheer enjoyment of creating advertising—was enough to overcome that relationship part. The high point was getting American Express back eleven months later.

Becoming CEO [September 1996] was an incredible moment for me, because to have worked in one place for twenty-five years and to have slowly gone up the ladder without any career aspirations, and then—and this is how it felt—to look around one day and say, "Oh, my God, I'm the CEO of a worldwide company," it was amazing to me. I still sort of can't take it in.

We have more than ten thousand employees. I do believe that you have to touch them. That just writing letters, doing videotapes, and sending E-mail is not enough. That I actually have to go out and spend time with them, shake their hands and talk to them and hear what's on their mind and tell them what I'm thinking about, and hoping and dreaming. I think that's crucial. One of the things that bothers me about business these days is there's a feeling that,

well, now that we have all this technology, we don't have to go out that much. I think it's terribly important. I'd say a third of my time, forty percent of my time, I'm traveling.

Advertising is suited to women in terms of opportunity, because I think that any business that is based on ideas—where you're selling ideas—they're so hard to come by that it's hard to have a gender bias. I'll take a great idea anywhere I can get it. So I think that makes advertising a place where women can do well, because they are judged on their contribution.

What I don't know yet is whether at some point later on I'd like to have another career, a different career, in public service. I've always been intrigued by the idea of having some significant role in government and trying that out as a career. It all intrigues me—whether it's Deputy Secretary of Commerce or Deputy Mayor of the City of New York.

When I speak at women's groups, people dismiss what I'm about to say now because it sounds so trivial and trite. I say, "The most important thing you can do as you pursue work is to do something you love." It's crucial. It's the key to everything. It's the key to balance, because you know you're going to love your children, and if you don't love your work everything's going to be out of balance. You're going to resent every minute you spend away from the thing you love, doing the thing that you're unhappy with. I think the luckiest thing for me is that early on, I found something I love.

KYLE MILLER, b. 1984,
eight-grader

I like have no idea what I want to do. Every day it changes. I don't even know half the jobs that I could be in. I don't think it feels like, Oh, my God, I'm a moron because I don't know what I want to be. I don't think many people actually know what they want to be at this age.

My dad owns a hotel and I've thought about working at the front desk. I mean, it's one thing that crossed my mind for like five seconds. I could own a magazine. I just thought of that. That seems like it would be awesome.

I think the career will come when it comes, and I'll find something good.

Kyle

dIANA LABRUM, b. 1944, pie baker

Diana raised seven children, put two husbands through school, and worked at jobs ranging from day care to bookkeeping until she found her niche: baking pies. The fragrance of a warm Labrum Family Pie, whether it's marionberry, strawberry-rhubarb, or Gravenstein apple, makes you want to inhale and inhale. But the thrill of connecting with her talent, and making $1,400 a weekend selling pies, has been bittersweet: a series of questionable business decisions toppled Diana off her path and back into bookkeeping.

Diana

my grandmother was famous for her pies. Her husband worked in logging crews and she'd go up and cook for the logging camps. Apple was her most famous pie.

She was a real grandma-lookin' grandma. I mean, a real grandma-lookin' grandma. She wore housedresses, had nylons knotted at the knee, had long white hair way down her back and wore it in a bun. I used to think it was gorgeous how she wrapped her hair. And she wore this union suit. She didn't wear bras or underwear. She wore this union suit that unhitched at the back to go to the bathroom. I was pretty fascinated by that as a kid. It was better than anything I'd seen.

She lived in a house that didn't have a refrigerator. It had an icebox. They had a wood stove. They had a pantry with flour bins. It was really pretty cool. She baked all the time.

The funny thing is, I didn't bake with her, and I didn't even bake with my mother, who was famous for her pies, too. She had restaurants. They were small, truck-stop lunch places. One was called the Pine Cone Café. She had three or four kinds of pies, cream pies. It wasn't until I started selling pies that I'd ask her how she got things to work, how she thickened things enough to be able to carry them, and what the racks were like that she built to carry them in her car.

I baked my first pie when I was thirteen. I was home taking care of my brothers and sisters. Mom always worked, and wasn't home that often at dinnertime, so from about ten on my sisters and I took turns making dinner. I still remember I made a lemon meringue for my first pie. It turned out really good. I made a lemon meringue pie and a chicken pot pie for the same meal. And it worked. My older sister tried to make a pie and it had these little globs of biscuit dough floating on the top. There were five of us kids, and no one else could bake pies. I used the recipe Mom used of Grandmother's. I guess it just worked from watching her.

> I don't feel very creative, but I do with pies. I'm almost apologetic saying this—I know a pie isn't like a painting—but to me it is.

I started baking pies professionally about eight or nine years ago. I had been an office manager for an architect, and I decided to stay home and be a farmer. (We were living on an island in the Pacific Northwest.) I planted about an acre, spent eight hours a day out there, weeding. On Saturday I'd go to market. I think I was making maybe fifteen dollars a week, and working just incredible hours. I mean, how much can you sell a cabbage for?

A farmer contacted me and asked if I'd sell his fruit at the market. I started doing that, and buying some of his fruit and making pies. The first week I made three apple pies and sold them, I think for $3.75. The next I made six. By the end of that summer, I was selling sixty, sixty-five pies at Saturday Market for $4.50 each.

There was another pie lady. I actually felt pretty guilty, because I ran her out of business. I just thought, There's enough business for both us. Finally, she came to me and said, "My brother told me your pies are so much better than mine."

All the praise I got from my customers felt really good. "These are the best pies I've ever had." "They taste just like my grandmother's!" Baking pies makes me feel good about myself because it's what I know I do well.

Making pies is a talent that not everybody has. And actually probably fewer and fewer people have, because people don't have time for homemaking things as much. The thing about my pies is that they taste like fruit. Commercial pies use fillings, something that comes in a five-gallon container and says Blackberries, and it's really globby, and it's already mixed with sugar, and they ladle that out.

I had some people complain that all my pies looked different. Well, they are. They're handmade. I don't feel very creative, but I do with pies. I'm almost apologetic saying this—I know a pie isn't like a painting—but to me it is. I like the idea of pie.

The next spring [1994], as soon as it was nice enough, I was out selling pies again on the weekends. All these different managers were calling, trying to get me to come into their markets. I was selling about two hundred pies a weekend, and they were up to $6.50, plus a hundred tarts for a dollar each.

I did it by doing a twenty-four-hour bake. On Fridays I started at four in the morning and baked until four in the morning on Saturday. I'd roll out four doughs, mix fruit for four, pour it in, put the lattice on, pop them in the oven, and start the next four. (My husband had turned a shed into a tiny commercial kitchen with three home-style ovens.) Rolling a crust uses a lot of back muscles, and after you've done it twenty or so hours, you're tired.

At six o'clock I'd drive out with a full van. Transporting the pies to market, the smell was almost overwhelming. We had to lower the windows. First, we'd go make a drop for my daughter. Amanda was eleven and was very good at selling pies. She was proud that we had this thing that was special. I'd overhear her whispering to her friends, "My mom's the pie lady."

I'd leave my husband at Redmond, and I'd go on to the University District. It was fairly ambitious. The farmers' markets in Seattle start in April and run through September. I was bringing in about $1,400 a weekend. Having been poor most of my life, it felt really good to see that much money. It was a wad of money, as you can imagine, in fives and tens.

I really love markets. You have to have been there to know, but there was a whole side of it that was a surprise to me. It's like, "The circus is coming to town!" Everybody's pitching tents, there's a real camaraderie among the vendors. I miss the markets. I liked the customers. You don't have that with bookkeeping. Baking a pie's almost like doing someone a favor. I had people come up and say, "That's so expensive. I'd never pay that for a pie." So, don't. But most of it was, "My God! Where were you last week?"

Years earlier my husband and I had put $2,000 down on a five-acre piece of land, and we'd talked this woman into

Baking a pie's almost like doing someone a favor.

selling us an old, old mobile home for $1,000 down. (We didn't even have a septic. We went up to town to go to the bathroom.) Our loan was coming up for a balloon payment, Joe had just been laid off, and we knew we didn't earn enough money to get a loan to build a house and pay off the land. So we decided to get our equity out and go to Oregon.

I told everyone we were going back to a simpler life, where we'd be able to live on my pie-making. Our thinking was that I'd found a way to support myself well, that it would go with me anywhere, so it didn't matter where we lived. I thought it was going to be easy.

We bought the house of our dreams. I love old things,

and it was a turn-of-the-century Victorian. I've never cared that much about status, but it was kind of fun when Amanda went to school and the kids said, "Wow! You live in that house!"

Our dream was to put in a Labrum Family Pie Shop. I ended up setting up a table in the foyer off the front door. I just plain left my front door unlocked, and people walked in and bought pie. Our vision was that the Labrum Family Pie Shop would be a gathering place. There was nothing like that in town, other than taverns. The pie shop went well. People were welcoming of me. But it didn't go well enough. I probably only sold five or six pies a day.

It all fell apart in slow motion. We put every dime we had into the house. Then Joe, who'd been working as a machinist, which he absolutely hated, got fired. And Amanda was miserably unhappy. It was such a culture shock to her. Ours was a darling, cute town, but Main Street was a block long and she had no friends.

After only six months it was crystal-clear that we had to put the house on the market. Bill collectors were calling. I was looking for jobs, finding I could only get $6.50 an hour as a bookkeeper.

It's hard for me to explain, but if something bad happens, I'm pretty good at rolling with the punches. I probably didn't let myself feel the full disappointment of that defeat. We sold our house and I got my job back immediately at the architect's office in Seattle. I'd done his books continuously for the last six years. (I gave away all my bookkeeping clients when I went to Oregon, except I took him with me.)

I was making $16 an hour. It wasn't bad money. It was okay except my boss expected to be the boss. I saw the job

as a temporary save until I figured out a better way. I'd really rather work for myself and start doing pies again. With the pies I found a niche for myself.

I lost my commercial kitchen in the move, and it's taken longer than I thought to get up to full steam. I don't think I could do a twenty-four-hour bake anymore, or would want to. When I'm doing it again, I'm going to try to find different ways, like freezing them, so I can make them all week, and other people can help me.

I just quit my job. I guess I hate working for people. My son said, "You quit?" I said, "The guy's an ass." And he said, "My mom always said if everyone you work for's an ass, then maybe it's you." I said, "Maybe your mom's wrong sometimes."

Recently I went out and stayed with my mom for a weekend. She has Alzheimer's and lives with my brother. I took my pie-making stuff out there. Baking was something we shared, and I thought maybe I could get through to her. She sat at the counter and watched while I made a marionberry and a strawberry-rhubarb. She really got into it. It brought me a lot of warm feelings to be able to do that, with Mom still able to enjoy it.

Amazingly, after dinner we sat around and reminisced. She's frail and thin, and she ate three slices. She probably forgot she'd eaten the first two, but she kept wanting more.

SHARON BARRETT, b. 1961,
golfer

My dad had me out on

Lots of children across America dream of growing up and becoming a

professional athlete. Few make it. Sharon did, and it was her father,

Boyd Barrett, who showed her the way. However, after sixteen seasons on

the high-profile LPGA tour, hers is still not a household name. Sharon's

is the story of how an elite athlete continues to contend with the grind

outside the Top Ten. And how such an athlete grapples with the decision

of when to retire and choose a different path.

Sharon

the golf course when I was crawling. He'd hit a putt, and I'd crawl out on the greens after the ball.

On weekends he worked in the pro shop at Cottonwood, a public golf course. For a high school math teacher, golf's an expensive sport, so he thought if he worked at the course, then his family could have free golf.

Early in the mornings he'd go out and set the pin placement on the greens. I'd be able to ride in a little cart and help him. That was always a lot of fun. I guess the neat part is that sometimes it was just the two of us. I wanted to be with him, and that's where he wanted to be. Today the most fun I have in golf is when I'm with my dad, tootling around the golf course.

He told my brothers and me that when we each turned eight we could get our own set of clubs and start taking lessons. The big problem was that my older brother had turned eight and gotten his clubs, and I had sixteen months to wait. I wanted it bad. I wanted to get started.

Prior to getting my own clubs, I had cut-downs—a seven iron and a putter. I'd go out and swing them and imitate anybody I saw, people on TV, my dad because he was a great golfer.

He taught me the grip, how to set my feet, how to carry my clubs—the proper way, so I didn't look stupid, so I looked like a player. I dabbled in it. I enjoyed it. But when I got to be eight, I got serious. I knew this was what I wanted to do for a living. I knew. Every day after school I'd run off to the golf course. Maybe it was just a dream, a little kid having a dream: I want to be a professional golfer.

My dad took me to an LPGA tour event at Whispering Palms in Del Mar. That's the Ladies' Professional Golf Association. It's the ultimate goal for a woman golfer if she wants to play professionally. I loved it. I loved the fact that women were playing golf and making money.

Right away after I got my clubs I played in my first tournament. It was ten-and-under girls, six holes on a par-three course. On the last hole I hit the wrong ball and got a two-shot penalty. When we added up the scores, I was tied for the lead, for first. The gal that won the play-off was older than I was. She was either nine or ten. But I left with a trophy and I thought, This is pretty good. First time up to bat and I bring a trophy home.

I got past the little-girl stuff pretty quick. I was getting into junior tournaments all over the country with all the best junior girls. I imagine I was getting a little uptight and Dad said, "Golf should be like a walk in the park. When it stops being that way, you've lost the purpose for being out there." He always told me to go out and have a no-brainer. He'd say, "Don't clog your head up with all these swing thoughts."

I went to the University of Tulsa on a golf scholarship. It has the best collegiate golf program in the country and I learned how to play in the cold, something I hadn't learned

in San Diego where I grew up. In my freshman year I won the first five college tournaments I entered. I thought I had a real good chance of being a tour player. I was gung ho. I was on a path. I left Tulsa after my first year because I felt I was ready to play professionally.

When I got my LPGA card I was only eighteen, which made me the youngest player on tour for about two years. To qualify you have to go through what we call a tour school. It's a seventy-two-hole tournament. If you're one of the low twenty-five scorers in that four-day tournament, you get your LPGA tour card, which means you're a playing professional. I tied for second at tour school, so I made full-exempt status, which meant I could play in 98 percent of the professional tournaments in the country.

After I got that tour card, I was thinking, I can't believe I can play next week with Nancy Lopez, Donna Caponi, Jan Stephenson—all these players I'd idolized. I was eighteen and had the privilege of teeing up with them. That just blew me away.

Driving home, my father said, "You know how many fathers would pay a million dollars for this card for their daughters?" Because you can't buy your way onto the tour. You've got to play your way onto the tour.

Dad decided he didn't want me traveling the country on my own, so for the first six weeks of my career he went with me, which worked out great. When he couldn't go, I stayed in private housing with families who want to house a player.

Teeing off in my first LPGA tournament—the West Virginia LPGA Classic in Wheeling, West Virginia—I was extremely nervous. For the first time I doubted whether I could hit the ball straight. I guess it was because I was in the ultimate league and these were the ultimate players in the world. Was my game up to that level?

In college and in junior golf, my whole career since I was eight and took that first trophy home, I'd been a winner. I'd been somebody to reckon with. People would say, "Sharon Barrett's here." I went from that to being a little fish in a big sea with all the best players that have ultimate amounts of experience they can pull from, and I didn't play that well. My first LPGA tournament I tied for sixty-third. That didn't feel good.

My rookie years I was at the golf course eight to ten hours a day, playing, practicing, practicing, practicing. See it, *read* it. See it, *hit* it. When it wasn't working, I always turned to my family, my dad, who was my coach. I questioned all the time, What's different? Players I'd beat in college would come out on tour and do great and make a bunch of money. I was stuck trying to figure out why it wasn't happening for me.

I tried other coaches. They had all the state-of-the-art bells and whistles as far as video equipment but they told me the same thing my dad did. I figured, Why spend beaucoup bucks to listen to them when I can go home to Dad?

I had a third. I had a couple seconds. I was getting in contention. Then, in '84, I won one. The Potamkin Cadillac Classic in Roswell, Georgia. I was twenty-two years old.

That was the ultimate experience. I thought I could live off that high for a while. But this is the LPGA. Nobody cares that you won last week. I was on the highest high and pretty soon it's like, Okay, back to work. That was a huge adjustment, too. I'd been used to winning a tournament and for a

month everybody going, "Hey, congratulations, good job!" That didn't happen. Professional golf is a roller-coaster ride.

My first four years—from '80 to '84—were an incredible learning experience. From the day I was eight years old my goal was always to win a tournament on the LPGA. Well, I won one.

Then I lost direction. From '85 to '90 my goals were unclear. I was out playing, but I wasn't enjoying it. It was not a walk in the park. I hated practicing. Out of two hundred active players on the LPGA, I was ranked about 160. I was mentally bruised from playing so poorly.

And when I'm out playing, everything's published in the papers, so everybody knows every round what I do. I'd go home and go out to the golf course and get hit by, "What's wrong? Why aren't you playing well?" This was from the locals, the men I'd known forever that had watched me grow up.

My life on the golf course was miserable because I was so hard on myself. But my life away from golf was wonderful. I met my husband at the lowest career point of my life, which is kind of interesting. I got married in '87.

In 1990 I played in ten tournaments and made $419. On the ninth hole in New Rochelle, New York, I was fifty yards off line, both right and left. I couldn't take it anymore and withdrew from the tournament. I said, "That's it. I'm done. I'm putting the clubs away." By the end of that season I was ranked 194 out of 198. (I can't believe four people had a worse year than I did.)

I retired for the first time and went into teaching at the Belmont Country Club. It's just outside of Boston. (We were living in Boston because my husband, who works in sales, had been transferred there.) For the first time in my life I had money coming in, a lot more than I was spending. I was reaping huge rewards mentally. Tour players have a way of making themselves feel worse—attaching their self-esteem to their stats, how much they made, where they are on the money list. Now I could detach myself from all that. I loved teaching the game. I loved working with the members and seeing their progress. I loved consoling them when they were having a tough time. Those two years away from the tour were great growing years for me as a person.

The end of my second summer at Belmont Country Club [1992], I woke up with this bug to practice my short game—chipping and putting. I hate practicing chipping and putting. So it was like, What is this feeling? It wouldn't go away. I went out and started practicing.

I played at an LPGA tournament in Boston and I loved it. I loved being back out with the gals on tour. I loved playing in front of people again. I knew at that moment that I wanted to come out of retirement. Playing golf is my job.

Out of thirty-five tournaments, I do eighteen a year now. For seven months I'm living out of a suitcase. Three weeks on, two off, something like that. I talk a lot on the phone with my family.

The biggest heartache so far is not playing up to my potential. I mean, I want to do it while my dad's still here. He's got acute asthma and the medications he's taken over the last seventeen years have taken a toll on him. I think that's one of the big reasons why I've gotten this second urge to kick into gear and work hard.

I'm one-hundred-percent confident that as soon as I can get the feel of this new swing, and get it to work under pressure day in and day out, then I'll be able to be competitive with the best in the world. Most of the great women golfers start peaking in their thirties. Right now I'm thirty-five, and it's a perfect time to play well.

I want to win. I want to be considered a top player. I want the position I had when I was in junior golf and college golf. I want to be Number One on the LPGA tour, or to be in contention to be Number One. I'd like to be the person that's in demand for interviews and appearances to represent the LPGA. I think I'd be a good ambassador for them.

If I contemplate my career and talk about missed cuts, then it can be quite the downer. But even when I talk about the hard times, I'm one of a couple hundred of the best women golfers in America. There are a lot of good players, great players, that have never won a tournament. And I have.

A lot of people over the years, especially members at the local golf course, think I should just pack it up, that I can't play under pressure. I've always said, I'll have my day when I'll prove them wrong.

1

UANA LACY, b. 1970,
probation officer

Growing up tough and hanging out in the roughest areas of Milwaukee, Luana was a child-at-risk. Now she wears the badge of a Nashville Juvenile Court Probation Officer and works with children and teenagers at risk. She says, "I see so much of myself in the kids I'm working with that it's almost like I'm reaching back and helping myself."

Luana

i work in the south Nashville area, in the Edgehill project. My office is an apartment turned into an office for me. It's subsidized housing. The apartments have cinder-block walls. There's no air-conditioning. A lot of people kind of use fans in the windows. They do have roaches, lots and lots of roaches.

When I first started, a few people said, "Exactly what do you do here?" Word kind of spread that I'm not a police officer. I don't have the authority to walk up to somebody smoking weed and arrest them. I'm not here to take anybody down. I'm not doing surveillance on the adults. However, I do watch out for the children on my caseload. The kids up to age nineteen that live in this area, if they get a felony or too many misdemeanors, then they come on supervised probation, and that's my caseload. I'd say 90 percent of the kids on my caseload are car thieves. My job is to kind of decipher what's going on in that child's life and expose him or her to some resources in the community that could put them on the right track.

With all of the apartments being so close together and all of my kids being so close together, there can be a sense of family here. Sometimes at just the right time, when school's letting out and the parents that are home come outside, sometimes they kind of get together and everybody's talking. You don't get that feeling in the suburbs where the houses are spread apart and there's no sidewalks.

I took this job August 1, 1995. This is the first job I've had that when I got my Sunday paper I didn't want to keep checking the classifieds to see what else was available. Why was I even holding that paper? I was actually enjoying the work I was doing.

I realized that I'd been working pretty much in the social services field for a long time, even before I was actually getting paid for it. In high school I worked as a peer counselor. I thought, I'm being a do-gooder, volunteering so I can put this on my résumé. It turned out that I got so much out of it.

> # This is the first job I've had that when I got my Sunday paper I didn't want to keep checking the classifieds to see what else was available.

I grew up in Milwaukee, where I was kind of a hanger-outer. At twelve I was already in a 34-B, so I thought I was grown. I rode around in cars that were stolen, which now a lot of kids on my caseload do. I fist-fought with other girls. I

started sex really early, at fourteen, because I thought being grown was having sex.

The ironic part was that I didn't end up in trouble with the law. One time I was caught with a weapon at school, which now kids get on my caseload for. My principal said, "Luana, you're a straight-A student, I don't know where this anger is coming from. Don't do it again. We won't tell your mother." That made it worse because I thought I could do whatever.

My father and mother argued a lot. I had a lot of anger at both of them for not getting it together and raising me. My mother stayed home when I was younger, and we had a wonderful relationship. She went back to work when I was in the second grade. Even though we needed the money, I got really mad at her for not being at home anymore and not fixing my french fries when I came in.

My grandmother got really sick [Alzheimer's], so we moved down to what appeared to be this little hick town in Mississippi. I thought I'd just take the run of things. But Mound Bayou was so small you couldn't do anything without anyone knowing. What I ran into there was so shocking. It's a one-hundred-percent African-American town, founded by former slaves. Living in that all-black town was my first encounter with racism. It wasn't your traditional black and white, but it was within the race. Even though the lighter-skinned girls that I hung around with were in my classroom and we were all in honors, I couldn't understand why these teachers kept telling me, "You're not fit for these girls."

I couldn't understand it until I got to college and took this sociology class called Black Rhetoric. That was a big, big step for me. That's when I started understanding more about my African culture, making the transition, trying to let go of the anger, and trying to move in a different direction.

Although I was on a path trying to better myself, I was in a violent situation. I didn't know it then, but I know now that my boyfriend was an abuser. It started with his wanting to spend more time with me. Then it went to, I don't like your hair that way, to, That dress is too short, only wear that when you're around me because other people might think you're easy. Eventually it led to physical abuse, which I put up with for a whole year. My dad didn't even whup me when I was little. That was the first time a man ever hit me, so I didn't know what to do with it. Once he visited me in my dorm room and pushed my head into the wall hard enough for my neighbor to call security.

At the end of my sophomore year I told my parents. I thought they were going to blame me for it. They didn't. They came and took me home. I thought it was over but he started watching my house, following me from place to place. One day I'd just dropped my mother off at work and stopped at a gas station, and he jumped into my car. He wanted me to drive to his sister's house, and I knew there was no one home. At that point I was pretty paranoid and I was carrying weapons with me—a revolver and a semiautomatic.

I had a restraining order on him because he'd broken into my parents' home. I thought my life was in danger. I thought it was either going to be him or me. I knew I didn't want it to be me, and I needed all the support I could get. If that meant getting a restraining order to get the legal system on my side, I did it. I actually thought if worse comes to worst and he actually does kill me, there'll be some documentation and there won't be any question who my murderer was. At the same time I thought, He's not going to get the chance to drag me off somewhere and bury my body and put my family through that. That was why I carried guns with me, in case of running into him.

I was driving and he was telling me, "I really hate to have to beat you up." When I didn't make the turn to his sister's, he threw the car in park. That's when I pointed one gun at him and told him to get out of the car. He reached right over and plucked it out of my hand. I knew I had the automatic, which I was a better shot at. When we got to his sister's, he was standing in the driveway, saying, "Don't make me pull you out of the car by your hair." I pulled the automatic on him. He wet his pants. The gun jammed. It didn't fire. What was worse was that there were neighbors all around and they did nothing. After the gun jammed, I screamed to the neighbors, "Call the police!" They just looked at him, and said, "Hey, y'all right?" I got back in the car and drove away.

The last time I ever saw him he was crying in court when the judge sentenced him to jail for breaking the restraining order. I transferred to another school and didn't tell any of my friends. I was afraid he might try to contact them. I wanted to kind of put an end to all that, leave that behind me. I felt lucky to be able to do that. A lot of people aren't able to just leave everything and start anew somewhere else. I knew then that I could survive anything, and that my life was forever changed.

It's hard to explain, but if I hadn't gone through that experience I don't think I would have ever considered taking a job in what is considered such a high-risk environment in the middle of a project. Today when I come up against domestic violence, I can definitely relate. That's for sure. And not just male-against-female, boyfriend-against-girlfriend type thing, but I've got insight in mother against daughter, sister against sister. Any kind of really angry, hostile,

I think I make a smidgen of difference every day. That's my ultimate goal—on a daily basis to make a difference in somebody's life—even if it's just my own.

violent crimes, I feel I have a little insight because I went through something pretty similar. I can kind of recognize the controlling personality in a lot of the family members that I work with. I can spot it a mile away. And I talk to a lot of girls who seem to be right at the beginning of a relationship that looks like the exact same relationship I was in. I tell them what they may come up against if what I see is right.

In college I'd been in advertising, but I never felt connected the whole time I was in those classes. It seemed so competitive. So me-me-me. Me going ahead. Me going up the corporate ladder. I thought about sociology and the Black Rhetoric class. It was the society part of sociology that I liked, trying to figure out what makes society tick.

In graduate school I did an internship at Cumberland Heights, an alcohol and drug rehab center. That's when I started realizing my niche. I felt more at home in the youth division and in the family division, especially. I got a job as a case manager at Serendipity House, working with children in foster care. I always call that my first real job because that's when I started knowing I was on the right track. I wasn't quite there yet, there was some little ingredient missing, but I was real close.

To be perfectly honest, I think I make a smidgen of difference every day. That's my ultimate goal—on a daily basis to make a difference in somebody's life—even if it's just my own. There's this girl. I'll call her Pookie. She's fifteen. She's not your average "I don't like school" kid. She's way beyond that. She came on probation for assault at school. She wasn't going to school, and every time she did go to school I'd get a call from the principal that she'd attempted to jump on someone or she *had* jumped on some-one. She frustrated me so bad that I'd say to my husband, "This is one I'm going to have to wash my hands of."

I started finding her little hangouts and catching her. She said, "You're the most nosy person I've ever met in my life. It's amazing, but I like you." I said, "If you like me, then listen to what I have to say. You can't do anything without an education." She said, "Help me. I don't like school." I went through her school list and told her she didn't have any fun classes. Now she's taking cosmetology and likes it. She still doesn't like school and is starting nighttime GED classes, but it's not quite as bad as it used to be.

I came home that day and told my husband, "Guess what? She was willing to sit down and talk with me. She said she likes me. It's so uplifting." My husband said, "You're crazy!" But that made me feel good, just her saying, "I like you." It was like, *yes!* It made me feel that maybe I do have a knack for talking with people and that with even the most hopeless situations there's a way out.

I have this big fat dream. I hate to sound so old-fashioned but I truly believe that our young men hold the key to reshaping our community. If they can find themselves first, and help one another, I feel kind of like we can start something new. Women are very important, too, but I guess it's because ninety-five percent of my caseload is male that I see more men going down a path that I don't think is positive at all.

Right after breaking up with my boyfriend I thought, This is a real bummer. If all guys are like that, I'm in big trouble. When I moved to Nashville, I started meeting a lot of men that really had it together, or at least seemed as if they were on the right track of having it together. They were strong, they were healthy, and they were positive thinkers. I married one. They have a lot to offer the younger men in our community. Sometimes I'll get my husband involved, and I feel when the two of us get together we have a stronger impact on the young men on my caseload.

I would love to see a safe haven where young men in our community can come and express whatever is on their minds to older men who have already gone that way and who've gotten it together. We have some organizations [100 Black Men of Tennessee] and outreach programs, but I don't see those programs reaching the kids on my caseload. I'd like to see a centrally located venue where this healing can take place. A lot of organizations have an office, but it's just that, an office. It's not a place of comfort. I'd rather see a house, something a little more personal. That's my dream for the future.

S ISTER MARY JOSÉ HOBDAY, b. 1929, educator

Sister Jo is just as likely to be found sharing the stage with the

Dalai Lama in Chicago, speaking about simplicity and spirituality,

or driving a Jeep in New Mexico, helping the native people learn

how to get the resources they need. Every five to seven years she's

had a moment of clarity, her work has changed, and her path has

led her somewhere new.

Sister Jo

i flunked kindergarten. I had a dull teacher. She was so religious about us drinking that warm milk and lying down when we weren't tired and tying shoelaces around chair legs. I had nine brothers and I already knew how to do all of that. I couldn't find anything that interested me except Officer Bob and his Harley-Davidson motorcycle. (I've always had a plus attitude for the law since, and I've always loved Harley-Davidsons.) Officer Bob came during recess and asked if I'd like a ride. So every recess, if the weather was decent, I rode around the block in his Harley-Davidson sidecar.

When school was over the teacher sent a note home with my grade and it said, Fail. She wrote: This child does two things well. She runs up and down the fire escape and rides around the block on a motorcycle with a policeman. I was so disgusted. She didn't even know the name of the motorcycle, and I'd called it a Harley-Davidson all year. I said to my mother, "I don't care. It was boring. I'm glad to get out of there." My mother said, "But you're not out of there, Jo. No one has been put on this earth to entertain you, my dear daughter. If you were bored all year, it's because you were boring. You are here to entertain yourself." She said, "You're going back to repeat that class until she lets you out." I went back and I was so cooperative I drove the teacher crazy. I force-fed the kids that warm milk, and within two weeks she passed me on to the first grade. That's how I got out of kindergarten. It taught me that I'm responsible for my life being interesting, and that if I'm bored, I'm boring. That was one of the best lessons I could have ever lived.

In the second grade I had a vision and learned what I wanted to be when I grew up. I had a wonderful teacher, Miss James. There were eighty-three children in the classroom. (I have to smile these days when fifteen is too many. Everybody had sixty–seventy kids in a classroom. One teacher. That

> My dad said, "Try a lot of things and figure out what you love. Then figure out how to make a living with it. Never start the other way around."

was a normal public school in Montezuma County, Colorado, in the 1930s.) Miss James was an old maid. She cut her hair short and comfortable. She was rather plump and she was, I'm sure, in her seventies, because she was supposed to have retired. But we just loved her. Her classroom was magic.

We had a spelling test one day and I got a perfect paper, which meant that the girls' team had won and we'd get to take half a day off from school. But some kid turned around and accused me of cheating because I'd forgotten and left the little spelling book up at the corner of my desk. I hadn't looked at it, but I looked guilty because this book was open on my desk. Open. Miss James said, "Jo, did you look at the book during the test?" I couldn't answer her. I shook my head and cried. She put her arm around me and said, "Don't worry. I believe you. The girls have won!"

What a wonderful world—to have somebody who could do something like that for your life. Somebody who could believe you. I decided then that I was going to be a teacher. That was a vision for me. The spelling contest was the last period of the day. The class had ended, but I'd caught something special and I didn't rush out. I was full of light and understanding, and I stayed a long time at that desk, so the vision wouldn't go away until I understood it.

It may seem unusual for a seven-year-old to act like that, but I've talked to children about things that have happened to them, and I don't think it's so unusual. I just think children don't have anyone to talk to about it, or it happens so fast. People have told me these things happen, and they push them aside. But I didn't push it aside. I was trying to hold on to it.

I was thinking how I'd learn to be the best teacher, like Miss James. I knew I had to make a serious effort and get right into it. I got money from my piggy bank and bought a spiral notebook and ruled it into four columns. I headed them: what I like about this teacher, what I don't like about this teacher, what the other kids like about this teacher, what the other kids don't like about this teacher. I kept books on all my teachers, all the way through college.

Until the eighth grade I was going to be a great teacher, that's what I said. Then I met another great teacher, Mrs. Kuenneth. She said to me, "So, you're going to be a teacher?" I said, "Yes." She said, "Why don't you be an educator, Jo?" I said, "What's the difference?" She said, "The size of the classroom. If you're an educator, the whole world can be your classroom. Teaching can be limited; education never would be."

We had so much teaching in our house. My dad was very good in geology and social studies and geography, things like that, and my mother was good in math and spelling. They were natural teachers. We had this big blackboard in the kitchen and Dad would say, "Okay, everybody to the board for geography tonight." He'd call out capitals and we'd write down the states. Or he'd call out states and we'd write down rivers, all of that. That was just to warm us up. Mother would have the math and spelling contests.

It was fun for us to learn. We had a lot of hoboes come to our house. Out on the porch we kept a towel for them, and a razor and a soap dish. Dad would say, "These men are living geography lessons. They've been all over the country looking for work. If you've got any questions, these are the men to ask." We had no church and only had Mass about once a month, so we had all these visiting ministers and mission priests. Everything was learning for us.

My dad said two things to all of us. He said, "Try a lot of things and figure out what you love. Then figure out how to make a living with it. Never start the other way around. Never start with money. Start with what you love to do." The other thing he said was, "Life is all about selling. You just

It was a surprise to me how much freedom I had when I entered the religious life.

have to decide what you want to sell. Sell ideas, sell yourself, sell wares." Those two themes stuck with me. I knew I wanted to sell ideas. Later, I knew I wanted to sell the possibility of spiritual values and truths.

My parents were both equally my role models. I wanted to think like Daddy and tell stories like Mother, and cook like Mother and sell things like Daddy. (He was a salesmen of professional shoes—he sold only to chefs and nurses, people who were on their feet all the time.) I loved both my mother and father. I thought they were unique. My mother was a full-blooded Seneca—Iroquois is our nation, Seneca is

one of our tribes. Daddy taught us to live by our head, and Mother taught us to live by our heart.

I was getting ready to graduate from Colorado State College—it was a five-year program and I had a double major in English and business. And the priest said to me, "How are you and John"—that was the guy I was dating—"getting along?" I said, "Fine." But I told him, "I don't want a good man, a nice guy. I want somebody who's got a spiritual path." He said, "Have you ever thought about being a sister?" I said, "You mean a nun? That's got to be the most abnormal way in the world to live—no men or anything. I'd never want to be a nun." He said, "You don't know anything about it. They do a lot of things you believe in. They run their own lives, they're teachers. Maybe you ought to look into it."

I did not want to enter religious life. But I was used to listening to wise people, and he was a wise man. That's how I was taught as a child. Listen to so-and-so, they know more than you do. So, I had that as a pattern, to have my ears perked up.

My mother had raised me as a Franciscan, so he suggested I go to a Franciscan community to look at it. I went to the public library and found that there were 103 Franciscan communities. I made out a questionnaire and sent it to them all. It was hysterical. I told Father, "If they don't answer every question 'yes,' I won't even consider them."

About ten wrote back and said things like, You don't ask the questions, we ask you the questions. The Sisters of Saint Francis of Assisi of Milwaukee were the only community that answered all the questions "yes," and they offered an invitation to call if I had questions. They even wrote a personal letter:

"Dear Jo, I can see you know absolutely nothing about religious life. . . ." It was signed "Sister Mary Esther," and my mother's name was Esther. I thought I'd better look into that.

I called and said, "I'm coming." She said, "Wait! Someone will come to see you." I was working in Estes Park, waiting tables in a restaurant and bartending at night. Two sisters came, the major superior and a member of the council. I'd been at a party at Estes Park, and I was all dressed up. I'll never forget—white skirt and white blouse and red shoes, red earrings and everything. They were very friendly, and the major superior said, "Well, so this is Jo. Spin around and let's see how you look." I was a grown woman and I thought that was a little odd, but I spun around. Then I said to her, "Now you spin around, so I can see how you look." She just burst out laughing. She said, "Here's one with a mind of her own!" We visited for a couple hours. See, they like to get a look at you, see if you're basically normal, healthy. See if you look like you'd fit into the community.

That September I made the decision to enter, to try it for a year. That was the key thing. I didn't enter to stay. I entered to look. I saw an awful lot of women doing what I thought were great things, living a simple, meaningful life, actually a poor life in terms of their personal things, having much time for prayer and study—everything that seemed important. Although I didn't appreciate all the aspects about it, Father had said, "You don't know anything about it, so keep your mouth shut for one year. At the end of a year, look at your whole experience. If there's not more life there than you've ever experienced before, get out and never look back."

I did that. I didn't sit and nitpick my first year; I threw myself into it. I found there were tremendous opportunities for life that I'd never seen before. And it satisfied me enough spiritually to go on. See, I had five years to live it and test it and see if it was right for me.

What appealed to me was that these people were living by a spiritual guide. And then I like the life of Saint Francis. Here was a man who was happy, who had nothing, who was a peacemaker, who was in connection with the animals. That's the way my mother had brought me up—that the animals were all my relatives, that the earth was my mother, and the sky my father.

We made our own choices as women—we ran our own money. Even though we had Rome and the clergy, that didn't affect our daily lives much. And you had the opportunity to keep studying, to keep learning. I just loved it. It was so vital. The first year you're a postulate—that means you are asking about the life. The next two years you're a novice— you are studying the life. And then you take temporary vows—you are living the life. At the end of eight years, you take final vows for life. That's when you take the vow of celibacy. The obedience didn't bother me, and the poverty— I always knew that the less you have in material things, the more power you have spiritually. Celibacy was the hard one.

I was almost twenty-eight and I went seeking counseling to a Jesuit down at Marquette University. He said, "The confessional is no place to talk about sexuality as a sister. Meet me out in the pews." I almost went home because I didn't want to talk about this face-to-face. But he came out and shuffled over—this old, old man, about eighty-five, with one little wisp of hair. I thought, Oh, God, I'm trusting my information on sexuality to this guy?

He put his arm around me and said, "Sister, we have enough anemic nuns in the Catholic Church. If you've got great passion, you've got the power to be a great saint." He said, "Sexuality is part of all life. It's part of your fullness as a human being. But you have to learn how to handle the physical part, and if you can't do that, you shouldn't take the vows." He said, "Celibacy's a gift. A lot of people don't know that, and they want to do it by gritting their teeth."

He said, "Sexuality, when it's expressed physically, is essentially an appetite. You have to understand your appetites. I want you every day at every meal to deny yourself something—just very small, it should go unnoticed, never tell anybody. If you like salt, don't take it. Every meal I want you to do that—to tell yourself that you have the power over that appetite." He said, "Do it for a year, and you'll have the data that you can do it. Now, whether you want to do it or not, that's your own choice.

"You'll always have the itches and the urges. Don't just run and take cold showers. That's not the answer. Get into doing something you love to do. Do something exciting and physical, get out there and do what you want to do." He said, "You'll always have them, if you've got a real healthy appetite for sex." And I still have. They don't bother me a bit. I just smile because I know they're natural, they're part of me, and I don't give in to them.

My major superior wanted me to go on for a master's, and the community was going to send me to Catholic University in Washington, D.C. I said, "No! I'm a Notre

Dame woman!" My brothers and I had listened to their ballgames all my life. They didn't take women, but they included sisters who were at the graduate level of study. I joked that we were neuter, that we were so well-armored in our habits

that we weren't any kind of a temptation to anybody.

Afterward, for about seven years, I taught high school and college, and in the seminary. When I was teaching at our private high school in Milwaukee, I offered a class in creative writing for juniors and seniors—with the guarantee that they would publish by the end of that year. And they did. The editor at the *Milwaukee Journal* did a double spread on the class. Educators around the state invited me to speak at conferences. Word began to spread, and my public speaking career took off. As my jobs changed, my speaking changed— it moved from the area of creative writing and education to spirituality and prayer.

Then I was asked to go into formation work, training the young women who enter the religious community. I did that until I was about forty. About five to seven years seems to be my average doing one thing. That's my style. It's happened all my life. About every seven years I get the next direction. I moved into working in areas of peace and justice, women in prisons, ethnic groups, and, because I'm an Indian, I was doing things with Native Americans, and people wanted me to speak from that perspective. See, that's how the public speaking kept building. I'm still booked two to three years in advance, and this is year thirty-six.

It was a surprise to me how much freedom I had when I entered the religious life. It was amazing to me. I was doing all this in relation to my community. I always asked my community, Do you want me to keep going out there and talking? Even if I went alone to start—to visit women in prisons and see the injustices, or the Native Americans on reservations to help them find new ways through the tangles—my community always supported me.

Next I'm heading for the Southwest. I've had invitations to work in Albuquerque and Santa Fe and Gallup. I'll probably just move into a house with no furnishings and wait and see what I'm led to do. Within a week or two I'll know what I'm supposed to do. I find wherever I go, the native people come to me because I know how to help them get the resources they need. I'm never doing the work for them. I'm for helping them find out how to do it for themselves.

When I'm on reservations I drive to where the people are. I have to drive with automatics now. I had non-Hodgkin's lymphoma. A year of chemotherapy for that destroyed those cancer cells, but the chemotherapy went astray and hit my left ankle bone. I've had seven surgeries on my ankle. This is my twenty-ninth cast, my fifth brace. It's just been one damn thing after another. I discovered I had cancer the week I was sixty-five, and now I'm sixty-eight. I'm going to have a permanently deformed left foot. I don't sit around and mope over what's gone wrong with my life or when I hurt. People say, "How do you keep going?" The doctor said I can stay home and feel sorry for myself, or I can continue to do the work I enjoy doing and have a little more pain. I choose a little more pain.

As a child, we always said a prayer when starting on a family journey. We'd call ourselves to consciousness by saying: *Our Lady of the Highways, be with us on this journey, for all your ways are beautiful and all your paths are peace.*

CARLYN ROBERTSON, b. 1992,
k i n d e r g a r t e n e r

I want to be a firefighter because I want to put out fires and wear red clothing and have red trucks and help people. I want a fire dog.

No! I want to be a policeman. Do policemen have dogs?

Did you know I can be anything I want when I grow up?

Carlyn

Afterword

by Kathy Sims

These profiles are a vivid reflection of women in today's society and are a great demonstration of what makes the fabric of a woman's career path special. They illustrate the different elements that can influence the direction of a career, from the personal to the professional. As these women bare their souls and tell their stories, the one underlying theme is that career is not just work. Career is the composite of one's life.

For generations of women, the two greatest obstacles to career success were a lack of support from society and the fact that their paths are less direct. Janet Marie Smith sums up this difference when she says that boys are often pigeonholed in their careers, and girls are not. That we have a book of women who found their way on unique and circuitous paths is not surprising; such paths are more typical for women than for men. From these stories we learn that what used to be thought of as major drawbacks to women in careers can now be seen as powerful advantages. These women were sidetracked by personal obligations, or by pursuing a career dominated by men, or by lack of role models, and it made them more resourceful, more self-nurturing, more career-tough.

I've chosen to focus on a few of the most basic career elements that shaped and influenced these women's paths:

Family and Personal Relationships

A fresh lesson to be learned from these profiles is that personal obligations and family relationships, whether or not they seem to have a negative impact on one's career progress, can be used to one's advantage. Doreen Stone, who was obligated to care for her ailing mother, revealed that when she photographs actors today she uses the skills she developed while trying to cheer up her mom. Marcia Beauchamp's lack of support from her family, who did not encourage her to pursue college, sidetracked her from realizing her obvious academic potential. But when she ended up at Harvard, she drew value from what she had learned from her years as a hairdresser.

Many times career counselors have a client who says, "My ambitions are unrealistic. I might as well give up. I need a job, any job, because I have to take care of my family." We can help these people see that, like the women in this book, they have an opportunity to benefit personally and professionally from the way they meet these obligations.

Joining with Others to Develop Your Career

Teamwork and team-building are terms we hear a lot in the business world, and a person's ability to work with others is absolutely crucial to her career development. Here we are presented with excellent examples of women who identified their own skills and then worked with others to create a successful business.

Teaming can take a lot of different shapes: Maxine Kelley and her two daughters came together to form a construction business; Jeannie Pepple runs an auction barn alongside her husband; and Mama La and her large family operate a chain of restaurants. Whatever the composition of the team, the idea is that when people work together, they can accomplish more than they could have individually. Another important aspect of teaming is that it can be more fulfilling, and more fun, to be working together toward a goal and contributing to another person's successful career.

Overcoming Obstacles and Meeting Challenges

There are people in this world who need to be challenged before they can move forward, whether the challenge comes from their work, as with Julie Brown, a fisherman, or from troubled relationships, as with Sunday June Pickens and Neepa Ved. A lot of people think that they lack direction, but when they're faced with something to overcome, it becomes very clear what they want to do.

A tool that's widely used and highly regarded is behavioral interviewing. Here the employer seeks examples of past performance to indicate future performance. Employers are looking for individuals who have overcome an obstacle or faced a challenge that's not necessarily the result of being an officer in the engineering club: "I went home for Thanksgiving and my dad's house caught on fire. Here's how I handled the crisis and still managed to return to campus in time for finals." Employers now understand that these kinds of experiences shape character and sharpen one's ability to respond in the workplace.

The hiring world is finally learning to accept the value of the nontraditional experiences that people, and women in

particular, are bringing to the marketplace. In the 1970s, career counselors encouraged women reentering the workforce to acknowledge their experience as mothers and volunteers; after all, that was part of the package they offered. But for many years that experience wasn't given much validity as preparation for employment outside the home. Today, however, we're finding that these experiences are increasingly valued and even encouraged in the labor market.

Role Models and Mentors

Every woman profiled mentioned people who influenced her. The person didn't have to be someone the woman admired; in fact it sometimes was a person they did *not* want to be like. Madeline Martinez had a not-so-happy childhood, but her father, who had a negative influence on her, was the person through whom she discovered her calling of massage.

Among the most valuable tools that career counselors give their clients are the methods and encouragement to identify role models. People used to think that it wasn't whom you knew or what you learned from them, but where the jobs were and how you applied for them. Now we know that all the right credentials in the world aren't as powerful as good role models or mentors in a network that grows.

It's unlikely that everybody is going to have a mentor, and I'm not saying that a mentor is necessary for career success. In fact, the opportunity to simply observe people perform who are in one's field of interest, or to ask them questions about their work, can be extremely enlightening. This is called informational interviewing, and I recommend it highly. In fact, the profiles in this book could be considered informational interviews at their most candid.

I suggest that people identify an individual who is already successful in the field they're considering. They approach the person, saying, "I'm not asking for a job. I'm interested in hearing what a day in your life is like, and how you prepared for this line of work." Of course, there can be a hidden agenda beyond gathering information. If the person is inspired by what she hears and encouraged by this individual to pursue that career path or course of study, then this interaction might result in a continuing relationship. The career-seeker might negotiate an internship, a part-time or summer position, or an ongoing mentoring relationship that could provide crucial guidance toward the chosen career.

The testimony of the women profiled in this book supports the importance of role models and mentors in shaping careers. However, a lot of these women acquired role models by chance. Counselors today stress that people don't have to wait for it to happen to them. An individual can hand-select and create these powerful influences in her life.

Career and Job Search Assistance and Resources

Career resources are available in a variety of venues and media, and can be just as effective for the satisfactorily employed mid-career person who needs career management as for the young person who hasn't a clue about her options.

We're witnessing an incredible transformation of resources for career guidance and employment information. About 70 percent of the information on the World Wide Web has some relevance to employment opportunities or career assistance. Most public libraries provide access to the Web, which is by far the greatest and quickest source of career information that has ever existed in one place.

Community Career Information and Search Assistance

Assistance from these sources is either free or available for a small fee:

The Urban League of most major cities offers free job development workshops, career counseling, and job listings.

Forty Plus, a nonprofit organization, has chapters across the United States. The services are targeted to experienced professionals in career transition, and are built around the support-group model of job search assistance.

Take Our Daughters to Work Day. Sponsored by the Ms. Foundation for Women and celebrated on the fourth Thursday in April, this national event helps the next generation of women by exposing girls to different areas of work.

Pastoral or religious centers. Vocational counseling is a major aspect in clerical preparation, and pastoral counselors are trained to offer vocational assistance.

The Small Business Administration gives targeted support to women in business and identifies grant and loan opportunities for women.

Some local college career centers extend to the general public the services they provide for their students and alumni, either free or for a small fee.

Career centers on university campuses have historically been underused by women. Only one woman in this book, Marcia Vaughan, mentioned using her college career center.

For many years the most visible activities of career centers (then called "placement" centers) involved corporate recruiting for business and technical candidates. Today's college career centers are diversifying the types of organizations that recruit, and are better publicizing opportunities for students of the liberal arts, education, and the fine arts. In addition to providing career counseling and instructional workshops, they offer print and multimedia resources and are able to deliver many services over the Web, so that people no longer have to visit their campuses to be connected to their career centers.

Books, Magazines, and Directories

Career and job search publications are abundant and easily accessible in libraries, bookstores, and newsstands. The challenge is in determining which combination of resources will be the most helpful.

The Career Guide for Creative and Unconventional People, by Carol Eikleberry, Ph.D. (Ten Speed Press, 1995)

Career XRoads: The 1998 Directory to Job, Résumé, and Career Management Sites on the World Wide Web, by Gerry Crispin and Mark Mehler (MMC Group, 1997)

Jobs '98, by Kathryn Petras, Ross Petras and George Petras (Simon & Schuster, 1997)

The National Business Employment Weekly Jobs Rated Almanac, 3rd edition, edited by Les Krantz (John Wiley & Sons, 1995)

The 1998 What Color Is Your Parachute?: A Practical Manual for Job-Hunters and Career-Changers, by Richard Nelson Bolles (Ten Speed Press, 1998)

World Wide Web–Based Resources (Accessible from Most Public Libraries)

The World Wide Web can help jump-start the career process because a person who is researching a career area has immediate access. You can click on a bibliography of career resources, and, in some cases, find the entire resource online, and you can go into chat rooms and conduct informational interviews with people who have described their areas of expertise. Start with a website that is designed to help organize your search for reliable career information, such as a college career center home page.

The Riley Guide (www.dbm.com/jobguide) is a guide to employment and job resources. It is compiled by Margaret F. Riley, an Internet recruitment consultant and frequent columnist for the *National Business Employment Weekly.*

JobWeb (www.jobweb.org) is a site for the National Association of Colleges and Employers, with selected directory information and career advice, job leads, and worldwide links to college and university career center websites.

Bridges (www.bridgesonline.com) is an on-line professional network for women, featuring profiles, forums for topical groups, job listings, a calendar of live events, and career "Power Talk" by interest area.

As director of the UCLA Career Center, **Kathy Sims** *supervises a staff of sixty career service providers. She is co-creator of the University Network, a national benchmarking group for directors of selected university career centers. Kathy experienced complete vision loss eight years ago, but she continues to show others the way.*

Acknowledgments

every good idea deserves a godmother, and the godmother for this project was Linda Phillips Ashour, the novelist. When this book that you hold so solidly in your hands was still just a wisp of an idea, Linda said to me, "I need that book, my mother needs that book, my daughter needs that book, and you have to hurry because she'll be graduating in two years. And, furthermore, my editor would love the idea."

That's how I lucked into having Robert Asahina as my editor. In his ineffably elegant way, Bob shaped and steered this project to its current form. I felt blessed working with him and his splendid team: Casandra Jones, senior editor, put in many long days and late nights, giving my manuscript the kind of TLC most authors only dream of; Melissa Crane, summer editorial intern, left Princeton on Fridays to see this project through to completion in the fall; Tiffany Cale, administrative editor, offered encouraging feedback when I sent another story off to New York; and Anne Sullivan, editorial coordinator, jumped in with great kindness to help with the later stages. Thanks also to copyeditor Ann Keene and proofreader Andy Goldwasser.

The book's fabulous look is due to the artistic vision of Ellen Jacob, creative director, working together with Gwen Petruska Gürkan, associate art director. This pair of alchemists transformed raw text and a stack of photos into a book so handsome I still love holding it and gazing at it. Ellen, who oversaw the press check at the printer's, invited me to be with her and scheduled the first books to come off the line on my birthday.

It's no wonder that I got everyone on the team a T-shirt that had LUCKY emblazoned across the front. That's how I felt getting to work with these folks.

Special thanks go to the behind-the-scenes creative people whose enthusiasm and energy extended the good cheer of this project from the editorial process out into the marketplace: Lori Garrabrant, director of sales and marketing; Karen McDermott, director of publicity; and Audrey Leung, director of subsidiary rights.

Many others helped this book along its way. My husband, Douglas Forde, belongs in a category all his own. Darlin' Dougal—a doctor, an internist, a professional listener—listened in his own expert and loving way to every word in every story as I read them to him, and he manned the home front and the dogs while I was away.

I extend a deep bow of gratitude to my first readers, Jennie Nash and Donna Dederer, who put their own work aside to read mine. And to Julie Wheelock, who raised overnight transcribing to an art form. A special nod of appreciation goes to Harold A. Lipton, whose careful counsel makes me feel I'm in good legal hands. And it's with pleasure that I acknowledge Linda Venis, director of the Writing Arts program at UCLA Extension, who gave me the opportunity to teach other writers and offered me a university setting in which to develop a workshop based on *A Woman's Path*.

From our first spicy lunch at a Caribbean restaurant, it was a pleasure working with Jill Johnson, the photographer. Her warmth and affection go a long way to putting at ease the people she photographs. Jill gives thanks to her assistants Tony DeRose and Denise Johns for going on the road with her; Ken Leslie, her runner; and Tina Corlone, our liaison at Nardulli Photo Lab in Hollywood. Jill also thanks her mentors and fellow photographers: S. Peter Lopez, Deborah Roundtree, Mark Laita, and Anthony Nex. And her husband, Eric, for supporting her in following her dreams, even if it meant she was hanging off a tugboat on the Columbia River. Finally, Jill thanks her parents for leaving that camera sitting next to her on that hot day in Michigan.

In a project of this scope, for which Jill and I traveled to more than twenty-five cities, hundreds of people caught the spirit of what we were doing. Sometimes they opened a door by saying, "You've got to meet so-and-so," and sometimes a door was opened to hospitality, an invitation to stay and enjoy a meal or spend the night. Without all the people who jumped on the bandwagon, this book would not have come to be, and it certainly wouldn't have been so much fun. Some of these people might be surprised to find themselves thanked publicly. They might think, I did nothing, really. But at exactly a crucial moment they supplied a lead or offered a thoughtful suggestion that helped give birth to this book.

To all these new and old friends across America, we give thanks: Kathy Stingley, Homer, Alaska; Chief Sonya Baker and Master Chief Doug Gorham, with the U.S. Pacific Fleet in San Diego; Harry Yamamura, Susie Hepner, Sheri A. Lee, John, Kristen, and Hannah Eby, Seattle; Chris Pinchbeck and Karen Black, Rockport, Maine; Harriet Hanson, with the Columbia River Bar Pilots, Astoria, Oregon; Linda Graf, Jill and Scott Douglas, Chicago; K. C. Cole, science writer, *Los Angeles Times;* Louise Steinman, PEN Center, U.S.A. West; Eileen Kreutz, Chicago Women in Trades, and Linda Beesley, President of Associated Builders & Contractors, Southgate, Michigan; Lou Vader, Nashville Juvenile Probation Court; Raine Wallace, Ellie Cahill, Ron Schlager, Tim and Mary Johns, Julie Logan, and Tamara Brown, Los Angeles; Dave McCullough, Atlanta; Barbara Dickey, Ogilvy & Mather Worldwide, New York City; Jane T. Dowd, New York City; Dee Soder, executive coach and president of Endymion, New York City; Connie Duckworth, Goldman Sachs, Chicago; Guy and Delores Roberts, Chicago; Jo Schiff, L.A. County Dependency Court; Ray and Hilda Johns, Miami; Ray and Jeannie Hartzog, Houston, Texas; Carol Applegate, Bonnie and Bob Gregson, Anne Dest-Gordon, and Pene and Will Anderson, Vashon Island, Washington; Lynn Byznski, editor, *Growing for Market;* Jean Dobbs, managing editor, *New Mobility;* Carolyn Mortimer, Cooper-Hewitt National Museum of Design; Sharon Jacobson, Los Angeles; Toni, Lamont, and Chris Johnson, Monterey, California; Wendy W. Finan, Johnson O'Connor Research Foundation, Irving, Texas; Joseph A. Nonno, reference librarian, Malibu, California; Morgan Schwartz, Crossroads School, Santa Monica, California; Marianne Maki and Girl Scout Troop 676; Jim Lew, Judy Thornber, and Diane Dahl, Chicago; Fay Jean Hooker, Harvey Wallender, Sean James, Denise Johns, and Jane MacLeish, Washington, D.C.; Helen Overly, Freda Raker, and Marge Taylor, McConnellsburg, Pennsylvania; Delores Edison, Baltimore; Lorraine Monroe, New York City; Mary Golladay, the National Science Foundation; Dr. May Berenbaum, Urbana, Illinois; Linh Lu-La and Paul M. Ringlaben, Kim Son Restaurant, Houston; Beth Lieberman, president, Women's National Book Association, Los Angeles.

For pals who extended encouragement early on, I'm thankful to Wendy Giese Barnhart, my sister, who sent a clipping, PERSISTENCE PAYS OFF, that's been tacked to my bulletin board for years; to Irvin Barnhart, my brother-in-law, who took the first photo for the book proposal, which prompted Bob Asahina, my editor, to comment, *"That's* the kind of photo I'm looking for"; my brother Jimmy Giese and his best friend, Susan Barry; my stepson, Doug Forde, who graciously introduced me to Chris Eiche; Gregory Forde, who honors me by calling me "Mom"; Susan Taylor Chehak, for her writer-to-writer generosity; Terry and Stan Hoffman; Sandy Rubel and Michael Cook; Alison Gardy; Elda Unger; Sheila and Allen Enelow; Bill Skinner; Carol Ross; and to Christel Uittenbogaart and her husband, the late Kerry Kosak. When I'd come home bubbling over with new stories, our good friend Kerry loved nothing better than coming over for dinner to hear about them. He died one week after I finished writing this book.

For laying the first stepping-stones on this path of mine, I extend a special thanks to my parents: my dad, Jim Giese, a sixth-grade dropout, an inventor, a self-trained engineer, showed by his maverick example that it was possible to invent your own path; and from the time I was knee-high to a card table, I learned from my mom, Gladys "Babe" Giese, and her pinochle group how important and life-sustaining a women's group can be. And so I thank my generous group of women friends on Vashon Island, Washington. I feel so lucky (there's that word again) that they continue to enfold me into their group when I return to the island: Valerie Willson, Vicki Adams, Penny Grist, Joanne Hammer, Mary Robinson, Mary Rothermel, and Jill Stenn. I also wrap a warm hug of gratitude around my dear friend Judith Searle for making her shrimp-and-rice salad and for inviting the women to that first gathering of our Women's Lunch Group in Los Angeles—Dale Pring MacSweeney, JoAnn Matyas, Luchita Mullican, Doreen Nelson, Amanda Pope, Janet Sternburg, Susan Suntree, and Carol Tavris.

About the Author and Photographer

Jo Giese

Jo Giese was an American studies major in college, and when working on her thesis she traveled around the country interviewing people about Frank Lloyd Wright's contribution to American architecture. She seemed to have a knack for one-on-one research, but she couldn't see how chatting with Wright's widow in her suite at the Plaza Hotel had anything to do with work in the real world. She thought it was a lark. As she says, "How do you know it's work if you've never seen anyone working like that?"

A few years later she was producing documentaries for public television, doing the same kind of work—talking to people, getting their stories. But she still didn't see a clear path for herself. She was still tortured by questions: How do you choose the right career? Or does it choose you?

If the average individual has seven or eight job changes in a lifetime, Jo had that many in her twenties, from newspaper writing in Houston to television reporting in New York City to consumer reporting in Los Angeles, always searching for the right fit. She has gone on to write for dozens of publications, including *The New York Times, The Los Angeles Times, Vogue, Ms.,* and *New Woman.* She also serves on the board of directors of PEN Center West and teaches in the Writing Arts Program at UCLA Extension.

It took twenty-five years for the *aha!* moment to sink in—for Jo to realize that her path, as circuitous as it's been, has a wholeness to it. While writing *A Woman's Path,* she learned that sometimes one's path is seen only in the wisdom of hindsight. And she has been comforted to realize that her preference for project-by-project work is actually more in step with the employment patterns of the future than the one-job-for-a-lifetime model of the past.

Jo Giese lives with her husband and two feisty dogs in Malibu, California.

Jill Johnson

Jill Johnson's path to photography began when she was four. Her older sister was playing a high school softball game, and Jill was fidgeting in the stands—until she saw her parents' camera, an old 100. She snapped a photo of her sister way out on the pitcher's mound. That was the last frame on the roll of film, and her parents told her, "Don't ever touch the camera again!"

Her dad gave her the picture she'd taken. "You couldn't even tell it was my sister," says Jill, "but to me it was the best thing I'd ever done." She still has that first photo framed in her darkroom.

She was hooked. When she was twelve she announced that she was going to be a photographer. Her parents thought she'd change her mind, but they started taking her seriously when she signed up for college classes at the Media Institute in Lansing, Michigan. Afterward she headed for Detroit to start assisting, photography's equivalent of apprenticing. But as Jill says, "In Detroit they shoot cars, cars, cars—and then there are trucks." She already knew that she wanted to shoot people.

To broaden her options, she moved to southern California, where she completed her degree at the Brooks Institute of Photography. After graduation she worked as an assistant, lugging other photographers' equipment and learning from them. She shot for a local college, businesses, and magazines until she got her first big break—photographing the women in this book.

One of Jill's favorite photo shoots was that of Diana Labrum, pie baker. Jill spent hours looking at the pies, lighting the pies, photographing the pies, smelling the pies. After the shoot Diana gave Jill and her assistant a marionberry pie. "It was the best pie I ever had," says Jill.

Jill Johnson lives with her husband in Monrovia, California.

Jo Giese would like to hear from you.

Everyone has a story, the authentic story of her life. If you're interested in learning more about how to tell *your* story, please write, enclosing a #10 self-addressed, stamped envelope. Jo Giese is also available for lectures and workshops based on *A Woman's Path.* Details will be sent on request.

Jo Giese
P.O. Box 6347
Malibu, CA 90264–6347